The Basic Handbook
of
Grants Management

The
Basic Handbook
of Grants
Management

ROBERT LEFFERTS

Basic Books, Inc., Publishers

NEW YORK

Library of Congress Cataloging in Publication Data

Lefferts, Robert.
  The basic handbook of grants management.

  Includes index.
  1. Fund raising—Handbooks, manuals, etc.
2. Grants-in-aid—Handbooks, manuals, etc.
3. Research grants—Handbooks, manuals, etc.
I. Title. II. Title: Grants management.
HG177.L43   1983   658.4'04   82-72400
ISBN 0-465-00600-0

To Morris and Ella

Contents

Contents

Contents

List of Figures

Preface

This is a book to help you manage projects—those time-limited service and research activities that are supported by grants and organized as special units of a larger organization to achieve specific objectives. The major focus of the book is on how to manage projects in the broad fields of human services, health, mental health, the arts and humanities, and the social and behavioral sciences.

It is exciting to get a grant! Exciting until you have to recruit staff, direct activities, fill out forms, account for funds, write reports, get the typewriter fixed, wait for a site visit, and seek refunding. These are the realities of project management. Most project directors and principal investigators are not managers. They are people with ideas, commitment, and know-how in a particular field. They want to provide a new needed service, demonstrate a better way to solve a problem, further knowledge, contribute to change. But they must also manage. This book is for them and for those who want to learn more about the management of grants and projects.

As I surveyed this field and talked with and observed people who were running projects, it became obvious that there was very little material available specifically on grant and project management. Most new project heads learn by trial and error and are looking for guidelines to help them manage more effectively and efficiently. Some actually believe that there exist a set of precise management techniques that could solve any administrative problem; a reflection of the mystification surrounding the field of management.

In response to these observations, this book is intended to meet the needs of both new and experienced project directors. It is designed to meet three main needs: the need to understand the nature of projects as a special kind of organization requiring a specialized managerial approach; the need to understand the characteristics of project management as a special form of administration; and the need to understand how to employ a variety of methods in project management.

The book is based on a conceptual framework that defines projects as a special type of organization which has five distinguishing characteristics: (1) emphasis on implementation; (2) focus on predefined goals and objectives; (3) time-limited duration; (4) relationship to a host agency; and (5) relationship to a funding agency. These characteristics generate a series of management functions that project managers must perform effectively, including how to (1) understand and respond to funding requirements; (2) maintain relationships with host and funding agencies, including effective reporting, site visiting, and other communication activities; (3) organize and direct the project's staff and activities to achieve project objectives; and (4) establish and manage financial systems, budgets, programs, and seek refunding.

Because of wide variation among projects in their size, purpose, activities, settings, and funding requirements, it is always necessary to adapt management methods to the needs of an individual project. The provision in this book of numerous examples of management techniques is to encourage project managers to use them as a basis on which to devise their own approaches; to trigger imagination; to provide a guide to development of your own creative and effective project management.

A handbook such as this is, in part, a chronicle of the experience of others. I am deeply indebted to the twenty funding agency officials who provided information and to the twenty project directors who generously shared their experience with me. In this regard, I want to acknowledge the particular help of Mathy Mezey, Fred Ringler, Stephen Rose, Jane Hazan, Daniel Fox, Susan Pickman, Robert Schneider, and Lynne Soine. Jo Ann Miller, senior editor of Basic Books, encouraged and criticized in ways that led only to considerable improvement. Susanne Torjussen's special secretarial skills more than matched the challenge of my need for help and search for clarity in preparing the original manuscript. Kay L. Dea's review of the manuscript was of invaluable aid in the process of revision.

Finally, I want to make clear my ideological perspective with respect to the central issue of exploitation that is inherent in the management of any endeavor in our society. Every project manager must make decisions about the personal needs of people involved, about the level of salaries to be paid, and about recognition and other rewards. The nature of project management, its emphasis on goal achievement and efficient use of funds, may push managers to treat people as secondary to these goals. I trust that in the use of the management methods that are presented, you will use them in ways that will help, not exploit, those with whom you work.

Robert Lefferts

The Basic Handbook

of

Grants Management

Chapter 1

Introduction: What Is Project Management?

The Growth of Projects

Since the first recorded government research grant of $20,000 to Samuel Morse in 1842 to test the feasibility of the telegraph, the history of grant-supported projects has been replete with concern over whether projects were managing their affairs efficiently and effectively.

The management of grant-supported projects is a specialized and relatively new part of the field of administration. Most project directors and principal investigators have little background in how to deal with the management aspects of heading a project. What needs to be done when a nonprofit social agency gets a foundation grant to start a new program for helping teenagers deal with the problem of drinking; when a university sociology professor receives money from the National Science Foundation to study the effects of television on people's attitudes toward different races; or when a county welfare department obtains a grant from the federal Department of Health and Human Services to demonstrate a new service to reduce child abuse? In each of these cases the organization sets up a project—a separate organizational unit, headed by a project director or principal investigator, having its own staff, budget, facilities, and relationships with a funder and other agencies.

Each of the cases involves a series of management problems that must be resolved:

How shall the project be organized?

What does the granting agency expect of the project; what are the requirements; and what methods can be used to deal with the granting agency?

How does the project fit into the larger host organization such as a university, a health department, or a social agency?

How can the activities that must be carried out be best organized and monitored?

What methods can be employed to be sure the project accomplishes its goals and completes its work on time?

How can the work of the project be evaluated?

How can the project monies be managed so they are used most efficiently?

What methods can be employed to be sure the project's accomplishments become known?

In the last fifteen years, due to the proliferation of grant-supported projects during President Lyndon Johnson's Great Society programs, these management issues have become increasingly important. The considerable increases in the availability of governmental, foundation, and corporate grants since 1965 has resulted in more and more service and research activities being organized as special projects in the fields of health, mental health, education, the arts and humanities, community development, social welfare, and the social and behavioral sciences. Even with the cutbacks in federal monies in the early 1980s, organizations of any size (hospitals, welfare departments, museums, health departments, universities, family service agencies, Catholic Charities) have one or more grant-supported projects that are organized as separate identifiable units and which do not operate as part of the organization's ongoing routine operations.

Most of these service and research endeavors are supported by grants from foundations, government agencies, and corporate funding sources. At least five hundred thousand such projects are funded each year. Many thousands of additional projects are organized and carried out by agencies and institutions using their own resources.

These grant-supported and nongrant-supported project activities take many different forms of which four are the most frequent: service

4

programs, such as a juvenile delinquency prevention program; research activities, such as a study to evaluate the effectiveness of a housing rehabilitation program; training programs such as preparing high school students to act as tutors; and cultural endeavors, such as community arts festivals. Taken together they represent an annual expenditure that exceeds some $40 billion. With relatively little notice, they have become a distinctive administrative innovation that has introduced a new dimension to organizational life in general and to the administration and management of organizations in particular. There is need to more fully analyze and understand the organizational implications of this development and, most importantly, how to effectively administer and manage them. This book is intended to meet this need.

The growth of grant supported projects has been dramatic. For example, from 1965 to 1980, foundation grants increased from $1.1 billion to $2.2 billion; corporate support went from $.8 billion to $2.3 billion; and federal funds for research and development to universities and colleges increased from $1.1 billion to $4.1 billion, and from $.7 billion to $2.2 billion among nonprofit agencies. By 1980 the annual federal nondefense budget for research and developmental projects was $17 billion; and at least an equal amount went to various training and service programs supported by grants.* Agencies that seldom received government or foundation grants (Girl Scouts, Boy Scouts, community theater groups, the local library, the community hospital, the community college) have all become dependent on these grants to offer particular services. Many organizations, especially universities, to a large extent measure their status by the amount of grant money they receive and by the attention paid to their grant supported projects.

By the beginning of the 1980s, the project approach was firmly entrenched as a useful programmatic and administrative device among nonprofit and government agencies alike. From the small rural school district to the large metropolitan medical center, it has become institutionalized as an integral part of the strategy of organizations to both maintain financial support and to promote their service and research activities.

---

* *Statistical Abstract of the United States,* U.S. Department of Commerce, Bureau of the Census (Washington, D.C.: U.S. Government Printing Office, 1980).

Impact of Projects

The administrative consequences of this development have been substantial as any administrator will testify. There is recognition, for example, that the influx of considerable funds from federal, state, and local government agencies into the private, nonprofit agency field for project support has blurred the traditional distinctions between public agencies and private agencies. Can a local, nonprofit family service agency that gets 60 percent of its total budget from government grants feel free to offer controversial services in the abortion field? Can a neighborhood improvement association that receives most of its budget from the city housing department consider itself a part of the movement toward purely voluntary citizen activities?

Accepted notions about organizational decision making and management practices have come to be questioned as the special characteristics and demands of project administration have begun to emerge. For example, the accountability a university's grant-supported projects have to funding sources such as the National Institutes of Health to report on project expenses is very different from the university administration's accountability to its own board of trustees that oversees its ongoing operations. Maintaining staff morale and deciding on staff deployment are different in a short-term project situation that may only last for one year as compared to the way staff decisions are handled in the long-term course of regular operations. Internal relationships, cooperation, and coordination between a project and the organization's regular departments such as its personnel department or accounting office must be developed. Conflicts and strains between a project and these other units often develop and must be managed and resolved. Maintaining satisfactory relationships with a governmental funding agency or foundation must sometimes be given priority over attending to other problems in order to avoid the loss of grant monies.

A new language, the language of projects, grants, and contracts, has been introduced into the culture of social institutions. "Soft money," "hard money," "cost sharing," "full-effort," "roll-overs," "cost reimbursable," are terms not to be found in the dictionary. A plethora of forms, rules and regulations, guidelines, executive orders, and procedures has come into being with the new language. "A–21," "OMB 110," "A–95," "human subjects review," are all things that grant administrators must understand and comply with. New professional roles have come into being and, not surprisingly, a new breed of professionals has emerged. The grantsperson, contract manager, project director, and principal investigator are management roles unknown to most standard textbooks on administration. And, as every project manager finds out, a substantial amount of time must be given over to the preparation and submission of financial and program reports to funding agencies.

One can ask, however, if this is not past history in view of the call for additional fiscal constraints and cutbacks in the 1980s. The evidence clearly indicates the answer is "no." The utilization of the grant and special project is strongly institutionalized in the operations of American social, political, and economic organizations inside and outside of government. While they adapt themselves to changing economic constraints and to shifting governmental policies and priorities, their basic mode of operations tends to remain intact. It should be remembered that in the mid-1970s the country experienced a severe recession and a reduction in grant availability from government and foundations. Programs were cut back. Grants were less available. Yet, the long-term trend shows an ever-increasing reliance on the project approach, with or without special funding, as a way to organize and deliver services and research. The past fifty years has seen many periods of cutbacks and uncertainty in the funding of programs directed at service or research related to the country's social conditions. These have always proved temporary with the only lasting change being some shifts in the kinds of activities that receive support or in the mechanisms for conveying funds such as the recent utilization of revenue sharing and block grants and shifting responsibility for administering certain programs from federal to state or local governments. To the individual or institution that has failed to get a grant or has lost resources, these findings are of little consolation and seem to be nothing more than rhetoric. However, the fact remains that the grant and project component of institutional operations is here to stay. And along with it is the demand for more effective project management. There is no question that cutbacks have resulted in increased competition among those seeking funds. As a result, successful management of a current project contributes to the ability of organizations to obtain future funding by establishing a track record that will attract new monies.

It should also be noted that under conditions of tightening fiscal constraints organizations attempt to avoid long-term commitments to the extent possible. This results in an increasing reliance upon the use

7

of special projects (with or without outside support) as a way to structure the provision of service programs and research. The project format is an effective device for organizations to employ in the face of uncertainty about the future. As one agency executive puts it, "I organize almost any new activity as a separate unit with its own staff and a completion date for its program. This avoids long-range commitment of funds and personnel. It has the advantage of allowing me to observe results before making a more permanent commitment."

In addition, the use of the project approach may well be part of a more basic change in American organizational life that is responding to the growing alienation of workers, reductions in productivity, and the apparent inefficiencies of traditional modes of organization. Alvin Toffler in *Future Shock* and *The Third Wave** has called attention to this development which he refers to as the growth in "adhocracy"; the use of temporary organizational forms such as task forces and work groups to accomplish specific tasks. The project approach is also consistent with the analysis of Bennis and Slater in *The Temporary Society* which develops the idea that time-limited, organizational arrangements have the potential for avoiding problems of social relationships that develop in more permanent organizational forms.† It is also consistent with the interest in new management approaches aimed at improving the effectiveness of operations such as quality circles and other approaches developed in Japanese industry and matrix management in the United States. In these approaches, workers are often assigned to temporary functional, task-oriented work groups at the same time that they maintain their regular ongoing administrative location, and thus may report to two different supervisors.

One of the more discernible trends in the grant field has been the shifting locus of governmental support for grant-supported activity. The federal government in the 1970s and continuing into the 1980s increased its use of so-called block grants to the states in the place of the prior categorical federally administered grant programs. In 1981, for example, twenty-three different federal health programs were eliminated and combined into a single lump sum allocated to each state for community health services. This trend will result in an increase in the extent to which the principal funding agency will be

---

*Alvin Toffler, *Future Shock* (New York: Random House, 1970), pp. 124–151; Alvin Toffler, *The Third Wave* (New York: William Morrow & Co., 1980), pp. 136–137.

†Warren G. Bennis and Philip E. Slater, *The Temporary Society* (New York: Harper and Row, 1968).

come a state agency and in some cases a local governmental agency. While this affects the process of making grant applications, its impact on levels of support and its implications for project and grant administration are not yet clear. The major impact has been related to the fact that the rules and regulations governing what a grantee can and cannot do and what kinds of reports must be submitted vary considerably among state and local agencies and, thus, add to the problems of project management. There may, of course, be a greater effect in the future, and administrative approaches may have to adapt to such changes. The history of domestic spending, however, would suggest that major changes will not occur other than the introduction of some new forms, some new agencies, some new rules, some new programs, and some new actors in the grants field.

The Problem of Project Management

Accompanying the growth of the grant industry and the increased utilization of the special project, there is a developing body of experience in relation to the management of these activities. It has become apparent to administrators in the public and the private sectors that there are many factors associated with grant and project management that are different from the problems involved in the day-to-day administration of agencies, organizations, and institutions. In spite of this recognition by practitioners, very little has been written or systematically tested in connection with this particular area of administration.

The largest group of literature related to grant and project management was published in 1975-1976 in the form of a wide variety of reports from various universities. These publications were the result of a series of studies funded by the National Science Foundation's program on Research Management Improvement. This material, however, is concerned with university-based research and is largely focused on the university-wide organization of research rather than management of the project itself. There is also a body of literature on project management in the industrial, space, and engineering field that is concerned with large-scale production projects such as the Apollo missile, but which is not applicable to the kinds of research, training, and service projects with which this book is concerned. A third group of literature is concerned with the organization, supervision, and control of scientific research teams, but it too does not deal with the problems of day-to-day project management.

In part, the lack of literature reflects a basic problem in the field of administration. Public administration, business administration, educational administration, and social administration are all applied fields that have little theory of their own. Like other applied fields such as medicine, law, or engineering, they rely upon various disciplines for theoretical guidance, and they attempt to utilize eclectically whatever concepts from these disciplines seem to apply to practice. The field of administration has traditionally looked to the disciplines of sociology, psychology, and economics for a theoretical understanding of organizations and for principles that apply to their management. Many of these ideas have been grouped together in an area known as organizational theory (that body of knowledge that purports to explain the nature of organizations). While much has been written in this area, it is characterized by a wide range of competing ideas: Weber's theory of bureaucracy, Thompson's ideas of organizational interdependency, Etzioni's analysis of compliance structures, Taylor's scientific management, Barnard's human relations school, to mention only a few.* The person who must manage a project finds little help in these theories and usually ends up developing management approaches that are based on experience and which utilize and adapt techniques from the broad field of administration.

Who's Who in the Project Drama

Good managers, like good motion picture directors, have to be clear about the cast of characters and their respective roles. The field of project management is complicated by the fact that there are a number of different titles for persons who perform the same or similar jobs.

First, there is the person directly responsible for running the project. This person will usually be called the project director or principal investigator. The person may also be known as the project coordinator, or just director or coordinator. In this book, the terms project director,

---

*For a good brief overview of these various theories, see Amitai Etzioni, *Modern Organizations* (Englewood Cliffs, New Jersey: Prentice-Hall, 1964).

principal investigator, and project manager will be used interchangeably to refer to the person, or persons, who head up the project.

Second, there are persons in the offices of the host agency who have responsibility in the grant field and are assigned to assist in the management of projects. These responsibilities may range from actually having all project personnel appointed as employees of this office (for example, a university-wide research foundation) to providing consultation on writing proposals. There may also be a separate grants management office that handles all of the fiscal affairs for a project. In addition, there may be a personnel office, a purchasing office, and a travel office. All of these will have forms to fill out and must process and approve project activities in their area. The people in these offices will have many different titles such as grants directors, directors, grants business managers, assistant directors.

Third, are the persons in the funding agency. In federal agencies there are two sets of persons. One set consists of those who are responsible for liaison and monitoring the project. These are the program people known as program managers, unit chiefs, project directors, contract managers, program officers. The other set are those persons who are concerned with financial management of the project and are known as grant managers, grant officers, and so forth. In foundations, the responsibility for program and finance may be assigned to a single person, such as the foundation director, program officer, program associate, staff associate, and so forth.

Organization of the Book

This book is based on the assumption that one can most fruitfully approach the problem of understanding and administering a project from a perspective that recognizes the practical, political, economic, and social realities that must be faced by project managers. One set of these realities grows out of the nature of projects as a special form of organization. Thus, in chapter 2 we begin by describing five major organizational characteristics of a project and assessing the administrative consequences, implications, and problems that result from these characteristics. The primary focus of the book is on the principles and methods that can be employed to assure more effective and efficient operations and facilitate the achievement of goals and objectives. In chapter 3 we examine the six specific functions that grant and project managers must carry out and show how these are consistent with and responsive to the special characteristics and management needs of these endeavors.

Chapters 4 to 9 deal with the specific methods and techniques of grant and project management. These chapters recognize that effective management depends upon the ability to understand and manage the interplay between *external* factors (for example, funder requirements, relationships with funders and host agencies, reporting requirements) and *internal* factors (for example, implementing program and research activities, financial control, managing personnel). Therefore, in chapter 4, there is a detailed examination of how to understand and comply with the rules, regulations, laws, and other external requirements imposed by funders that provide the administrative and political context within which projects must operate. In chapter 5 the methods that maintain satisfactory relationships with funders and host agencies are reviewed. Because formal and informal communication and reporting usually is the key to maintaining relationships, chapter 6 is devoted exclusively to the planning and implementation of an effective project reporting program.

One of the most critical (and anxiety producing) events in the life of the special project is the site visit by funders and other outside agencies. Chapter 7 describes a series of techniques for the implementation of successful site visits.

In chapter 8, a major area of internal concern, the management of program or research activities, will be examined. This chapter describes the methods that can be employed to establish and implement the structures and processes to enhance the effectiveness of program management, ranging from staff organization to adopting techniques such as MBO (Management By Objectives) to the project situation. One of the most critical areas in the management of projects is fiscal operations. In chapter 9, the principles and methods to assure more effective financial management are described.

The book concludes with a glossary of terms and appendixes of reference material.

Chapter 2

The Characteristics of Special Projects: Management Implications

---

Five Characteristics of Projects

A project is the result of some person or group having developed a plan and then acquiring the resources to carry out a particular set of services or research activities. Usually a proposal has been written and submitted to a foundation, governmental, or corporate funder; a grant has been awarded; staff have been assigned; and activities are gotten underway. The project is generally organized as a separate unit that is part of a larger host organization. A social research project lodged in a university on the effects of alcoholism on family life, a department of social services foster care program for emotionally disturbed children, and a hypertension screening program in a hospital are typical examples of these arrangements. The larger host organization has varying degrees of overall responsibility for handling the project's operations, ranging from bookkeeping to performing an evaluation of its effectiveness. Technically, the grant for the project is made to the host organization which has the final accountability to the funder for the proper use of the money.

Occasionally, a project may be free standing; that is, it is not a part of a larger organization since the grant money has been obtained for the purpose of setting up a new agency. This is the case when, for example, a foundation gives a grant to a group of citizens incorporated as a board of directors for a new day care center, a neighborhood improvement association, or a women's health clinic. In addition, some projects are set up without special grants by assigning existing staff and other resources to the project. The material that follows applies to these situations as well as to the more usual grant-funded projects.

To develop an approach to effective management of projects, it is imperative to go beyond such a rudimentary description of projects and to identify the salient characteristics of projects that have major consequences for administrative practice. Anyone who has been associated with projects knows they are quite different from other types of organizations, and that they present an unusual range of administrative and management demands and problems. The problems of project management are different from those involved in operating a hospital, a county department of health, a symphony orchestra, a museum, a mental health clinic, or a social agency. One project director puts it this way: "I am always thinking about the foundation that funds us, the YMCA in which we are located, the need to help the project go full steam ahead, the project goals that must be met by the end of the year, that application for new funds, the reports I need to write, and the broken xerox machine, or other crises that are slowing us down."

What is different about projects from other organizational forms? As one observes projects and talks with project personnel, it becomes apparent that there are five major characteristics of projects that distinguish them from other organizations and which provide the context for most of the activities involved in project management:

1. An emphasis on operational implementation; they are under pressure to "get the show on the road."
2. A focus on achievement of a set of predefined goals and objectives; they are expected to show specific results.
3. Their time-limited duration; they start and end on specific dates.
4. Their almost total dependence on an external supporting organization for financial resources; the foundation or government funder controls the money the project needs to operate and imposes a variety of requirements on the project.
5. The fact that they are part of a larger host organization that has varying degrees of responsibility for project operations and has policies and procedures with which projects must comply.

That projects have major characteristics that vary significantly from the characteristics of ongoing organizations provides the basis for identifying project management as a discrete form of administration that requires its own distinctive knowledge base and methodology. In the remainder of this chapter the characteristics of projects will be described and analyzed from the point of view of their implications for project management. It is the consequences of these characteristics that define most of the activities of project managers and which also give rise to the major problems that must be overcome in the process of project management. In this regard, it is important to note that the characteristics of projects are complex and are interrelated. Thus, no simple cookbook of techniques will suffice for responding to these characteristics. The ingenuity, creativity, and ability of project administrators are constantly challenged by the problems generated by the different nature of the special project. An understanding of the characteristics of projects helps to contribute to the refinement of administrative skills and the more conscious planning and selection of managerial approaches and methods.

A Structural Approach

It is important to recognize that all five characteristics have one thing in common. They all are structural. They all have to do with how projects are organized and how they carry out their functions. Stressing the structural nature of project characteristics has some major implications for project management. It explains that most administrative problems are more the result of organizational arrangements and processes than they are of the personalities, behavior traits, or values of the persons who are involved. This is not to deny that individuals and values make a difference and create problems. Obviously, they do. However, a structural approach emphasizes that project performance is chiefly determined by how the arrangements and activities that are related to these five characteristics are managed. Administrative practice is focused on concrete conditions that one can do something about instead of dwelling on the often unmanageable (in the project situations, at least) aspects of individual behavior. Further, it is consistent with the recognition in the field of organizational analysis that structural factors are major determinants and set the parameters for a good deal of individual behavior in organizations.

An example of this was provided by the following. A project funded to promote economic development in part of a large city was required by the government funding agency to include participation by residents of the neighborhood in deciding what specific companies the project would try to attract.

A two-person staff, professionally trained and experienced in economic planning and development, had conducted marketing and feasibility surveys that showed priority should be given to attracting small electronics firms involved primarily in assembly of parts. They were overruled by the residents who favored attracting commercial businesses to a shopping center. Because of the structural arrangements such as the funder's requirement for participation, the staff's expertise was, in effect, challenged. Further, because the project was structured to complete the initial phase within three months, there was not sufficient time for the staff to educate and persuade the residents to the staff's point of view.

The major problems that occur in project managment of how to organize a staff, how to manage a program, how to assure financial efficiency, and how to get results are generated by the structural characteristics of projects. While it is true that managers and workers may sometimes be ineffective or that there are personality clashes among staff or that workers have legitimate complaints, these are problems inherent in all social and economic enterprises. They are human events that can be painful and time consuming and must be dealt with and resolved. In so doing, managers must be mindful of the feelings and interests of those involved and treat them with respect and as humanly as possible. But this is not the foundation upon which one can develop an approach to project management other than to devise organizational means for their prevention or solution. Thus, for example, the structural approach to personnel management is not so much concerned with the process of supervising a worker or with how to interview or dismiss a worker as it is with the establishment of organizational arrangements to facilitate communication, provide for consultation with staff, manage overloads, avoid burnout, coordinate the performance of personnel, and provide for an equitable evaluation system.

It should also be stressed that these five characteristics are highly interdependent. For example, the emphasis on implementation is related to the fact that the project is time limited. The emphasis on goal achievement is influenced by the expectations of the funding agency upon which the project is dependent for financing. While each characteristic will be discussed separately in the material that follows, this is done for ease in analysis since we cannot say everything at once. Their partialization is to a degree artificial since in practice they overlap and interact with each other.

Characteristic One: Emphasis on Implementation

Projects are under great pressure to "get the show on the road." The Latin roots of the word project are *pro* and *facere*, which not surprisingly mean "to throw forth." The primary concern is with implementing a definite set of activities and tasks that usually have been previously outlined in a funding proposal. Financial support and other resources have been allocated to the project based on what, in effect, was both a promise and a plan contained in the proposal. Projects have a legal responsibility to use the funds they receive for the purposes set forth in a proposal or grant award notice. The continued flow of funds and the credibility of the project and the host organization are highly dependent on getting the project into operation. Whether it be the tasks involved in evaluating a health program, or producing an experimental drama, or conducting research, or establishing a training program, the project staff's first preoccupation is with getting the work started.

The activities involved in implementation usually fall into three phases. First, is the preparatory phase comprised of the tasks involved in planning and preparing for operations. Second, is the operational phase which involves all the tasks to carry out the operations. And third, is the completion phase consisting of the tasks required for completing the project.

Each of these three phases of implementation present different management problems. The major preparatory tasks include recruiting and hiring staff, obtaining equipment and offices, planning activities and, in the case of research projects, refining the design and preparing instruments. Managing these activities presents different problems from those of managing the actual operations such as the delivery of a training program, data collection, or counseling troubled teenagers. Similarly, completing a project, preparing final reports and disseminating them, disposing of equipment, closing offices, informing other organizations of the termination of services present management problems of a somewhat different nature.

Given the pervasive pressure for projects to carry through these activities, it should be no surprise that principal investigators, project directors, and project staff are sometimes regarded by others as short-tempered or tough. Project personnel must frequently work long hours, make fast decisions, and move ahead with a minimum of planning as the result of the preoccupation with implementation. The preparatory phase may often be cut short. Program planning and the recruitment and selection of staff must be accomplished as quickly as possible—sometimes too quickly to be thorough. The project must move to its operational phase and must get its act together with a minimum of delay.

The pace and character of project activities is different from the more settled ongoing operations of the host organization. Starting up a one-year project in a YMCA to study teenage drug abuse, for example, requires considerably faster action to recruit and orient research staff, refine the study design, and print questionnaires than does the day-to-day operation of the typical YMCA branch. Because of the pressure to move ahead, projects may make many demands on host organizations for resources, equipment, and administrative services such as the speedy processing of staff appointments and getting people onto payrolls quickly. This can result in friction between the host agency and the project which can, in turn, make severe demands on the time and energy of project managers and staff. Thus, a major management issue for project administrators is, on one hand, to assure that implementation can be moved ahead and, on the other hand, to mitigate the stresses, the inefficiencies, and ineffectiveness that can arise from the emphasis on implementation. Understanding that these problems are primarily the result of the pressure to implement enables one to more effectively prevent and ameliorate them than if they are simply seen as behavioral problems that get termed "lack of cooperation by host agencies," or "projects wanting special treatment."

The tasks involved in the completion phase of a project, including its phasing out or planning for refunding and preparing new grant proposals present another set of management problems. More often than not, many of the problems here are generated by waiting until the last minute before starting to handle these tasks. Effective project managers recognize at the beginning of a project that there will be an end point that must be planned for ahead of time.

The Characteristics of Special Projects: Management Implications

All phases of implementation are heavily influenced by the nature of the project proposal submitted to the funder. Proposals set forth the project's plan for implementation and delineate what the project objectives are, what the activities will be, and the staffing plan. Implementation activities must be geared to the proposal specifications and at times these force a project director to take actions that may not represent what he or she would prefer to do. For example, you may prefer to employ a psychologist in a youth counselor position, but if the proposal specified the employment of social workers, you are expected to follow that plan.

Characteristic Two: Focus on Goal Achievement

Closely related to the emphasis on implementation of activities is a second characteristic of special projects which is their focus on the achievement of predefined goals or objectives. Projects are expected not only to "get the show on the road" but also to "produce." Projects are always under pressure to show successful results.

Projects are usually based on proposals that were submitted to funders which included a set of specific objectives or accomplishments that the project was designed to achieve. A proposal for a job training program for released criminal offenders may have as one of its objectives "to increase the number of ex-offenders who become employed." A proposal for a hospital-based program to use volunteers to help homebound patients has as one objective "to train 100 volunteers." Projects are expected to deliver on these promises.

Project administrators share with funding agencies and host agencies a need and a desire to be able to document their achievements. Refunding and continuation of projects are often based on an assessment of the extent to which objectives are being reached. In addition, the prospects for getting a grant for a new project are highly dependent on establishing a successful "track record" of achievement in prior efforts. Even in the case of long-term basic research projects, which are generally more process than output oriented, the focus on showing certain kinds of achievements or progress is a pervasive force. For example, refunding decisions for such projects are often affected by the number and type of journal publications that have been produced by the investigators.

The personal and professional commitments of the project leaders and staff also contribute to the concern with realizing objectives and showing results. Professional advancement is enhanced by a record of accomplishments. Certain management approaches that enjoy popularity among some granting agencies such as MBO (Management By Objectives), PPBS (Program, Planning, Budgeting Systems), and PERT (Program Evaluation Review Techniques) have further contributed to the use of objectives as the criteria for the measurement of success.

What are the administrative consequences of the goal–achievement orientation of projects? Certainly one of the most troublesome possibilities is the pressure it can create to sacrifice the quality and even the integrity of project activities. This is somewhat analogous to the problems of the sacrifice of product quality that arise in the private sector among firms that focus only on short-term rather than long-term profit situations. When cars are designed and built with the first priority of being able to market them, safety may be sacrificed. Similar problems may occur when service and research projects become overly concerned with their outputs. Attention to the processes that are involved in carrying out service, training, or research projects may be minimized in favor of concentrating only on results. There have been extreme examples of such consequences reported in the press, ranging from the falsification of research data to the manipulation of training programs and test results to satisfy the objectives that the project was set up to achieve.

One notorious example of this occurred in the case of an educational project in Texas public schools to improve the performance of school children on reading, writing, and math tests. The private firm that had a government contract grant to run this project was found to be training children in the correct answers to the written tests that were going to be given rather than in the broader improvement of these basic skills.*

This emphasis on goal achievement can also result in problems in other aspects of the management of project operations. Audit problems can be created if budgets are overspent or manipulated in order to shift money into those activities that will show short-term results. Examples of this have occurred in training projects that have only accepted trainees who show good promise of succeeding; and in mental health projects that shift resources from individual counseling to

---

* *New York Times,* 27 October 1978.

group counseling in order to meet their objective to serve a larger number of clients.

Staff morale may be adversely affected if the assessment of staff performance is done by using their contribution toward goal achievement as the only measure of their effectiveness rather than by evaluating their total performance. Public relations efforts aimed only at showing achievements may become an end in themselves.

The impact of the focus on objectives upon project administration is further complicated by the trend toward stating program objectives in narrow behavioral terms that are subject to quantitative measurement. While this is not so true of research projects, it has become increasingly applicable to service and training projects. For example, it is not sufficient to state an objective in terms such as "improving the quality of nursing care in nursing homes." Rather, one is expected to state such an outcome in measurable behaviors that serve as proxies for "quality" such as "increase the number of visits per patient by 25 percent." Such a statement, of course, does not necessarily measure quality since what is done in a visit may or may not improve the care of a patient. This practice can easily push projects into redefining their programmatic activities in much more narrow terms than originally intended and, as a result, important findings and services can be ignored or entirely overlooked. Thus, project heads must establish systems for program management and monitoring that have sufficient flexibility to measure the achievement of narrow objectives and to also facilitate the broader less measurable, but nevertheless, important aspects of the project's work.

At the same time, and in a more positive light, the goal-achievement emphasis can provide project managers with a set of benchmarks to keep track of progress; to assess productivity; to modify activities, if required and, to document and report achievements. In addition, a sense of commitment on the part of project personnel to shared goals can greatly contribute to the quality of the work experience and improve job performance, satisfaction, and morale.

The proper use of explicit goals as a basis for administrative decision making can also lead to a reduction in the extent to which arbitrariness or irrationality might enter into decisions about resource allocations, staff deployment, and program activity priorities. It is much clearer, for example, to make and explain administrative decisions regarding staff deployment and work loads when a research study has a specific output goal of "interviewing 1,000 residents" than if the goal is expressed in vague terms such as "interviewing a sufficiently large sample."

There are certain obstacles that are inherent in all social organizations that managers must overcome as they seek to maximize the achievement of a project's substantive goals. For one thing, employees give their first priority to their own job security and advancement. Keeping one's job and improving one's salary are legitimate goals for a worker. They may or may not be consistent with the project's programmatic objectives. Administrators, for example, often gain their reputations and are rewarded for expansion of their operations and for acquiring grants rather than for programmatic achievement. These factors coupled with the limitations of the state of technological know-how in providing services and conducting research tend to reduce substantive goal achievement possibilities. Project managers must be realistic about the goal-achievement aspect of administration. The information they gather on the project's program or research activities should not be limited to progress in achieving objectives, but should reflect what is really going on in the project. Managers who institute management information systems (MIS) need to know who is being served, what is happening to participants, or what is the quality of research information that is being obtained. They need to be prepared to modify objectives and institute changes in project activities based on the realities of project experience. They need to be able to negotiate these changes with funders and host agencies. And they need to be able to document the strengths and weaknesses in operations and provide accurate reports on progress to host agencies and funding agencies that include, but are not limited to, the achievement of objectives.

Characteristic Three: Time-Limited Duration

Perhaps the most obvious and concrete characteristic of the special project is that it has a well-defined temporal life. Projects start on the given date and end on a given date. Project timetables are usually developed prior to project implementation and have been set forth in grant proposals or in the very early planning phase of the project's implementation. These timetables generally list all the main activities and when each is to start and be completed: for example, staff is to be recruited by the end of the third month; interviews are to be finished by the sixth month; final reports written by the twelfth month. Project administrators are responsible for seeing that the timetable of tasks is adhered to as closely as possible. This can enhance both the implementation process and the goal-achievement process. Completing a task on time, such as the organization of the curriculum for a training program, certainly contributes to the project's need to become operational as fast as possible. Recruiting trainees on time certainly contributes to achieving one of the project's objectives.

But there can also be negative consequences of the requirement to adhere to timetables. For example, the opportunity to use a developmental approach in which the future activities are largely built on the experience with preceding activities as part of the process of implementation is limited. This means that flexibility and the ability to respond to changing conditions is reduced considerably. Managers can become overconcerned with implementing scheduled activities and fail to respond to the actual experiences that the project is confronting in its operations. Managers may not pay sufficient attention to what is happening to project participants or to handling individual and group interests involved in the project. "Running the trains on time," a frequently used phrase in the language of project administrators, can become an end in and of itself. Project staff members who had no role in the development of the project's timetable may regard management's emphasis on completion dates as unrealistic or arbitrary, and their work may be adversely affected. Insufficient attention to necessary preparatory and planning activities and the temptation to employ inefficient shortcuts are other possible negative consequences of the time-limited nature of project operations. For example, the failure of one mental health project in the field of sex therapy to adequately proofread a report due to the funding agency on a given date had so many errors in spelling that it placed the project's refunding in jeopardy.

At the same time, the achievement of time-related targets can provide project staff with an important sense of accomplishment (and often a sense of relief as well). Financial efficiency can be furthered through prudent management and control over the timetable of events. There are a variety of time-oriented management techniques that have grown up in recent years, including the use of Program Evaluation Review Techniques (PERT), activity and performance scheduling, Gantt charts, and milestone charts. The time-limited character of the special project requires that managers understand these techniques and the extent of their effectiveness, and use them as tools in planning and control of the project activities.

Characteristic Four: Relationships with External Funders

Research and service projects that are supported by grants from foundation, governmental, or corporate sources have relationships to these funding sources that have major implications for project administration. The form and substance of these relationships are different from the other kinds of relationships that ongoing organizations have to external groups such as a state budget office, newspapers, and cooperating agencies. They need to be understood and managed if projects are to function effectively.

The management problems that the project-funding agency relationship generates grow out of four specific aspects of this arrangement:

1. Projects are almost entirely financially dependent on the funding source(s) and must maintain this support throughout the life of the project in order to operate. There are usually only one or two funding sources involved, and the major focus of the project's external relationships is on these relationships. Though other external relationships are present, they are of lesser administrative (as contrasted to programmatic) significance.

2. Projects are subject to a set of specific rules, policies, regulations, and conditions that are imposed on them by funders and with which they must comply in order to obtain and maintain the flow of resources. These may sometimes involve requirements that apply to the full range of project operations including its policies and practices regarding finances, personnel, activities, and procedures.

3. Major changes in project budgets, programs, and personnel that are necessary cannot be made unilaterally by the project since they often require the approval of the funding agency. In addition, the financial and program accountability of projects is subject to external requirements of funding agencies which frequently engage in their own auditing and assessment of a project's operations.

4. Projects must maintain satisfactory relationships with funders as necessary to facilitate renewal or continuation of funding for the project, or to gain support for new efforts by the host institution and/or the project staff.

These factors create a special set of circumstances for project directors and principal investigators that make considerable demands on their time and energy. The political and managerial skills that are required are different from those involved in directing the substantive aspects of the project's programmatic or research activities. Many administrators find this aspect of project administration burdensome and diversionary to their main interests and may not see it as germane to the "real" work of the project. Completing a monthly financial report to a state health department that is supporting a drug abuse counseling project is not nearly so interesting to a project head as the "real" work of working with drug abusers. The effective administrator must, as a first step, revise this position and accept the fact that the relationship with the funder is a high priority part of his or her job. Indeed, the requirements of funders can often be utilized to enhance the work of the project in a variety of ways. For example, the preparation and submission of required periodic financial and program reports or the planning and conduct of site visits can also serve to improve the coordination of project activities and to help staff members understand the importance of their individual work in the total project effort.

Characteristic Five: Host Agency Relationships

The vast majority of projects are located within a host agency which is a larger organization such as a university, a hospital, a social welfare agency, a school system, a health department, or city/county government. Host agencies provide the immediate organizational setting that influences projects in a myriad of ways and have management implications for project administrators. Projects are expected to adhere to the philosophy, policies, and procedures of the host agency. These may or may not be consistent with the effective operation of the project. The administrative problem is to negotiate them satisfactorily in order to maintain the smooth operation of the project. A project lodged in a medical school, and aimed at providing self-care instruction to women, for example, must find ways to relate its work to the school's more traditional gynecological program for training physicians in order to avoid criticism by physicians within the school that might threaten the project's continuation.

All large host agencies have detailed grant administration policies and procedures that may or may not correspond to those of funders but with which projects must comply. Host agencies also have many short-term and long-term programmatic and financial interests and goals. A youth service agency may want to expand its services to new parts of the city; a university may be trying to start a new law school. Projects are expected to function in ways that contribute to those interests or, at least, not interfere with the host agency's plans. Of course, host agencies may have rules and requirements related to finances, personnel, and procurement with which projects must comply.

Host agencies tend to regard special projects in rather contradictory ways. Certainly the additional resources, the recognition, and the substantive importance of a project are seen as institutionally desirable assets. But, the project may also be viewed within a host agency as an intruder, as an activity that drains rather than contributes resources, as a privileged operation, as a threat to stability, or as a liability. Project administrators must deal with all of these factors in order to maintain effective working relationships and assure stability in project operations. Project administrators have a special set of responsibilities to adhere to host agency policies and procedures, to keep host agencies informed of project activities, to contribute to the interests of host agencies, and to provide them with benefits.

Maintaining satisfactory working arrangements with host agencies is also critical because projects are dependent on host agencies for a variety of services. Financial management, the keeping of project accounts, personnel, records, purchasing, and payroll are functions often performed for projects by host agencies. They may also provide space and equipment for project staff.

One of the most complex aspects of the project-host agency relationship grows out of the fact that many aspects of the relationship with funding agencies are handled by the larger host agency. This is because grants and contracts are almost always made to the host agency, not to the project, per se. The formal contract or agreement is between the host agency and the foundation or government funder. Sometimes there may be little or no direct involvement of the project staff in these matters. Host agencies interface with funding agencies in terms of negotiations regarding overhead or indirect costs, employee fringe benefits rates, and even the type of research procedures that are to be followed. These are areas in which the project may be caught in the middle between host agencies and funders. When, for example, the central research administration for a university negotiates a higher indirect cost rate with the federal Department of Health and Human

Services, each individual project director in the university will have to submit an increased budget to its funding source when applying for a grant.

As noted earlier, it is tempting for the project administrator to avoid these issues since they may be regarded as not being central to the substantive service or research operations. The unfortunate result of such a stance can more often than not be the imposition on the project of host agency-funder agreements that become barriers to a project's smooth operation. Funders and host agencies alike have their own agendas and may also lack sufficient understanding of the realities of the project's program or research procedures and requirements. The result, unless project administrators are actively involved, may be the striking of agreements that are not consistent with the project's needs. Project administration, therefore, requires a strategy for managing not only direct project-host relationship, but for influencing host agency-funder relationship in ways that are in the interests of the project.

Location within a host agency also has important implications for management of the project's staff members. Since the project is time-limited, staff members are concerned with their longer-term professional futures. They often regard the host agency as a potential future employer, and their work within the project is affected by this. A counselor in a one-year project to provide services to persons facing retirement that is located in a large social service agency may have his or her eye on the possibility of a regular full-time job in the agency. In addition, in the case of some projects, regular staff of the host agency may be assigned to the project as part of a cost-sharing arrangement. Salaries of project administrators themselves may be partly or fully paid by the host agency. This results in a duality of identification for such staff. Unless there are carefully worked out agreements or understandings between the project and the host agency, the project's ability to assign and utilize its staff resources when and where they are needed can be adversely affected.

While many problems are created by the relationship with a host agency, there are also distinct strengths in this arrangement that project administrators should seek to maximize. For one thing, the resources and services of host agencies particularly in the area of financial management and the provision of facilities and equipment relieve the project administration of a considerable amount of effort that would otherwise be spent in time-consuming management details. Another important aspect of the host-agency arrangement can be the utilization of the larger agency's standing (for example, its accreditation or licensing, it size, its stability, its history) as a way to further legitimize the project.

One additional aspect of project-host relationships that project administrators must deal with is in connection with issues of ideology. All organizations adopt certain belief systems that justify their activities and decisions. In the human and health services field and in the social and behavioral sciences, these belief systems are usually connected to how problems are defined, what kind of service or research theory and technology is preferred, what kind of administrative structures are desirable, and how best to structure relationships and power among the participants. Projects, of course, develop a set of beliefs in the same areas. However, since projects are frequently developed to be innovative, to test new approaches, and to break new ground, they often may be based on ideological paradigms that deviate from those of the host agency. As a result, it is not unusual for there to be underlying ideological tensions between projects and host agencies. Project administrators must manage these tensions so that they do not develop into unresolved conflicts that threaten the ability of the project to carry out its mission.

One example of this is a mental health project that is located within a graduate school of social work. The project staff, including students, work with patients who have been released from mental hospitals and are living in boarding homes. The project's purpose is to demonstrate new ways to aid in the rehabilitation of these ex-patients. Its program is based on the ideology that ex-patients are subject to a variety of political, social, and economic oppressions, and that their situation is largely the result of not being able to cope with a legitimate sense of alienation from society in general, and work, family, and other social situations in particular. The school, on the other hand, while sponsoring the project, trains students to work with patients from a causal explanation that identifies psychological and interpersonal dysfunctions of individuals as the principal cause of mental problems that lead to hospitalization, and the rehabilitation of ex-patients is therefore best accomplished through psychotherapy and counseling. The innovativeness of the project is a challenge to the host agency's, in this case the school of social work's, explanation of the causes of mental illness as well as the kind of treatment necessary. The project director in this situation must constantly interpret the project's ideology in a manner that will maintain the school's continued support, must build allies and a constituency that support the project, and must use the project's resources in ways that benefit the school.

Throughout this chapter, we have shown how the five characteristics of special projects result in a myriad of demands on project managers. In the next chapter, we shall describe the functions and the roles of project managers as they strive to effectively manage the consequences of these characteristics.

Chapter 3

The Functions and Role of Project Managers

How can a project director or principal investigator begin the implementation of a new project? How can he or she divide up the multitude of tasks that must be undertaken into a manageable plan—recruiting and selecting staff, organizing the staff, starting program or research activities, establishing procedures with the host agency personnel, purchasing and accounting offices, setting up a system for financial management, obtaining office space and equipment. The list seems endless.

Or once in operation, what does a project director do when faced on a Monday morning with a telephone call from the federal grant officer questioning the project's request for shifting $5,000 from salaries to travel; or a university research administration staff member unhappy because she was not sent a copy of the original request; or the failure of the typewriter rental service to deliver a machine needed to type a new grant proposal; or two research assistants out sick; or no heat in the offices?

Project administration is complex, and a multitude of problems and responsibilities faces every project manager. Effective administration requires a strategy that project managers can use to guide them through the maze of demands on them. Demands on project directors come from the expectations and requirements of funding agencies; the policies, philosophy, purposes, and procedures of host agencies; one's own sense of professionalism, ideology, and interests, and from the day-to-day problems of managing the staff, budget, facilities, and program activities of the project. There are no sure-fire formulas for success for project management; it is certainly as much an art as it is a technical craft. However, there is sufficient knowledge and experience about project administration to substantially increase the chances of successful administration through informed action. While every project director or principal investigator develops his or her own strategy and style of administration, certain common characteristics are apparent in terms of the functions that project managers perform and the role they play. The material in this chapter provides a framework for both new and experienced administrators to further refine and develop their approach to administrative strategies and methods. This will be done by describing the major functions that project leaders must carry out and the role they may play in performing these functions in an efficient and effective manner. Subsequent chapters include more detailed methods and techniques for carrying out these functions.

Developing an approach to project management that is based on the functions of project administration has a distinct value. It facilitates the grouping of the myriad of specific activities of project directors into a few manageable categories. The project director is no longer dealing with what may seem to be an endless series of random events, but instead is developing a way to simplify and partialize administrative activities so that action can be better planned and more conscious.

Six Functions of Project Administration

There are six functions that project administrators perform. These six functions include the wide range of managerial tasks that all project heads actually carry out. Depending on the particular substance of the project's program, its size, and the particular kind of funding and host agency that is involved, there may be variations in the relative importance of a given function and in the amount of time spent on each function. Nevertheless, all project administrators engage in all of these functions. These include the need to:

1. *Understand and respond to requirements* that are imposed by host agencies and by funding agencies in order to assure that the flow of resources and the integrity of the project and its operations can be maintained.
2. *Organize the project's staff, activities, and processes* in a manner that will

.

31

expedite the implementation of the substantive programmatic or research activities of the project and of its management.

3. *Lead, direct, and control* the project's programmatic, administrative, and financial activities and processes so that they are efficiently and effectively carried out and completed.

4. *Communicate and report* on performance to funding agencies, the host agency, the project staff, project participants, and external groups.

5. *Resolve internal and external crises* and problems in ways that reduce interference with the pursuit of the project's activities and goals.

6. *Develop plans for future funding* of the project or related activities, or for its incorporation into other activities, or for its termination.

These six functions are all generated by the characteristics of projects outlined in chapter 2. These relationships are shown in figure 3-1.

FIGURE 3-1

Relationship of Project Characteristics and Management Functions

Project Characteristics		Management Functions
		Organize Project
Emphasis on Implementation		Lead, Direct & Control Activities and Finances
Focus on Goal Achievement		
Time-Limited Duration	generate	Resolve Crises
Relationship to Funding Agency		Respond to Requirements
Relationship to Host Agency		Communicate and Report
		Plan for Refunding

The six project management functions overlap because of the interdependent nature of administrative decision making and action. Each decision and act has or may have effects that go well beyond the immediate situation. There are seldom any benign or isolated acts in the administrative process. Sound administrative strategies are built on this fundamental principle and managers must take these interdependencies into account in order to identify the most likely consequences of their actions. Administration is fraught with uncertainties, yet, administrators must act. To the extent that administrators can reduce uncertainty, effectiveness is increased. In order to move in this direction, we shall, in the chapters that follow, make reference to how the various management techniques that are set forth serve to fulfill one or more of the functions of project administration. For example, in describing how to plan and conduct a site visit in chapter 7, we shall show how these activities are related to performing four functions: (1)

complying with funder requirements; (2) directing and controlling programmatic or research activities; (3) reporting on project performance; and (4) refunding of the project.

This approach to administration takes into account some of the salient concepts from the body of knowledge known as general systems theory. These concepts include the recognition that human systems such as projects are essentially "open" systems that, while they establish boundaries to distinguish themselves from their environment, are still dependent on their environment for resources. In addition, projects are also subsystems of a larger entity, the host agency, and therefore subject to considerable influence from this source. At the same time, the project itself is comprised of functional subsystems, mainly a managerial subsystem and a program or research subsystem. The overriding role of managers is to control and manage relationships with the environment and the functioning of these subsystems. This must be done in a way that assures the flow of resources at the same time that it reduces external interference in order to preserve the stability necessary to implement the project's activities and achieve its goals within a time-limited period.

Function One: Understand and Respond to Requirements

All projects are subject to a series of requirements that are imposed by both funding agencies and by host agencies. These include rules, regulations, and guidelines in the following areas:

Personnel procedures—including hiring, affirmative action, personnel rank or grade, employee benefits, personnel policies and practices, salary levels, trainee costs.

Financial management regulations—covering bookkeeping systems, audits, procurement and purchasing, insurance coverage, cost-sharing arrangements, subcontracting, allowable costs, travel, payment of consultant fees.

Programmatic guidelines—including conforming to program activities as set forth in funding proposals, approval of research instruments, human subject review procedures, animal care and treatment, patents and inventions, copyrights, publication and dissemination of information, publicity, safety precautions, eligibility requirements covering participants who receive service or training, the level of effort to be maintained, numbers of persons to be served.

Reporting requirements—including progress and final reports, reporting changes in personnel, budgets or activities, site visits, participation in evaluations, and financial reports.

One of the most frequent sources of difficulties that arises in the course of project administration is the failure to adhere to these requirements. This is especially true in the areas of financial management procedures, personnel procedures, purchasing and procurement, reporting and dissemination of information. Project directors are usually trying to be as efficient as possible and as a result may initiate actions that do not comply with the procedures used by funders or host agencies. This results in time-consuming efforts to correct them at a later time. It also results in heightening the stress between the project and the host or funding agency.

This is illustrated in the case of a project run by a state agency in a rural area. This project was to demonstrate how discharged mental patients could improve their functioning in the community and develop marketable skills by living in and managing a small farm residence for twelve people and growing vegetables for local restaurants. The project began in the spring and needed various seeds immediately. The project director called a local seed company and ordered over $900 worth of seeds. The state purchasing department refused to pay the seed company since the order did not go through the department. It was straightened out after two months of paper work and negotiation requiring hours and hours of the project director's time that should have been devoted to training the residents in planting and growing methods.

The requirements within which project administrators must operate may impose certain procedures that must be followed even though they may seem unnecessary. For example, a training project needed to purchase tape recorders to record group sessions and purchased three recorders at $150 each out of its equipment budget. The university purchasing office refused payment because the items should have been charged against its "consumables" item because to be charged to equipment an item must cost $300 or more.

Such problems arise more in the case of projects lodged in large governmental bureaucracies or those funded by federal and state agencies (as compared to foundation funding) since these agencies have many more rules and regulations to which project operations must adhere. Many of these cumbersome procedures originally developed many years ago during periods of "reform" in order to reduce fraud and favoritism, and to increase accountability and protect against abuses that occurred in earlier years.

Project directors tend to want to just file away statements of requirements from funders, especially if they are very long. They are under pressure to implement activities and do not want to divert attention to other details. In the long run, however, project administrators will be able to move ahead with implementation and to maintain more satisfactory relationships with host agencies and with funders if they take the time to carefully review statements of policy and procedures and to comply with the "letter of the law" as set forth in these regulations.

There is considerable variation in the nature and extent to which requirements are imposed by funding agencies. Foundations and corporate funders have fewer formal requirements than do governmental agencies. And among the various governmental agencies, there is considerable difference in the requirements that they impose on projects. Projects that are funded under contracts as compared to grants are also subject to differing requirements.

For example, in the case of two projects to provide training for alcoholism counselors in how to involve the families of alcoholics in the rehabilitation of the alcoholic person, one was funded by a contract, the other by a grant. The project funded by the grant was required only to submit a final descriptive report of its program to the funder. The project funded by a contract was required to submit monthly financial and program reports before the state agency that was funding the project would release its quarterly payments to the project. In addition, both projects found it necessary to retain psychiatric consultants which had not been anticipated in the original proposal. The grant-funded project did this by using $1,000 from its budget for secretarial services which turned out not to be necessary. The contract-funded project had to wait three months before the contractor approved a similar change in its budget because the contract required submitting any change of this type in writing for formal written approval prior to expending the money.

It should be noted that by stressing compliance we do not mean that project heads should not attempt to maximize their interests by using other methods that are more adversarial such as negotiating and bargaining as described in chapter 5. Rules and regulations are always subject to interpretation, to negotiation, and to deviation. They can often be bent one way or another depending on the skill with which projects build relationships, develop constituencies to support the project's position during negotiation, and exercise whatever political power and support they can to act on their behalf. For example, an expression of interest in and support of a project's work by a congressperson or senator is appropriate and helpful.

Function Two: Organize Staff and Activities

Earlier we discussed the dual emphasis of projects on the implementation of activities and on goal achievement. In response to this, project managers must rather quickly devise and put into place the organizational structures and processes to facilitate effective delivery of programmatic or research activities.

Typical tasks involved in this function are described in a report of the first two weeks of the activities of a new project to develop a county-wide program to help schools serve learning disabled youth more effectively:

> I had a staff of eight persons to work with the eight different school districts in our county. The original proposal had indicated that one person would be assigned to work with each district. But, as we discussed the work that needed to be done it became apparent that intensive work was needed in each district in specialized problems such as teaching methods, how to organize classes, how to assign and evaluate work of learning disabled students, how and where to refer them for special services, and how to involve and work with their families. Thus while there were many advantages to assigning one person to each district in terms of establishing good relations with the district and providing continuity in contact and service to the district, I decided to organize the staff into two technical groups (teaching and use of community resources) and rotate them among the eight school districts.

Projects that involve six or more people generally require that the project personnel be organized into two or more units that have different responsibilities and activities. One of the major questions facing a project head is how best to organize the project in order to achieve its research or service objectives, or what has been referred to as the "embodiment of purposes into an organizational structure."* There are a

---

*Philip Selznick, *TVA and the Grass Roots* (New York: Harper & Row, 1966).

variety of factors that affect decisions regarding organizational arrangements for projects. These include: (1) the policies and norms followed by the host agency regarding organizational structures, job titles, unit titles, and the like; (2) how the particular tasks that need to be performed fall into logical or homogeneous groupings based on such factors as the functions to be fulfilled, the technology or methods involved, types of persons to be served or studied, or the geographical distribution of tasks (in the case of projects that are dispersed over a geographical area); (3) the political interests and philosophy of the project administrator and key project staff with respect to how power and control over resources and decision making should be distributed within the project; (4) the particular objectives of the project and what it seeks to accomplish; and (5) the resources that are available in terms of money, personnel, and time.

Because organizational structure is the result of these competing factors, a wide variety of organizational arrangements are found in actual practice. (In chapter 8, some typical models are illustrated). What usually happens is that structures are established that attempt to make accommodations between the factors. For example, a principal investigator may want to maximize his or her control over the day-to-day research processes by establishing a tight administrative hierarchy. All major research decisions must be approved by the investigator, and research activities are closely supervised in order to maintain quality control. However, the research methods involved may be such that a great deal of autonomy must be exercised by each individual member of the research staff if data acquisition is to be maximized as is the case of qualitative research, participant observation, or "snowball samples" in which respondents are suggested by other respondents. The administrator must devise a structure that will take into account these conflicting needs and play a role that is sometimes quite direct and other times quite laissez-faire.

In spite of these dilemmas every project administrator must move ahead and get the project going. These tasks include:

1. Recruitment, orientation, and deployment of staff.
2. Designation of subunits, or in the case of smaller projects, the assignment of staff to specific roles.
3. Acquisition of physical space, facilities, and equipment; assigning them to personnel; and establishing rules for their use.
4. Adoption of procedures for financial management within the project and with the host agency financial management personnel.
5. Adoption of procedures to guide communication and interaction among the project staff.

6. Adoption of programmatic or research methods and procedures.
7. Institution of management procedures for purposes of decision making, coordination, control, and supervision.
8. Delegation of authority and of responsibility to other staff.
9. Formation of boards and committees and the designation of their roles.
10. Adoption of procedures to control the flow of work, timetables, filing, and storage and retrieval of information.

Function Three: Lead, Direct, and Control Activities, Personnel, and Finances

The third function of project administration is to provide substantive and managerial leadership, direction, and control in order to be sure that the project is running well. Having once established the project's organizational structure and procedures, it is this activity that occupies the major share of the time and energy of a project administrator. It includes being responsible for the programmatic and technical supervision of activities, the management of staff, and the supervision of financial and office procedures.

The typical activities of a project director in relation to this function are exemplified by the following calendar for one day in the life of the administrator of a project to provide counseling and other services to the parents of seriously underweight, prematurely born infants who were to be hospitalized for extended periods of time.

9:00–10:00	Staff meeting
10:00–11:00	Conference with Chief of Pediatrics re: training of residents
11:00–12:00	Training session with residents on social and emotional aspects of hospitalization and separation
12:00– 1:30	Lunch with hospital director on coordination of project with hospital purchasing department
2:00– 3:30	Meeting with project evaluation staff to review patient impact survey
3:30– 4:00	Interview with applicant for counselor position
4:00– 5:00	Review project budget with hospital finance director

Depending on the size and type of project and how responsibilities have been allocated among the project staff, the project director's or principal investigator's leadership role will vary considerably. In those projects in which the project head is also the leading substantive expert, he or she may exert leadership and spend a great deal of time on the day-to-day research or service activities. Much of the managerial detail such as report preparation, record keeping, and budget control may be delegated to another staff member or assistant. In other cases, a project administrator may have more of the managerial role and subsequently spend a lesser amount of time in providing substantive leadership. In either case, however, the project administrator's role is to be an integrating force: the human glue that holds the project together, the person who facilitates the work of others, and the source of final decisions in relation to administrative issues. In addition, it is the project director or principal investigator who carries the burden of maintaining relationships with the host and funding agency during the course of project operations and of final accountability for the project's operations to these agencies.

To be effective in this leadership role, project managers must demonstrate their competency in the managerial and/or substantive area. They must also maintain satisfactory communication with the members of the project staff. If this is not done, the ability to control research or program activities will be severely hampered. Project managers then attempt to exert leadership on the basis of the political power they have as the chief administrator. When this occurs, the manager is not regarded by the staff as a leader but only a "boss" to be gotten around.

The leadership role of the project manager is greatly enhanced when he or she is seen as one who acts in the interests of the project staff and its operations. Project administrators should take great care to communicate their activities in this area to the project staff. Project staff want to be sure the project head is on their side, advocating their position with the host agency, funding agency, and other external bodies.

Demonstrating the effectiveness of the manager as the leader and director of project activities also serves to improve relationships with funding and host agencies. It is not unusual for projects that are actually doing good substantive work to fall into disrepute with funders because the project has not communicated the adequacy of its administrative leadership and direction. To some extent, project administrators must "market" themselves. Not in the crude sense of market manipulation through high pressure or irrelevant advertising, but rather, in the sense of establishing an identity and style of administration that is made known to the various project constituencies, especially to funders and host agencies, by reports, site visits, and other communications.

Leadership styles vary, from managers who attempt to be autocratic to those who attempt to promote democratic participation in decision making and function in a consultative way with project staff and other constituencies such as host agency staff. Maintenance of morale is dependent on the extent to which staff feel informed, valued, respected, and rewarded. Project administrators regardless of their style must convey their regard for these qualities to their staff in concrete and visible ways, not just through words. Public recognition of staff, flexibility in the use of time, salaries, and other benefits are examples of how this may be demonstrated.

In addition to leading, the project manager must keep things under control and assure quality of performance by directing and supervising the project's staff members and activities. The content of such supervision and direction varies widely depending on the technical nature of project activities. Supervising research activities is quite different from directing a training project.

For example, the content of a staff meeting with the staff of a research project may be concerned with progress in completing interviews and data assembly. A staff meeting in a training project may be devoted to the progress in developing training materials and enrollment in training sessions. Both meetings are concerned with the general subject of productivity in the implementation of activities. But the head of the research project must have a first-hand substantive understanding of the procedures involved in conducting research interviews and must know the methods for overcoming any problems in locating respondents, gaining their cooperation, scheduling call backs, completing interview instruments, and the like. The director of the training project must understand the process of locating curriculum materials, designing instructional materials, and the use of multimedia techniques.

Finally, the project director is responsible for financial and business management, including (1) assuring that the project is properly integrated with the financial and business management of the larger host institution and also has its own internal financial control and accountability systems; (2) assuring financial management is consistent with funding agency requirements; (3) controlling expenditures; (4) initiating budget changes; (5) reporting on financial status; and (6) coordinating financial and program operations. It has been pointed out that project managers must become acquainted with the general principles of financial management and accounting. He or she does not have to be an accountant or financial management expert to effectively discharge this role, but does need to understand the language and the basic methods that are utilized.* Methods for effectively carrying out these activities are described in chapter 9.

Function Four: Communicate and Report on Performance

Projects, like other social organizations, depend on communication in order to function. In this regard, projects have two distinct arenas in which they must carry out effective communications. One of these is the internal communications among the project staff in order to facilitate the effectiveness of the various programmatic, research, or training activities in which the project is engaged. The second is the external arena which involves communicating with the host agency, funding agency, and other organizations to which the project is related and on which the project is dependent for the money and other resources and for the legitimation necessary to maintain itself.

The role of project managers in performing this function involves directing five major sets of activities:

1. Communicating with funding sources
   (a) Preparation and submission of formal reports on finances and program in order to comply with requirements
   (b) Preparation and submission of formal and informal reports on project performance in order to create better understanding of the project's operations, problems, and achievements
   (c) Planning and conducting site visits
2. Communicating with host agency
   (a) Preparation and submission of reports on finances, administration, and program to comply with formal requirements and procedures
   (b) Informal communication including written reports and personal contacts to enhance understanding of project operations, problems, and performance
   (c) Formal and informal communication with other units of host agency in order to coordinate efforts and develop collaborative arrangements where necessary
3. External communication with other agencies and organizations
   (a) Preparation and submission of reports to meet requirements of regulatory agencies and groups (e.g., local health department)

---

*See, for example, James T. Kenny, "The Accounting Responsibilities of the Project Administrator," *Grants Magazine*, vol. 3, no. 4 (New York: Plenum, December 1980) pp. 227–231.

    (b) Formal and informal communication to further understanding of project operations and to build constituencies and support among community organizations, professional groups, and the like

4. Internal communications among project personnel

    (a) Planning and conducting staff orientation and training programs related to understanding the project's purposes, procedures, and operations

    (b) Consultation with staff with respect to administrative and programmatic decisions

    (c) Arranging for staff participation in problem solving with respect to administrative procedures and solving of substantive and technical problems

    (d) Keeping staff informed about what is going on, problems, and progress

    (e) Providing information to project participants (e.g., research subjects, trainees, program participants) in connection with project purposes, operations, and progress

5. Communication regarding project achievements

    (a) Preparation of final reports on research or program

    (b) Dissemination of final reports to funders, host agencies, scientific and professional community, community organizations, and the like

The project director or principal investigator is the person who has the final responsibility to see that there is a planned program of internal and external communications and to make sure it is carried out. Communication is the basis upon which the relationships that are necessary to maintain the project and implement its activities can be developed. Project administrators must be highly visible in these efforts. Interestingly, the project administrators who successfully carry out this function seem to be the ones who are also successful in their efforts to develop and obtain funding for new projects.

Function Five: Control Crises and Problems

No organization, especially a project, functions without many short-term crises and problems—a research interviewer quits, the foundation or government check does not arrive on time, a duplicating machine breaks down, a funder disapproves a needed budget expenditure or change, papers are misfiled, a computer program is not sufficiently debugged. Many of them are minor. But, for any project with the pressure to complete its work within a given time period, these "normal crises" can easily become major barriers unless they are overcome quickly. It is no surprise, therefore, that successful project administrators usually report that they take an active role in the solution of these problems. Project managers are called upon to deal with many minor problems that would often be dealt with by other staff persons in typical ongoing organizations. In large projects that have a number of administrative staff members, the project heads may be spared having to deal firsthand with these events. However, the wise administrator stays on top of minutiae such as these and insists that other staff report on the solution of any problems that may interfere with the implementation of the project's work and schedule.

Function Six: Prepare for Refunding

One of the most crucial functions that project administrators spend their time on is the preparation of proposals for refunding of the project or for a new project. The formal preparation of refunding and continuation proposals and applications may actually absorb a relatively small amount of the project administrator's time during the course of a typical one-year project. However, it is an activity that demands a great deal of effort and produces more than a little anxiety.

It is important to realize that there is much more to the refunding process than the preparation of the formal proposal. All contacts by the project with a funder and host agency may eventually influence a refunding decision. The effectiveness of the project's operations and the results it obtains also have a potential bearing on the refunding possibilities. The number of publications (and citations) that emanate from project work are important criteria for refunding of research projects. The impressions that funders get of how well the project is being managed with respect to its finances and administrative procedures also influences funder decisions in terms of future funding. Thus, in effect, the refunding function is one that tends to permeate all aspects of project operations and, in this sense, is of utmost importance as a component of project administration.

Refunding is affected by the result of evaluations of the project's activities, the extent to which it is achieving its objectives, and the efficiency of its operations. These evaluations may take the form of formal research evaluations, or they may be based on site visits from funders, or may simply be reflected in project progress and final re-ports to funders.

In addition to refunding, project managers also play a role in devel-oping sources of nongrant financial support for project activities after the grant runs out. Many funders require that funding proposals in-clude a plan on how this continued support will be obtained. Project heads are usually involved in implementing these plans which may include developing fund-raising events, charging fees for services, getting host agencies to include the project as part of their ongoing operations, and so forth.

In the remaining chapters, the methods and techniques to carry out these six functions are described in detail. We begin in the next chap-ter with the first function—that of understanding and complying with requirements.

Chapter 4

How to Understand and Respond to Requirements

The first component of a program of effective project management is to understand and develop methods to respond to the requirements that are imposed on projects by the granting agencies and host agencies. Whether it be a foundation, a government agency, or university, the ability of a project to assure the flow of funds and other resources necessary for its survival is dependent upon the proficiency with which the project staff is able to deal with these requirements. Ironically, this is the area of project management to which many project directors and principal investigators pay the least attention. Funder requirements, especially those imposed by federal and state agencies, may be embodied in long, boring, and detailed documents that are peppered with a profusion of bureaucratic and legal language. At first glance much of this material appears irrelevant to project leaders and tends to be quite intimidating. Often the project administrator simply hopes that someone else (the university's research administration, the host agency's executive director, the city's budget office) is taking care of these bureaucratic and technical affairs. And, often they are; but only in part. It is a serious managerial mistake to avoid spending the time and effort to develop a thorough understanding of the grant requirements. To fail to handle them expeditiously will only result in problems for the smooth operation of the project. Any project director who has had a grant payment held up because a financial report was not submitted knows this only too well. While every project head secretly hopes for a completely unconditional grant, such an autonomous luxury is seldom, if ever, a reality.

All major areas of project operations are subject to the requirements of funders and host agencies. These requirements are discussed in this chapter and include: record keeping and accessibility; monitoring and reporting on performance; audits; role of project directors/principal investigators; publications and publicity; copyrights; inventions and patents; protection of human subjects; approval of research instruments and forms; cost sharing; equipment; changes in program, budget, and personnel; transfer of grants; procurement; financial administration; cost principles; conflict of interest; and civil rights.

The tasks that project administrators must carry out in relationship to grant requirements include being able to first obtain all the relevant requirements and identify their significance for the project. They must establish efficient methods to assure compliance with requirements. In doing this, they must deal with inconsistencies between written requirements and the way they are interpreted by granting agency personnel. In addition, they need to deal with discrepancies among the various requirements and to overcome requirements that are not in the interests of the project. They must resolve differences that develop between the project, the granting agency, and the host agency over issues related to compliance. Finally, they must keep track of changes in funder requirements that might affect continuation or renewal of their grants.

It should be recognized that funder requirements are legally binding on the project and that most have the effect of law. Administrators must regard compliance with these regulations as a serious matter. At the same time, projects are legally protected against arbitrary regulation and against acts by grant personnel that are not authorized by written regulations. Grantees have a number of rights in the relationship, including rights to appeal, grievance, and remedies. Requirements, therefore, are something to be managed in the interests of the project. They are seldom as precise as they appear and there is, in practice, considerable latitude in the way they can be applied.

Where Grant Requirements Come From

Successful management of grant requirements is in part dependent on one's attitude toward these requirements. Understanding that requirements do not come out of thin air (although they often seem to) and are not really "arbitrary and irrational" (although sometimes you are quite sure they are) is the first step in getting on top of this aspect of project management. In this section, therefore, we will discuss the way grant requirements have developed in recent years.

The giving of money or goods in one form or another is as old as the history of people. Early giving was on a person-to-person basis. Organized religion introduced a third party, the church, into this process. And eventually, the state or the government began to exercise control over the giving of others and became a source of funds itself. The legal and institutional roots of the contemporary system of grants in the United States can be located in the Statute of Charitable Uses passed in England in 1603 during the reign of Queen Elizabeth. Part of what is referred to as the Elizabethan Poor Laws, this landmark act codified a variety of prior acts and provided, among other things, the authorization for government to be increasingly involved in aid for charitable purposes.

In the United States, organized governmental disbursement of funds to various kinds of state and social service groups dates back to the colonial era. The provision of government aid in the form of some type of grant, however, was a miniscule aspect of governmental activity until the mid-1800s when certain acts were passed to make grants to charitable and educational institutions and to industrial and commercial interests. These included acts to legitimatize the provision of land by the government to the developing private railroad system (sometimes at the expense of Native Americans) and to provide land for agricultural schools which gave rise to what are now known as land grant colleges and universities. In 1865, Congress established the Freedman's Bureau, which many consider to be the first government "welfare" agency. The Bureau provided financial aid to found black schools and educational institutions and to support other programs. By 1900, the provision of cash grants was well established in the federal government. Public funds were also beginning to be used to aid private charitable institutions. A study in New York City, conducted in 1978, identified forty-six health and social agencies, founded between 1822 and 1899, that were still in operation. In 1900, only eight of these agencies were receiving government aid. By 1978, all of them were receiving aid for special projects, or for the provision of specific services to clients, or both.*

---

*Nelly Hartogs and Joseph Weber, *Impact of Government Funding on the Management of Voluntary Agencies* (New York: Greater New York Fund, 1978).

Foundations also began to be established in the 1800s by the very rich "robber barons" of the day. There were eighteen known foundations in existence prior to the turn of the century when the organized foundation as we know it today came into being. In the early 1900s, Andrew Carnegie established several large foundations and these became the prototype for other foundations which were established by rich and powerful families, including those of John D. Rockefeller. These foundations served the dual purpose of supporting philanthropy and protecting the large fortunes that were being amassed by these families.

During the reform era of the early 1900s, government programs and, to a somewhat lesser extent, private charities became the target of reform efforts to correct the many abuses, frauds, and inefficiencies that were identified. The present far-flung system of regulation, rules, and requirements in the grants field is the result of attempt after attempt since 1900 to correct abuses among government and foundation grant programs, and to prevent private interests from benefiting at public expense.

The growth of foundation and government grant programs has been steady during the 1900s. The period of greatest growth has been since World War II. The most dramatic increase in the support of nondefense domestic programs has occurred since 1965. Today there are more than 25,000 foundations, 90 percent of which were organized after 1940.* Most of the 1,000 domestic assistance programs of the federal government were established in this same period.[†] Thus, the current pattern of regulations and requirements in the grant field has developed piecemeal over a relatively short period of time. It is little wonder that the kinds of requirements and procedures facing most projects often seem to be poorly formulated, irrational, or irrelevant.[‡]

Problems associated with grant regulations have been recognized in the U.S. Congress for some time. During the 1970s, the Subcommittee on Intergovernmental Relations had under consideration various legislation to improve the government's grant practices. The Internal Revenue Service has acted to correct deficiencies in the operation of some foundations. The Office of Management and Budget has attempt-

---

The Foundation Directory, 8th Edition (New York: The Foundation Center, 1981).

[†]*1980 Catalog of Federal Domestic Assistance,* Office of Management and Budget (Washington, D.C.: U.S. Government Printing Office, 1980).

[‡]*Summary and Concluding Observations, The Intergovernmental Grant System: An Assessment and Proposed Policies,* Advisory Commission on Intergovernmental Relations (Washington, D.C.: U.S. Government Printing Office, 1978).

ed to provide some degree of uniformity and simplification in the grant administration practices of federal agencies and of grantees. However, as of the 1980s, most observers still consider the situation unsatisfactory.

The federal government and, to a lesser degree, state governments are the key actors in the grant requirements arena. The government plays two major roles in the area of regulation. It sets up and enforces requirements that guide its own grant programs, and also exercises control over the foundation field, particularly through the tax laws and their enforcement. State governments must approve the operations of foundations, which must also have the approval of the IRS to maintain their tax-free status. In addition, foundations must report their activities to the IRS and to state agencies. With the passage of the Tax Reform Act of 1969, foundations have been subject to increasing regulation in connection with the disposal of their income. As federal, state, and local governments have expanded their grant programs, they have promulgated an ever-increasing quantity of rules and regulations to govern the use of the funds these programs provide.

The Sources of Federal and Governmental Requirements

The requirements that grant-supported projects are subject to have their roots in a number of particular sources. The broadest source of these requirements is the U.S. Constitution and court interpretations and rulings. All laws that authorize the formulation of regulations for grant programs are ultimately based on constitutional provisions particularly those in the Fifth Amendment (due process) and the Fourteenth Amendment (equal protection under the law).

Another source of grant requirements is the general legislative provisions and executive orders that apply to all government operations such as those related to civil rights and freedom of information.

A third source is the agency-wide regulations that affect all programs within an agency. Many of these are included as subtitles of the *Code of Federal Regulations* such as Title 45, Public Welfare, Sub-title A, which applies to grant administration of social welfare programs within the federal Department of Health and Human Services.

A fourth source is the specific legislation that authorizes a particular grant program. These legislative provisions may also be incorporated

49

into a fifth and major source of requirements, which are the rules, regulations, and guidelines issued by the granting agency. These may cover a group of programs within an agency as well as individual programs. For example, the Public Health Service issues a set of grant administration policies that cover all of the various grant programs within the Public Health Service, and each individual program within the Public Health Service issues further specific guidelines.

A sixth source is the circulars and regulations that are issued by the Office of Management and Budget (OMB), such as circulars A102, A110, A21, A-122, A95.* While congressional studies have found that these OMB attempts to establish government-wide grant requirements have been effective, their legal status is not clear since these regulations are technically issued by OMB to other federal agencies. These agencies in turn incorporate them into their own requirements and into the *Code of Federal Regulations.*

A final source of requirements imposed on projects supported by federal grants is the specific conditions that are attached to an individual grant and which are written into the formal Notice of Award or are expressed in a grant agreement, letter of agreement, contract, or some other written document that applies only to the specific grant. In this regard it is also important to keep in mind that the approved project proposal or application material that was submitted to obtain the grant represents, in part, an agreement between the grantor and the grantee agencies. In some cases, particularly when a project is funded under a formal contract, the proposal may be appended as part of the contract, or it may be referred to as part of a grant award.

Grants and Contracts

The two major instruments for conveying funds to support projects are grants and contracts. Government grant programs use both; foundations and corporate funders seldom use contracts. While there are certain clear differences between the two, there is also a good deal of misunderstanding and lack of clarity regarding the relative impact they have on project operations. It is generally believed that, from the standpoint of project administration, the grant mechanism is prefera-

---

* These circulars are reviewed in appendix D.

ble since it involves a lesser degree of control over research, training, and service activities. This belief is largely based on the basic distinction between grants and contracts. That is, contracts specify an end product or service that the contractor must produce in order to receive the funds. These products may take the form of written materials such as a research report, training materials and curriculum, or a manual. Sometimes the "product" is expressed in units of service to be provided, such as serving 500 older persons or providing 1,000 hours of instruction, or 5,000 patient visits. Grants do not usually include such a provision. Grants are focused on supporting the process involved in a research, service, or training program.

However, a number of congressional studies have been conducted which raise questions about this distinction. They have pointed out that grants may have requirements imposed on them that are tighter than contract provisions, and that contracts may be administered as loosely as any grant. The popularity of the grant mechanism dates back to 1958, when Congress was considering how to respond to the scientific and technological position the United States found itself in following the Russian launching of Sputnik I. At that time, Congress passed the Grant Act of 1958 (PL 85–934) which authorized all federal agencies that had the power to enter into contracts to substitute grants if they wished. It was thought that this would provide an incentive for more speedy and efficient conduct of the research and development efforts that were seen as necessary to catch up with the Russian scientific superiority in the space field.

In actual practice both grant-supported projects and those supported by contracts may be subject to a degree of supervision and control that ranges from slight to substantial. The enforcement of requirements under which both operate are subject to considerable latitude, depending on the decisions that are made by the granting agency. Grantees and contractors must abide by many of the same requirements of the federal establishment, but these are found in different source documents. For example, when the government conveys funds by using a contract, the contractor is governed by the provisions of the Federal Procurement Regulations, the Armed Service Procurement Regulations, and special provisions that are attached to the individual contract. Recipients of grants are subject to the requirements of the *Code of Federal Regulations* (CFR), the regulations of the particular agency and grant program, and conditions that are attached to the individual grant award by the granting agency.

Contracts are almost always used when the government is procuring services from profit-making firms. They may also be used to obtain services from nonprofit organizations and, on occasion, with other governmental units such as a planning commission. Contracts are always used in cases where a formal request for proposal (RFP) has been issued that invites the submission of proposals that are required to meet certain specifications designated by the contracting government agency. Grants are usually used to support research, service, and training programs that are based on proposals that are either unsolicited or which are in response to government-issued program announcements and guidelines. Most governmental support for research through major agencies such as the National Institutes of Health and the National Science Foundation is in the form of grants. However, some shift in this pattern has occurred in recent years as the Public Health Service and the Institutes have opened the door wider to support research and training by profit-making organizations. In these cases, contracts are used. Similarly, the Department of Labor and state and local manpower agencies support training programs in private industry by contracting with individual firms.

Congressional studies have found that the conditions under which some federal programs decide on whether to use the grant or contract mechanism are not particularly clear and have often been quite arbitrary. As a result, for many years Congress has attempted to clarify the conditions under which different mechanisms should be used. In considering such legislation, many abuses of the contract and grant system have also come to light and many of them have been attributed to the lack of clarity and the conflicting regulations that govern their award and administration. Finally, in 1978, Congress passed the Federal Grants and Cooperative Agreement Act. This legislation established three main categories for the support and procurement of services and the support of research training and service activities:

1. Contracts would be used in cases where the services that are to be provided are for the direct use of the government or for ultimate public use. Bridges, roads, and military equipment are obvious examples of cases that would be covered.
2. Cooperative Agreements would be used in cases where the contractor is carrying out a government program and where there would need to be substantial involvement of the government in the performance of the activity. A technical assistance project to assist the implementation of a government program to provide technical assistance to rural economic development organizations where both contractor personnel and government personnel are involved would be an example of this kind of situation.

3. Grants would be used to support activities that have public purposes but do not provide direct services or goods for the use of the government and where little or no governmental involvement would be involved in the performance of the activity.

The implementation of this legislation was made the responsibility of OMB and obviously involved a considerable amount of planning. By the time the Reagan administration took office in January of 1981, these new procedures had still not been fully implemented.

This act reflected the confusion about the nature of grants that became exacerbated as the result of the substantial increase in federal grants of all kinds since 1965. There is no standard system to guide the relationship between granting agencies and grantees, and thus these relationships are subject to considerable variation and are often characterized by uncertainty. Some granting agency managers will try to push to the limits their authority in relationship to grantees, but most tend not to do this. Whether the project is funded by a government grant or by a government contract does not appear to be the determining factor in such matters.

Regardless of the basic causes of such problems in relationships with granting agencies, the prescription for what the project administrator needs to do is still the same: know the regulations and use them in the interests of project effectiveness and efficiency!

TYPES OF GRANTS

There are a number of different types of grants. The most frequent type of grant used to support research, services and training activities is the project grant or training grant. Project grants provide for a total set amount of money to be paid the grantee for work whose scope and estimated cost have been defined in a proposal or application. Grants of this type include research grants, demonstration grants, training grants, and program grants.

Another main type of grant is the formula grant and grant-in-aid which provides funds for rather broad purposes on the basis of some formula that is specified in legislation such as population, unemployment rates, or poverty rates. These grants are used primarily to transfer funds from one level of government to another, usually from the federal government to states or municipalities, or from states to municipalities or school districts.

Similar to these grants are the revenue sharing grants and the block grants, which developed in the 1970s for the support of community development programs by the Department of Housing and Urban Development (HUD) and social services programs by the Department of Health and Human Services (HHS) under Title XX of the Social Security Act. In 1981, the Reagan administration increased the use of block grants to the states and local governments when Congress approved new block grant programs to support activities in health, welfare, and housing.

This means that many projects must turn to state agencies rather than federal agencies for support. This results in the necessity for projects to conform to state rules and requirements, many of which will be in the early stages of formulation due to the newness of some of the block grant programs. Block grants are always made to the states or local governments; they are not used for the direct federal support of nonprofit agencies. Rather, nonprofit agencies must seek these funds from state or local government.

Another type of grant that is used particularly among colleges and universities is the institutional grant that provides funds on some type of formula basis to institutions and may take into consideration the existing pattern of grants in the institution.

TYPES OF CONTRACTS

There are two general types of contracts that are used. One is the fixed-price contract and the other is the cost-reimbursable contract. They differ primarily in the arrangements that are specified for paying the contractor. The fixed-price contract is used where the cost of the work can be accurately estimated ahead of time. The recipient guarantees to perform the work within the contract period and receives a fixed amount of money regardless of the actual costs. Sometimes these contracts include a provision for a price revision which provides an opportunity to negotiate the price up or down (within certain limits) upon completion of the work.

Cost-reimbursable contracts provide for the recipient to be reimbursed for the costs that are actually incurred up to certain ceiling amounts that are specified in the contract. These are referred to as allowable costs. A variation of this type of contract is the cost-plus-fixed-fee contract. This type of contract provides for reimbursement to the contractor of the allowable costs plus a fee which is usually expressed as a percentage of the total costs (for example, 8 percent of total costs). This kind of contract is used with profit-making firms. Such contracts are not used with nonprofit organizations, colleges, or universities.

How to Understand and Respond to Requirements

Contracts usually have two sections; one section contains the standard requirements and provisions that govern all contracts, usually called "boiler-plate" provisions. The other section contains special provisions that pertain to the specific contract. This includes specifications for the product such as a research report or the service such as technical assistance to be provided. It also includes the specific time period for completion and provisions regarding the project staff that are expected to work on the contract such as, who the principal investigator is to be, and the total amount of staff time (for example, person-years) that the project is to utilize.

Foundation Requirements

Foundations, unlike government agencies, seldom have elaborate statements of requirements to which grant recipients must comply. This does not mean, however, that the foundation-funded project is completely free of requirements. Many projects take place within host agencies that have other activities that are federally funded and, therefore, many federal rules apply to all aspects of the host agency's operation, including foundation-sponsored activities. Many host agencies, particular state and local governmental agencies, and universities have incorporated requirements into their own operations that parallel the scope and complexity of federal requirements. Many of these publish a project directors' handbook or similar manual.

In addition, there are many federal, state, and local laws that apply to a foundation-sponsored project, such as those in the area of equal opportunity in employment.

In general, a foundation will require:

> The funds must be used in accordance with the scope of work and budget submitted by the grantee in its proposal or application.

> The funds must be used for charitable purposes in the sense that the project activities are consistent with the charitable or educational purposes of the foundation itself.

> The grantee must obtain foundation approval or at least inform the foundation of any changes in the proposed work or budget before such changes are made.

> The grantee must submit periodic and final reports on their finances and substantive activities to the foundation for review.

The funds for grantees may be held up in cases where the foundation has some question about the project performance or the extent to which it is adhering to its originally stated purposes and scope of activities.

The foundation may call for an independent audit of the grantee's operation when the foundation believes it necessary.

It should be clear from the foregoing, which is based on a survey of the requirements of a group of larger foundations, that grants from foundations are not simply gifts with no strings attached. At the same time, the experience of most persons in the field of project management is that a project has much less of an administrative burden placed upon it with respect to compliance with requirements when the project is foundation funded as compared to government funded.

Host Agency Requirements

Host agency requirements for projects vary greatly according to the type and size of the agency. Most large governmental agencies and public universities and colleges at the state or local level will have formal requirements that parallel those of the federal government.

Large, nonprofit host agencies, such as private universities, which are recipients of substantial federal or state funds will also have their own requirements that parallel the federal requirements. However, sometimes nonprofit host agencies tend to have less cumbersome formal procedures to be followed in complying with these regulations. For example, a change in procurement procedure can often be quickly negotiated with the agency's purchasing department, when some item of equipment or a publication is urgently needed for a project, while such an action can take weeks or longer in a governmental agency.

Typical Requirements

Because federal requirements often provide the framework for most other requirements, they are the primary source used in the following description of typical requirements. While each individual funding program may have certain special regulations, the following list cites the requirements that are almost always covered. It is based on an analysis of the various OMB circulars, sections of the *Code of Federal Regulations*, grant administration policies from a number of agencies in the Department of Health and Human Services, the National Science Foundation, HUD, two large state agencies that have substantial grant programs, and a survey of twenty large foundations.

Project administrators can use these descriptions as a checklist of the areas in which they should be sure to acquaint themselves with the specific rules of the funding agency and host agency. As noted earlier, always make a written request to the agency for its written requirements. Keep a written notation of the response that is received. While the argument that you "weren't told" or "didn't know" usually has little or no legal standing, it is useful to have a record of whether a funder did or did not respond to your request since this can be used in the process of negotiating with funding agencies and host agencies.

RECORD KEEPING AND ACCESSIBILITY

Grant-supported projects are permitted to follow their own practices in keeping their financial and program records as long as they conform with certain minimum guidelines. Records must be kept for a three-year period after completion of the grant period. They must be accessible for audit and examination.

Contrary to public opinion, the provisions of the Federal Freedom of Information Act (the right to see public records) do not apply to the records of grantees, nor do the provisions of PL 93–579, the Federal Privacy Act of 1974 (the right to know what is in your personnel file). These acts apply only to the records and files of federal agencies. However, most states have their own versions of freedom of information and privacy act provisions which do apply to projects. Also, host agencies usually have policies, pertaining to a project, that correspond to the provisions of these acts. Until faced with some crisis, most project administrators fail to find out what the state laws and host agency policies are in this area. All it usually requires is a telephone call to the agency's legal counsel or state attorney general's office to obtain them.

The confidentiality of records on case material is governed by individual state laws and host agency policies and is sometimes assured through provisions embodied in a particular funding act. All project records, like those of any other agency, are subject to court subpoenas and must be produced.

The U.S. General Accounting Office (GAO) conducts audits and studies of federally-supported programs and, as an agency of the Congress, has the right of access to all records of a federally-funded project. So does the granting agency and any organization retained by the government to conduct evaluations and audits. Host agencies, on the other hand, may have policies that conflict with the federal position regarding access to records, and, as a result, there have been innumerable problems over this matter. In most cases it is possible to negotiate an acceptable compromise with the federal agency. An example of this is the case of a university-based project supported by the Public Health Service to provide services and conduct research related to families experiencing sudden infant death syndrome. The GAO, as part of a congressionally-mandated assessment of these programs, wanted to review case records of families being served and conduct its own interviews with them. The university took the position that this violated its confidential relationship with these families and would impair its future relationship with them. A compromise was struck that called for the university's project staff to contact the family to see if they were willing to be interviewed; the GAO followed up only if the families agreed.

Most funders and agencies involved in evaluations are usually understanding of such situations and are amenable to negotiated solutions even though, technically, they usually have the right of access to all records. In such negotiations, the project must be firm in its position and have a rationale for it that makes sense.

MONITORING AND REPORTING ON PROGRAM/RESEARCH PERFORMANCE

Granting agencies expect that grantees will monitor their performance to assure that adequate progress is being made to achieve the goals of the project. At a minimum, a project is required to submit some type of final report on its activities and performance. Most federal programs require this report to be submitted by the time the financial status report must be submitted which is usually ninety days after completion of the project.

Many granting agencies also expect that periodic reports, usually quarterly, will be submitted. Projects supported by contracts that have been awarded in accordance with the government's formal procurement standards will have to submit monthly progress reports. In addition to written reports, some projects may be required to provide periodic oral briefings to grant agency staff. And, of course, progress reports need to be presented at the time of site visits. Project heads should always check with the granting agency to ascertain the exact requirements for performance reports. In some cases, the granting agency or foundation may not have a formal reporting requirement but the program officer or grant manager will indicate that reports should be submitted at specified periods. Since granting agency personnel can change, any agreements of this kind should always be obtained in writing.

There is no standardized federal (or foundation) format for program reports. However, at least four kinds of information are almost always called for in such reports: (1) what activities took place during the period covered by the report; (2) what was accomplished in relation to the project's goals; (3) an explanation of any problems, slippages, or unusual events affecting the project's performance or budget; and (4) plans for overcoming problems and for future activities.

Any reports that are submitted to federal and to most state agencies will be subject to the federal or state freedom of information act. Since they potentially may be released to the public, the inclusion of information on clientele or individuals should be avoided.

In addition to regular periodic reports, grantees of federal programs are also required to report any matters that occur between scheduled report dates if these events have a significant impact on the project budget or program, or impair its ability to achieve its objectives.

Progress reports should be kept brief and typically are submitted in duplicate (contract-supported projects may require additional copies). The submission of programmatic, technical, and scientific reports is always the responsibility of the project director or principal investigator, as contrasted to financial reports, which may be prepared and submitted by the host agency's financial unit that administers grant funds. Program reporting is an extremely important activity since failure to adhere to funder requirements in this area may hold up the receipt of grant funds from the granting agency and may also impair applications for new or continuation funding.

AUDITS

All government-supported projects are required to cooperate with the government's right to audit. Many foundations also reserve the right to audit a project's finances or require the project to assure that an annual audit is conducted by a certified public accountant. Most audits are conducted upon the completion of a project, but may be conducted at any time. Federal agencies and state agencies usually have their own auditing units to perform routine audits. In some cases, a private auditing or accounting firm may be retained to conduct an audit, especially if there are serious problems related to financing of a program. The Department of Health and Human Services has its own auditing arm which performs the audits for almost all of the research, training, and service projects supported with federal funds through HHS. Audit activities are usually limited to the financial records and units of the host agency, and project personnel may have little or no involvement in this process. In cases where projects are free standing (that is, independent of a host agency), the project's own records are audited and project personnel will be directly involved. The involvement of project personnel depends largely on the extent to which financial records and management responsibilities are centralized in an overall host agency unit, such as a research foundation or research administration. Federal regulations stipulate that host agencies that are regular recipients of grant funds are expected to have their own internal audits conducted at least every two years.

Regardless of the fact that audits are primarily the responsibility of host agencies, project heads should ensure that any auditing problems will be avoided. As part of their role in directing and controlling project activities, they should be certain that all project records, expenditures, and income are well documented and up to date. They also must be certain that the project is operating in accordance with the funding and host agency financial administration procedures, especially in connection with procurements, disbursements, purchasing, and personnel actions (the areas where most problems occur). Preparation for the audit is something that project administrators need to see as an appropriate ongoing responsibility, not one that gets discharged at the last moment when the audit itself takes place. In chapter 9, systems to ensure proper financial management, control, and records are described.

PROJECT DIRECTORS/PRINCIPAL INVESTIGATORS

The following excerpt from the NIH Guide for Grants and Contracts (vol. 9, no. 8, 6 June 1980) is typical of federal requirements regarding project heads:

B. *Background*: Code of Federal Regulations, Title 42, Part 52, defines a principal investigator as "a single individual designated by the grantee in the grant application and approved by the Secretary, who is responsible for the scientific and technical direction of the project." The regulation also stipulates that applications for grants must include the "name and qualifications of the principal investigator and requires that he or she continue to be responsible for the conduct of the project for the duration of the project period . . . "

D. *Policy*: The single individual identified by the applicant institution as the principal investigator in an application for research project grant support must be the person who has the major responsibility for the scientific and technical direction of the project. Any proposed change of the designated principal investigator must be approved in advance in writing by the NIH awarding Bureau, Institute, or Division . . .

Some government funders, and most foundations, do not impose such rigid regulations regarding assurances as to who the project head will be and his or her qualifications. Nevertheless, projects should always keep funders informed in writing of any changes in project heads.

PERSONNEL

While changes in project directors or principal investigators may need to be submitted in writing and approved in writing by the granting agency, a fuzzier area has to do with changes among other members of the project staff. Federal regulations usually refer to "key people" as another group for whom replacement or changes must be approved. If the notice of the grant award names or identifies these key project people, it is necessary to obtain prior approval for changes among this group. A résumé and/or biographical sketch that explains and emphasizes the qualifications of the proposed replacement should be prepared and submitted to the granting agency along with the request.

PUBLICATIONS AND PUBLICITY

Special Report Requirements. Many government awards require specific end products in the form of reports that describe what content must be covered, the format, and the number of reports. These requirements are included as special provisions in the notice of the grant award or in the contract.

Acknowledgment of Support and Disclaimers. Grantees are encouraged and, in some cases, required to make the results of their activities available to the public. In so doing, they are expected to acknowledge that the work was supported by a grant and from what granting agency. Some funding agencies also require a disclaimer that the information does not necessarily reflect the views of the supporting agency.

Reprints. Submission of reprints of publications or articles that result from the work of some grant-supported projects are sometimes required. The Public Health Service, for example, frequently includes this requirement.

COPYRIGHTS

Grantees are often free to copyright material developed from work that is done under a grant. This is not true for work done under contracts, however. In these cases the copyright is usually to be held by the technical grantee which is generally the host agency (for example, a university or hospital) rather than the project, per se. Large host agencies have their own policies regarding copyrights as well. Government grant programs expect that a copyright of this kind will exclude any limitation on governments's use of the material. If there is to be commercial distribution or sale of copyright material by the grantee or project staff, it is not unusual that the granting agency will have to give approval to this arrangement. The reason for this is to attempt to see that activities supported by public funds are not converted into profitable activities for private persons or interests.

Many host agencies allow individual project personnel to hold copyrights to material but, like the federal establishment, prohibit any restriction on the host agency's own right to disseminate project results. There are no standardized government-wide regulations or standards in the federal government regarding copyrights and royalties. They are prescribed, therefore, by each individual granting program. Foundations, on the other hand, seldom impose restrictive requirements with respect to copyrights.

The lack of uniform standards and the conflicting interests of the various parties involved (that is, the grantor, the host agency, the project personnel) have led to many serious conflicts and much litigation in connection with copyrights. Project heads should not enter into publication agreements with publishers without carefully checking on the policies of both the granting agency and the host agency. Project directors who anticipate publication should clarify the copyright policies that will apply to the project at the beginning of a project and negotiate the arrangements that will be in their best interest.

INVENTIONS AND PATENTS

A complete written description of inventions developed as part of the government-supported project usually must be submitted to the granting agency. Grant agency policies and host agency policies vary considerably in connection with patents and, as with copyrights, there are frequent disputes in this regard. If it is expected that patent issues will come up, these matters are best negotiated with host agencies and grantors at the time the grant itself is negotiated. Some large host agencies, such as universities, have separate standing institutional agreements with the Department of Health and Human Services, and patent rights are determined in accordance with such agreements. Principal investigators should ascertain if this is the case in their institutions. If not, HHS, for example, reserves the right to determine whether patent applications shall be made and to decide on the disposition of patent rights. The National Science Foundation research grants are subject to a patent and invention clause and, like HHS, it reserves the right to determine if a patent application should be filed and the disposition of rights. Many universities have a policy whereby they own patentable inventions developed in grant-supported projects and provide for a percentage of gross royalties to go to the inventor.

HUMAN SUBJECTS RESEARCH

Research activities of any kind that involve human subjects and are supported by federal grants are subject to a set of policies, regulations, and review procedures that are intended to protect the persons who are the subjects of the research. Many state and local health, welfare, and educational institutions have developed additional policies and procedures to implement the federal rules and to apply these procedures to all research whether federally funded or not. The basic federal regulations are set forth in the *Code of Federal Regulations,* Title 45, Part 46, Protection of Human Subjects.

Any researcher would agree that human subjects must be protected from physical, social, psychological, and economic risks, and that their rights and welfare must be safeguarded. When the elaborate rules and procedures that have developed in order to assure this protection are not understood and followed, the result is a considerable loss of time (and money) to the project. The energy of principal investigators that should be spent on substantive research activities is unnecessarily diverted.

The key to dealing with human subject requirements is to be found in understanding the role and function of Institutional Review Boards (IRBs) and of the federal review process. IRBs are required of all institutions receiving federal research funds, and these groups must review all grant applications involving human subject research prior to submission of federal funding agencies. The federal review staff and panels, in turn, must be satisfied that adequate review has taken place by the IRB and that the project has an adequate protocol to ensure the (1) informed consent, (2) privacy, (3) confidentiality, and (4) safety of research subjects. In carrying out the research activities, it is essential that the written protocol approved by the IRB and the funder is followed by the project. Any subsequent changes in the protocol must be submitted to the IRB and the funding agency. Similarly, all applications for renewals or continuations of research projects must again be reviewed by the IRB and submitted to the funder as a prerequisite to receiving additional funds. Most large host agencies have standard forms for use in the review process and all federal research grant applications call for this information to be included. The federal form for human subjects information is in appendix B.

CLEARANCE OF RESEARCH INSTRUMENTS AND FORMS

There is a good deal of misunderstanding regarding the federal requirements that specify when a federally-funded research project must obtain clearance from OMB for forms to be used to collect data. Federal rules stipulate that when an instrument is to be used to obtain data from ten or more people, it must obtain prior clearance from OMB only if:

1. The project is supported by a contract (as distinguished from a grant).
2. The research project is being conducted for (or jointly with) a federal agency. (In these cases, the project will almost always be operating under a contract, not a grant.) A typical example would be a study by a consulting firm under contract with the Department of Labor to evaluate a federally-sponsored job training program.
3. A grant-supported research project has been authorized by the federal

agency to tell respondents that the information is being collected for the federal agency.

Since the vast majority of research grants do not fall into these categories, OMB approval is not necessary unless this is a specific condition attached to the notice of award. In those cases where clearance from OMB is required, it is the responsibility of the granting agency to obtain approval. Thus, forms should be submitted by the project to the grant or contract officer; not directly to OMB.

OMB clearance can take a number of weeks and can slow down a project considerably. Thus, project directors are well advised to send forms in early and to push granting agencies as hard as possible to try to speed up the process.

COST SHARING

Federal research grants often are subject to cost-sharing or matching agreements. Cost sharing or matching is the value of the in-kind contributions and any other costs of a project that are not borne by the granting agency but by the project itself, host agency, or other third party. These cost-sharing or matching requirements may not be met by another federal grant, however. Cost sharing is generally met by the value of donated services of host agency personnel, supplies, facilities, and equipment.

Typical of cost-sharing arrangements with respect to personnel is the inclusion of time of regular members of the host agency staff. For example, a $500,000 training project in one university was required by the federal and state agencies that funded the project to share in 20 percent or $100,000 of the cost of the project. This was accomplished by assigning regular full-time faculty members to work on various aspects of the project. Thus, a professor in computer sciences whose university salary was $35,000 was assigned to give 20 percent of his time to the project's data collection activities which provided the amount of $7,000 as matching funds. Ten other faculty were similarly assigned to meet the total $100,000 of matching that was required.

The OMB circulars define the general guidelines for computing cost sharing or matching for different types of grantees. For example, cost sharing for nonprofit agencies may consist of such things as charges incurred by the grantee, project costs financed with contributed cash by nonfederal agencies, project costs represented by donated services of personnel, project costs represented by donated real or personal property. All contributions (cash or in-kind) must be verifiable from the grantee's records. They may not be from other federally assisted programs. They must be necessary and reasonable to accomplish the project's objectives, and of the type that would be allowed under federal principles that govern allowable costs.

The federal cost-sharing policies are spelled out in the OMB circulars shown in appendix D and are discussed in chapter 9.

EQUIPMENT

Since passage of the Grant Act of 1958, the title to equipment approved for purchase under a grant by academic and nonprofit institutions usually, but not always, stays with the grantee, which is technically the host organization. In the case of profit-making organizations, title is usually retained by the grantor. Some agencies, (for example, the Public Health Service) may reserve the right to require that a grantee transfer title of equipment costing over $1,000 to the government. Projects that are not lodged in host agencies seldom are allowed to keep title to equipment. Project administrators should obtain a written statement from the granting agency regarding the title to equipment and the procedures for its disposition upon completion of the project. In order to avoid any confusion, the project should keep a written inventory of all equipment purchased.

PROGRAMMATIC CHANGES

Significant changes in a federally-funded project's program, objectives, scope, or any subgranting arrangement must be requested in writing. Approval for such changes must be in writing from the grants officer or unit head in the agency's Washington, D.C., or regional office. In requesting changes, it is important to show how they are consistent with the original purposes of the grant and will further the achievement of the project's goals.

BUDGET REVISIONS

Project budgets are usually approved by grantors on a line-item (such as, personnel, equipment) basis, and projects are expected to live within these allocations. Deviations must have prior approval if they involve transfers from one item to another. Such approvals must be requested and approved in writing (see chapter 9 for sample letter).

TRANSFER OF GRANTS

Sometimes a principal investigator or project director will take a new position that involves transferring to a new institution. Transfer of the grant-supported project he or she heads to the new institution may take place only upon a written request to the grant agency, written agreement of the original institution to give up the grant, and submission of a new application (for the remainder of the grant period) by the new institution.

PROCUREMENT

OMB circulars describe the basic procedures and requirements that apply to federal grantees who procure supplies, equipment, or services. These rules allow grantees to use "their own procedures" for procuring goods and services. However, grantees must assure "open and free competition" in the procurement process. In addition, they must follow a code of conduct that will eliminate any conflict of interest for persons who are engaged in the award and administration of procurement or of subcontracts. Various granting agencies have additional specific requirements that apply to procurement and these should be requested at the outset of the project. All large host agencies will also have their own rules and procedures for procurement that projects must follow. Failure to adhere to host agency requirements is a frequent source of irritation between projects and host agencies. Following the prescribed procedures and consulting ahead of time with the purchasing department can help avoid many of these conflicts.

Typical of the procurement standards of the federal government are requirements that grantees' have procedures that assure:

1. There is avoidance of purchasing unnecessary or duplicative items.
2. A determination will be made as to whether purchasing or leasing is most economical and practical.
3. Solicitations include a clear and accurate description of goods or services that are to be purchased.
4. Positive efforts to utilize small businesses and minority owned businesses be made.
5. "Cost-plus-a-percentage-of-cost" contract methods are not used.

6. There be some type of price or cost analysis in connection with every procurement action.
7. In the case of purchases over $10,000, there be a complete record and file of the basis for selecting the contractor or vendor, justification of a lack of competitive bids if they are not obtained, the basis for the cost, and follow-up on the contractors conformance with purchasing specifications and requirements.

FINANCIAL REQUIREMENTS

The most elaborate requirements imposed by funding agencies are in the area of financial administration. For this reason, a detailed, separate discussion is devoted to this in chapter 9. However, at this point, it is sufficient to call attention to the general aspects of financial administration to which projects must comply with funder requirements. These include:

Banking Arrangements—projects are permitted to follow the regular banking procedures of the host agency, and separate bank accounts are not required for the projects.

Financial Management Systems—grantees must maintain financial management systems that meet federal standards with respect to (1) financial reporting, (2) accounting records, (3) internal controls, (4) budgetary controls, (5) advances and disbursements of funds, and (6) allowable costs.

Subgrant Management—some projects may need to have part of their work performed by another organization. In these cases, they enter into a subgrant or subcontract arrangement. When this is done the subcontractor is subject to most of the same requirements that affect the grantee.

Bonding and Insurance—grantees must ensure that their employees are bonded and have proper insurance coverage. Grantees may follow their own requirements and practices with respect to the bonding of employees and insurance coverage. However, if there is an absence of coverage, the granting agency may require the grantee to obtain a reasonable degree of fidelity-bond coverage.

COST PRINCIPLES

Federal requirements include a set of principles to be applied in determining whether costs incurred by a project are allowable. Allowable costs are those expenses that are incurred by a project and that will be reimbursed by the grantor. Different principles apply to different types of grantees as follows: Cost Principles for Educational Institutions (set forth in OMB Circular A21); Cost Principles for State and

Local Governments (set forth in Circular FMC 74–4); Cost Principles for Hospitals (set forth in OMB Circular A 110); Cost Principles for Nonprofit Institutions (set forth in OMB Circular 122); and Federal Procurement Regulations (set forth in Title 41, *Code of Federal Regulations*, applies to profit-making organizations).

These principles identify the factors that are used to determine if a cost is allowable. They include whether the cost is reasonable in the sense of being necessary to the project and not excessive. In addition, certain costs are not allowable (that is, the project will not be reimbursed for them). Included among such costs are bad debts, costs of preparing proposals, or fines. But most costs are allowable if they meet the conditions that are in the cost principle statements.

CONFLICT OF INTEREST

Federal grantees must have written guidelines for staff that indicate which outside staff activities are proper and improper in order to avoid conflict of interests. Large host agencies generally have institutional policies that pertain to this issue and that cover all personnel including project staff. It is wise to get these from the host agency and distribute them to all staff members.

CIVIL RIGHTS

Federal grantees must comply with a number of laws, amendments, and executive orders pertaining to civil rights.

1. Title VI of the Civil Rights Act of 1964, barring discrimination by any federally-supported project
2. Section 504 of the Rehabilitation Act of 1973, barring exclusion of the handicapped
3. Title IX of the Education Amendments of 1972, prohibiting discrimination in any educational program

Grantors expect that projects will conform with these provisions. In applying for grants, projects often must include written assurance of compliance. Samples of the provisions and forms that are used for this purpose are included in appendix B.

Trends and Implications

In spite of attempts to introduce "deregulation" into the federal grant process during the Carter and the Reagan administrations, the trend over the past fifteen years has been steadily in the direction of more control by grantors. These controls have focused mainly on financial management and personnel issues.

In order to assure compliance with federal rules, most large host agencies such as universities, hospitals, and city and state governments have developed equally elaborate sets of requirements to which projects must adhere. This in turn has lead to increased emphasis on the quantitative aspects of project performance, especially financial management issues which are the easiest to quantify. And, as a corollary to this development, the role of government audits and auditors has increased. Some organizations that are operating a number of grant-supported activities have had four or five different government auditors present at the same time. Some have even set aside a special office for the use of auditors. Project administrators have frequently experienced the audit as a frustrating matter since they often regard auditors as having a minimum of understanding of the substantive nature of the project's research, service, or training content. Such understanding, they feel, is necessary to any rational assessment of budget, financial management practices, and performance. In addition, project administrators sometimes have engaged in a series of negotiations with the grant agency's program staff regarding the project's operations only to find that auditors have no knowledge or appreciation of these agreements. The audit system, on the other hand, sees these criticisms as confirmation of its ability to be objective and to examine financial operations from a fair and equitable position based upon the records and information that are available.

The implications of these developments for project administrators is clear: be sure that records of activities and finances are in order and up to date, and prescribed procedures and format are followed! Establish a written record (sometimes called a "paper trail") of administrative activities that might prove to be challenged or controversial!

This does not mean that the project administrator must be a bookkeeper or accountant, but it does suggest that administrators must take the time to familiarize themselves with the areas in which problems might arise and to be sure that procedures are in place to provide the evidence that project operations are adhering to requirements and standards of the granting agency and of the field in general.

How to Keep Track of Government Regulations

Given the wide range of requirements that may apply to a particular project, how can one possibly keep track of what is relevant and important? The most comprehensive source of applicable requirements is the *Federal Register*, which is a long, fine-print publication of the federal government that is published daily and is expensive. Naturally, no project administrator has the time each day to study the *Register*, but for a few dollars a year, one can obtain a monthly summary listing of changes in federal regulations; a monthly index of all the material that has been covered in each issue of the *Register* is also available. Many large universities and agencies that have central grant and research administration units have staff people that review the *Register* in some detail. They keep the faculty and administrators informed of material pertinent to their interests.

The importance of the *Register* as a source of information was dramatically illustrated early in 1981 when the Public Health Service published proposed changes in its regulations that would make private profit-making firms eligible for part of its $2.2 billion research grants program. These funds had been almost exclusively granted to nonprofit institutions, particularly universities, to support research activities. The proposed change could result in the loss of millions of dollars of support for academic insititutions. Yet, hardly a voice was raised from the academic and scientific community because, as the head of one organization of scientists puts it, "no working scientist reads the *Federal Register*." Such distain for paying attention to the workings of the federal bureaucracy can be a costly mistake.

The most effective way to identify the pertinent regulations is to request them in writing from the granting agency staff person who is designated as the program officer, grant manager, or contract officer.

Project heads can also make use of the resources of central grants administration or research administration offices that exist in most larger institutions by requesting the staff of those units to keep the project informed of all material regarding funder requirements.

There are a number of national organizations that specialize in providing manuals, newsletters, and institutes in the grant administration field that cover developments related to agency requirements (some of the well-organized services are listed in appendix A).

If there is any one group of documents that can be used to tune into the kinds of requirements that affect most government-supported research, training, and service projects, it is the OMB circulars. Some of this material is shown in appendix D for reference purposes. The circulars are subject to changes by the OMB, and project heads should obtain the latest version.

Conclusion: How to Manage

Project administrators are confronted with a number of problems in connection with requirements. They need to find out what requirements pertain to their project and what they must do to comply with them. While most granting agencies can provide this information, it is not unusual for a grantor to be unaware of all of the requirements that affect a given project. The requirements, particularly of federal grant agencies, have developed in a piecemeal and haphazard way, which has resulted in a good deal of complexity and considerable confusion.

Also, projects are subject to not only the requirements of the grantor, but to a set of requirements and procedures that are promulgated by the host agency. Some of these may be inconsistent with grantor requirements.

Another problem is that many requirements appear to be barriers to the ability of the project to implement its activities, achieve its objectives, and operate within its prescribed time period.

Project heads can minimize the pitfalls associated with the need to comply with requirements if they: (1) pay attention to the *Federal Register*; (2) request the regulations and requirements that affect the project in writing from the governmental grant agency, foundation, and the host agency; (3) use the resources of central grant and research administrative offices; (4) subscribe to one or more of the national resources that publish current reports on regulations and explain their implications; (5) review the OMB circulars affecting grant administration; (6) pay close attention to the conditions attached to grant awards and to the special provisions attached to the contracts; and (7) adhere to the plans and procedures that were included in the proposal that served as the basis for the support of the project.

From the standpoint of the project administrator, there is not much that can be said about requirements that can place them in a positive light. They are, however, a reality of project life. The wise administrator accepts this fact, learns as much as possible about requirements, adheres to them as meticulously as possible; and, at the same time, recognizes that some requirements can be waived or are subject to considerable latitude in their interpretation and application. Armed with this information, project heads can often negotiate with granting agency personnel to have requirements applied in ways that will further the interests of the project. This requires the maintenance of effective working relationships with funders and host agencies—a subject we turn to in the next chapter.

Chapter 5

How to Manage Relationships with Funding Agencies and Host Agencies

Why Be Concerned?

A project to aid migrant workers funded by a foundation has had its funds cut off because the foundation has not seen any appreciable results. A government-funded research study of the causes of school vandalism is about to be visited by the government program officials who are concerned about the slowness with which the project has recruited staff. A special training program for child welfare workers has been asked to submit a detailed report on how its curriculum is emphasizing the prevention of institutional placement by the state agency that supports the program. A university research administration has refused to approve the purchase of tape recorders for a foundation-funded program to recruit minority students into engineering programs. A federal grant officer has called to find out why last month's financial report has not been received.

These are some of the kinds of problems that projects experience in their dealings with funders and host agencies. In each case the problem could be avoided or resolved if the project had more satisfactory relationships with the governmental and foundation program officials with whom the project works. Successful project managers understand that among the special characteristics of a project are its relationships with a funding agency and with a host agency and that they must carefully manage these relationships. They know that these agencies may have a major influence on the project's operations because of the control that funders and host agencies may exercise over the various resources that the project needs, such as money, personnel, facilities, and legitimation. Most of the problems project administrators run into can be traced to differences among the project and funders and host agencies over the policies and procedures related to the management of these resources.

It is important to understand that the vast majority of funders start with the belief that the funder-project relationship will be cooperative and relatively free of any serious problems. This is particularly true among foundations as exemplified in the following responses to a survey of foundations conducted as part of the research for this book:

> The grantee-funder relationship is difficult to describe, for it differs in every case. I would not describe these relationships as "a problem area," for in most instances they constitute an important and positive aspect of grant-making. The most productive relationships evolve when the channels of communication are kept open; problems tend to arise when grantees and funders do not communicate.
>
> —The Vincent Astor Foundation

> Problems between the Foundation and its grantees are minimal. When they do arise they generally stem from the grantee's misinterpretation of the program's working priorities as related to the project proposal. In other words, if the program that begins to develop after a grant is made takes a significantly different tack than what the grantee originally proposed, a difficulty is in the making.
>
> —W.K. Kellogg Foundation

> Although I do not regard the grantee-funder relationship as a problem area, certainly the relationship varies considerably among various divisions of The Rockefeller Foundation.
>
> —The Rockefeller Foundation

The maintenance of effective working relationships demands that project administrators view this as a set of activities that must be carefully planned and implemented. The failure to take this approach is an error of omission made by many project managers and results in having to deal with relationship issues as a series of crises that are reacted to after problems develop.

The development of a planned effort requires an understanding of two things. First, what kinds of typical problems can be anticipated, and second, what different management practices can be used to prevent or resolve such problems.

The remainder of this chapter will be devoted to exploring these two interrelated areas. In doing this, we shall outline the specific kinds of problems that occur in connection with each of the five resources that projects must obtain and which funders and host agencies control or influence. These include: financial resources; staff; participants; facilities, equipment, and supporting services; and legitimation and approval.

We shall also discuss how to use three management strategies to prevent or resolve the problems that develop, including: compliance; cooperation and cooptation; and negotiation, bargaining, and appeal.

Being Systematic

The first step in developing more effective approaches to managing relationships with funders and host agencies is to recognize that the problems occurring in this area are much more systematic and predictable than they are random or idiosyncratic events. This enables one to become clearer about the nature of specific relationship problems and the range of management techniques that can be employed. This clarity can be furthered by using or adapting the chart shown in figure 5–1, and the worksheet shown in figure 5–2.

Thinking in terms of this chart helps to move away from the tendency to regard the whole matter of relationships as a broad, vague area and instead realize that the problems are more specific, identifiable, and usually follow a definite pattern. The chart and worksheet enable you to keep track of what strategy has been most effective in connection with each particular type of problem. It enables you to differentiate what works with different funders (in the case of multiple-funded projects) and with the host agency.

For example, a Public Health Service grant manager writes to inform the project that it is the PHS's understanding that when the project grant was negotiated the assistant project director was to be employed on a one-half time basis rather than for three-fourths time. The project director identifies this as a problem regarding staff resources

FIGURE 5-1

Relationship Problem Areas and Management Strategies

Relationship Problem Area Regarding Resources	Management Strategy			
	Compliance	Cooperation/ Cooptation	Negotiation/ Bargaining	Mediation/ Appeal
Finances				
Staff				
Participants				
Facilities, Equipment, and Services				
Legitimation				

and notes that there have been other examples of this funder raising questions about staffing patterns. The project director may engage in a series of different strategies to deal with this. The director may try being cooperative and comply. He or she may try to negotiate some type of compromise settlement, or, he or she may appeal to a higher authority such as the chief of the unit in which the grant manager works. Considering these choices in terms of the chart, the director may find that prior staffing problems have been resolved in the interests of the project by engaging in a process of negotiation rather than by simply complying with the funder's wishes or by engaging in conflictual strategies such as appealing to the grant officer's superiors. At the same time, it may be found that with the same funder, issues regarding the project's budget (financial resources) have been best resolved through some other strategy such as appealing to the PHS unit chief. As patterns like these emerge in dealing with a particular funder or host agency over resource issues, the project director is in a position to use his or her time more effectively and efficiently by not wasting effort on methods that seldom seem to work.

In the case of a multiple-funded project where money is being received from two or more funding agencies (for example, a government agency and a foundation) for different aspects of the same project, the chart and worksheet also help to identify the pattern of issues that are

FIGURE 5–2
Project-Funder Relationship Worksheet

Project Name _____   Funder _____
Project Director _____   Funder Staff Involved _____

Problem Area (Under each item note the specific problem, date, how it came about, who was involved)	Action Taken (Describe and note the strategy used: compliance, etc.)	Resolution (Describe the outcome)
I. Finances		
II. Staffing		
III. Participants		
IV. Facilities, Equipment, and Services		
V. Legitimation		

raised by different funders. One funder may consistently question budget management practices, another may be concerned more with issues of equipment acquisition and use, another with the need to document achievement of program objectives. Once again, a project director can make more efficient use of time by concentrating administrative effort on the management of a particular resource in ways that will preempt the funders' ability to raise serious issues and problems. This may involve some rather simple but important steps such as making more conscientious use of obtaining bids on equipment to be purchased or providing more frequent financial reports to the funder.

Typical Kinds of Relationship Issues

FINANCIAL

The most obvious and most critical resource that a project must have is financial support. And, once funds are obtained, their flow must be continued and maintained in order to meet financial obligations (paying salaries and vendors). The following are the typical issues in this area over which a funding agency, host agency, and project often disagree:

> Since project budgets originally submitted in a proposal are often revised during the process of negotiating the grant, there are later differences as to what is the actual approved line-by-line operating budget for the project.

> Whether the project is staying within the total approved budget amount and/or will continue to do so over the life of the project.

> The extent to which cost-sharing arrangements and in-kind contribution agreements are being adhered to by the project and by the host agency.

> Whether financial reports are submitted on time and are properly completed so as to conform to the funder's or host agency's prescribed financial reporting forms.

> Whether changes in the budget such as transferring funds between different line items (e.g., using travel money for salaries), increasing salaries, or modifying items have to be approved ahead of time, and whether such approval has been properly obtained.

> Whether there is overspending or underspending in specific line items in the budget for salaries, supplies, transportation, equipment, and the like.

> Whether accepted accounting and bookkeeping principles and methods are being employed by the project or host agency for the control of expenditures and the maintenance of proper financial records.

The justification for various expenditures and procedures that come to light during the course of an audit.

STAFFING AND PERSONNEL

The vast majority of funds that projects receive are used for salaries of personnel. The next most frequent set of relationship issues that develop (after the financial ones) are in connection with staffing arrangements and personnel procedures. These include:

The extent to which the project correctly follows the various rules, procedures, and forms of host agencies and funding agencies that apply to the recruitment, selection, and appointment of staff.

Whether affirmative action and equal opportunity plans and procedures have been implemented in the recruitment and selection of staff.

Whether salary levels, benefits, consultation fees, and personnel practices that apply to project staff are consistent with those of other projects, or with units of the host agency, or are consistent with those that prevail in the particular field in which the project is operating.

Differences regarding the level of effort (i.e., amount of staff time) that should be expended on different project activities.

The extent to which the project consults with host agency administrators in cases where host agency staff are being considered for appointment to the project staff.

Justifying the qualifications of project staff to host agencies and funders.

Differences regarding the extent of participation, level of effort, and role of host agency staff who are assigned to the project as part of a cost-sharing arrangement.

Instances of pressure on the project to employ a particular staff person, or a person with particular characteristics, or from a particular professional or other group.

PARTICIPANTS

Most projects require participants as research subjects or respondents, or as participants in service or training activities. Host agencies and funders can influence the selection of subjects and participants in indirect and direct ways that may create problems in relationships. These problems usually grow out of differences between the project, host agency, and/or funder over the following issues:

The adequacy of the project's plan to protect human subjects involved in research activities.

The slowness of the host agency's and funder's human subject review groups to approve the project's plan for human subject protection.

Slowness in the approval of survey instruments when this is required by a host agency or by a funder.

Differences regarding what population groups the project should reach or give priority to, particularly in relation to age, sex, ethnicity, socioeconomic class, or geographical location.

The extent to which a service or training project serves persons who, while needing service, do not fall within the funding agency's definition of who is to be served or who were not mentioned in the project's proposal description of who would be served.

Differences over whether the project is attracting participants away from other host agency activities or, conversely, is funneling persons into host agency activities that result in overburdening host agency programs.

An example of how project-funder relationships are affected in relation to the selection of participants in project activities is illustrated by the following situation. A project was established to provide education and counseling to women with children going through separation or divorce and was funded by a local foundation. When it was learned that some of the women being served were lesbians, the foundation became concerned with its "image" and began to indicate it might withdraw its support. The project director and two of the lesbian women met with the foundation officials and explained that the lesbian women were highly respected professionals in the community. The project was continued. But, there are other cases that have had a different resolution; a project, to maintain its relationship with a funder, has denied service to persons it felt it should serve.

FACILITIES, EQUIPMENT, AND SERVICES

In order to function, every project must have certain facilities and equipment, such as typewriters, office space, office supplies, duplicating equipment, computer facilities, and word processors. These resources may be provided in a number of different ways. Funds for their purchase or rental may be included in the project budget. In other cases, they may be provided by the host agency. It is not unusual, for example, for host institutions, especially those that receive indirect costs or administrative overhead out of the project budget, to provide office space, utilities, and other facilities. In addition, projects that are lodged in large host agencies are provided with a variety of central services by the host agency such as bookkeeping, purchasing, payroll, and financial management. Furthermore, host agencies and funders have certain regulations that apply to the disposition of the title to equipment, supplies, books, and the like that the project purchases with funds from grants and contracts.

These various arrangements frequently result in certain problems that affect the project-host agency-funder relationship. The most frequent types of problems are:

> Differences between the host agency and the project regarding the adequacy of the office space, equipment, and other facilities that the host agency makes available to the project for its use.

> Differences over the relative importance the host agency attaches to the project's need for space, equipment, and facilities as compared to the importance placed on the needs of other units within the host agency.

> Issues regarding the relative merits of purchasing certain equipment versus rental of the equipment.

> Failure of project personnel to follow all of the prescribed procedures and forms of the host agency in the purchasing and procurement of supplies and equipment.

> Differences between the project and the host agency regarding the amount of time that the project can afford to wait for the acquisition of space, supplies, and equipment.

Relationship problems over space allocation often occur in the case of large established host agencies and projects. One project, serving substance abusers and lodged in a large youth-serving agency offering mostly recreation services, is an example of this problem. The agency director had agreed to the project because it was worthwhile and brought in a grant of over $200,000. Most members of the agency's fifty-person staff knew little about the project. The staff insisted the project be lodged in an old annex building rather than in offices in the new main building, which the agency director had agreed to assign the project director and her staff. Only after a year of operating in the annex under very unsatisfactory conditions did the staff realize that the project was not going to interfere with their work and was not going to result in less available space for their use in the new building.

LEGITIMATION AND APPROVAL

The final resource that projects require is to have their activities legitimated and approved. Projects acquire this legitimation in both formal and informal ways. The sponsorship and approval of the funder that is implicit when a grant is made to the project is the most obvious source of legitimation that a project receives. Similarly, the agreement of the host agency to include the project as part of its total operation is another source of legitimation.

This means, of course, that funders and host agencies have a potential source of power over a project since withdrawal of their support is always a possibility. However, a project itself has a counterbalancing source of power in the relationship with funders and host agencies. They also need to be legitimated; and, the projects they support serve to provide legitimation for them. After all, funders are in business to allocate their money. The project makes this possible. Foundations and government funders need projects to legitimate their own operations both in terms of their social purposes and the legal obligation that they have to dispose to their funds. In addition, host agencies are evaluated, in part, by their ability to raise grant and contract moneys. The project is tangible evidence that they are being successful in such efforts. Furthermore, every funder and host agency wants to be able to point to the work of their projects as evidence of their own effectiveness.

In the course of this reciprocal relationship, some major problems can occur, however. These usually include:

> Differences over the extent to which the project's activities are consistent with the objectives of the funding agency and/or host agency in terms of who is being served, the kinds of services being offered, and the amount of service being provided; or, in the case of research projects, whether the research procedures being used, the scope of the research, and the analytic methods being employed are consistent with the funder's or host agency's expectations and orientation.

> Issues with the host agency regarding the extent to which project's philosophy, ideology, or purpose and objectives are consistent with the host agency's interests.

> Differences in connection with finances, personnel, facilities, and administrative practices that become so magnified that the funder or host agency threatens withdrawal of support or sponsorship.

An example of the way that one project dealt with the problem of legitimation by its own host agency is shown by the experience of a project based in a large community hospital. The aim of the project was to demonstrate the need for providing personal care services to chronically ill persons who had been discharged from the hospital.

The hospital's board of trustees and administrator had agreed to the project because it appeared that it would result in freeing up more beds for acutely ill patients. Many of the chronically ill patients did not need to remain in the hospital but were occupying a bed because of the lack of home care services. To accomplish its goal, the project needed to gain the cooperation of a number of other agencies in the community to provide transportation for patients, nursing care, housekeeper services, and the like. The hospital administrator, however, refused to write a letter to these agencies indicating that the hospital wanted them to participate. The administrator said to the project director "there are some of our doctors who don't like the project and I don't want to antagonize them." The project director had to seek legitimation elsewhere, in this case by getting the head of the community's health planning council to write the letter.

Other Relationship Issues

In addition to the preceding relationship problems which revolve around resources, there is one other area that is frequently reported by project directors as a source of problems. This occurs in cases where the project must deal with multiple administrative layers of the same funding agency or multiple units within the host agency. The problems that arise in these situations have to do with different or conflicting interpretations of policies and procedures that the project receives from these different sources. For example, a university-based mental health project receives a grant from the central office of the State Department of Mental Health which is in the state capital. The project activities, however, are monitored by one of the regional offices of the state agency. The project receives various forms to complete on its volume of service from the central state office. Questions regarding how to complete the forms are directed by the project to the regional office staff with whom the project has developed a close working relationship. The regional office says it has no knowledge of these forms, however. The regional office staff person tells the project to ignore the forms, admitting he is doing so, in part, out of pique with the central state office for failing to keep the regional office informed. The project is caught in the middle. It is faced with the dilemma of finding a way to resolve this problem in order to maintain the support, approval, and cooperation that it needs from both the regional office and from the state office.

How to Manage and Resolve Relationship Problems

In this section of this chapter we shall describe the different methods that project directors can employ to resolve the kinds of problems that were just described. Three specific methods will be discussed: compliance; cooperation and cooptation; and conflict strategies.

COMPLIANCE

Compliance with the regulations of funders and host agencies is the most frequent and routine way of managing these relationships. It represents, as outlined in chapter 4, developing methods to adhere to the requirements of these agencies. It is satisfactory so long as (1) differences do not develop between the project and funder of whether, in effect, the requirements have been adhered to by the project, or (2) the requirements do not seriously impede the project's operations. When neither of these two conditions prevail, the project director has two choices. One is to acquiesce to whatever the funder or host agency is asking be done. The other is to attempt to bring about a change or modification in the position of the funder or host agency. This latter course of action calls for a recognition that the problem of relationships has now become redefined as having a political component. That is, it is a problem that has to do with the exercise of authority and power as part of the process of negotiation, bargaining, and conflict between the project and the other party. As part of such processes one makes use of facts and logical argument. Having reached this stage, it is important to recognize that the context for the use of such substantive information is basically political. Politics is not used here as a negative term, but rather a descriptive term that denotes that there are conflicting interests among the parties involved that must be resolved. Such situations should not be regarded as zero-sum situations in which there is only a "loser" and a "winner." On the contrary, a major skill in managing and resolving differences is in the attempt to define a problem and its resolution in a way that does not result in a total break of the relationship that can occur when the "winner-loser" situation is defined as the "name of the game."

COOPERATION AND COOPTATION

The main result that a project seeks to achieve in managing relationships with funders and host agencies is to gain the understanding and support of these bodies for the project's operations and positions.

But, agreement cannot always be achieved on all issues. Thus, the project's goal is to develop an atmosphere in which disagreements are handled in terms of as much reciprocal respect as possible and recognition of a shared or mutual interest between the parties involved. This may sound like an idealistic goal; but most projects achieve it in large part. One of the most effective ways for a project to accomplish this is to engage in activities that promote cooperation as the result of communication. As pointed out earlier, this is usually achieved through judicious and effective compliance with requirements. But compliance may not always be in the interests of the project and there are other techniques that may be employed to gain the support of funders and host agencies that are all based on furthering project, funder-host agency communication. These are: provision of information, personal contact, consultation, marketing, and gaining additional funding.

Provision of Information.   By providing a stream of information to the funder, a project can assure that the funding agency is aware of the activities, accomplishments, and problems of a project. Techniques to do this include sending funders:

Clippings of newspaper, magazine, and journal articles about the project reprints of published articles from journals and other periodicals authored by project staff

Descriptions of presentations by project staff at conferences, meetings, and community groups

Copies of project newsletters, brochures

Notice of awards or honors received by project staff

Copies of studies and reports issued by the project

Copies of pertinent internal reports such as monthly summaries of activities and of descriptions of the demographic characteristics of participants

Copies of letters from "satisfied customers" and letters of commendation from professionals in the field who know of the project's work

Personal Contact. Important as the written material may be, it is no substitute for personal contact with staff members of funding agencies and host agencies. An effective and natural way to do this is to make a visit every two or three months to talk with the staff person(s) about the project in order to bring them up to date on what is going on. Such visits should supplement the official contacts with the funder that go on in relation to compliance with regulations or as part of site visits. Keep these visits businesslike but informal. Be sure you have real things to talk about since no one appreciates contrived contacts that do not have substance.

Typical of the items that can be discussed are (1) changes that may be occurring or anticipated in the project activities or staff, (2) problems that may be cropping up, and (3) progress in implementing activities and achieving objectives. Use anecdotes and examples to be sure the staff person knows exactly what you are talking about.

Consultation. Another form of personal contact that helps to maintain positive relationships with funders is to seek the consultation of funder staff in connection with project activities, refunding, publicity, problems, and the like. Asking for funder advice or technical assistance should not be regarded as a sign that the project is floundering or ineffective; and, should never be approached in this way. Seeking advice must be sincere, must be related to a concrete problem, and must be something with which the funder can be of real help. A typical example of this is the variety of questions that surround project publicity that the project can bring to a funder. Does the funder want to be mentioned in a newspaper or journal article? How would they like to have the description of their participation worded? Would a funder staff person like to be quoted in a press release? Is it desirable to mention the amount of the grant in an article?

Marketing. In a sense the use of cooperative and cooptive strategies to further project-funder relationships is a form of marketing. This means you must (1) know your audience, who are the key persons with whom relationships must be built, what are their interests, background, and role; (2) present the project in ways that are convincing as to the project's efficiency and effectiveness; (3) show how the project is connected to and promotes the interests of the funder and host agency.

Attracting Additional Funding. A final point in connection with gaining the support of a funder has to do with demonstrating that the project is actively seeking other funds. In the words of the Rockefeller Foundation: "The Foundation . . . expects energetic efforts by grantees to secure additional and subsequent funding from other sources."

Nothing pleases a funder more than evidence that programs they support are viable enough to attract other resources. One of the most important things that can be done to strengthen relationships with a funding agency is (1) to make concrete plans to obtain additional support from fees, other foundations, the host agency, or through fundraising efforts; and (2) provide evidence that these additional resources are actually being received.

CONFLICT STRATEGIES

Regardless of how skillful a project director manages relations with funders and host agencies, there will be times when the interests of the project and funder and host will conflict and where one party or the other is not initially prepared to revise its position. In these cases, the project can employ two main strategies. It can attempt to bargain and negotiate, or it can turn to mediation, appeal, and even litigation.

A state university-based project, funded by the local public school system to conduct research on the nature and extent of vandalism in local public schools and make recommendations for reducing acts of vandalism, faced withdrawal of the school's cooperation when it became apparent the research was going to lay most of the blame on school practices rather than on student behavior. The head of the study, a former police officer and a sociologist, decided to take on the public schools directly and enter into a confrontation with the schools. The project publicly announced it was going to submit its report to an outside panel of three education experts for an evaluation of its research methodology and analysis. The experts endorsed the soundness of the report. The public schools withdrew their criticism and continued funding the project, even though, in the final analysis, they paid little attention to the report's recommendation.

Another project, funded by a federal agency to study the adequacy of emergency rooms in seven local hospitals, was told by the agency program manager that he was going to recommend withdrawing the agency's support prior to the completion of the study, because his staff had concluded from a site visit that the study had not paid sufficient attention to analyzing cost-effectiveness factors in its data collection and analysis design. The project director quoted to the program manager the section of the federal provisions that establishes a project's right to formally appeal a postaward decision and said he was going to pursue such an appeal. Interestingly, the federal program manager was not aware of the existence of an appeal procedure. He called back the next day to say that funding would be continued.

These are all adverserial strategies. The first, bargaining and negotiation, is carried out between the project and the host agency or funder. The second set of strategies involves a third party such as a mediator or an appeal board, committee, or person. Litigation is very seldom employed, and, since it involves the use of attorneys and the courts, it represents a complete break in the relationship between the funder and the project.

Bargaining and Negotiating Techniques. Project directors will sometimes have to negotiate differences between the project and funders. The result of these efforts is usually some form of compromise. For example, one project insisted to a federal funding agency that it needed $2,000 in additional travel money and proposed that it use a transfer of unused personnel funds in its budget for this purpose. Initially, the funding agency's grant manager refused the request. The project responded by further documenting its need and by raising the question of whether it could effectively carry out its goals without these funds. The result was that the funder and the project agreed on the transfer of $1,000 instead of the initial request of $2,000. This example illustrates a number of important "do's and don't's" that should be considered in the process of bargaining and negotiation.

DO

Provide written documentation of your request or position with a sufficient amount of factual data to convincingly support your claim.

Get the other party to agree on at least the initial facts such as what the approved budget figures are, or what the objectives are, and certainly on what exactly the project is requesting or wants.

Be patient, keep the door open for further presentation of material and communication.

Keep extraneous and unrelated items out of the negotiation process.

Be prepared to bargain, to give up something in exchange for something else, to "make a deal."

Show the other party how your request can be in their interest, or at least identify where the funder's interests and the project's interests overlap.

Take things a step at a time.

Identify what items cannot be reconciled, if any. Set them aside and try to agree on the things that can be reconciled.

Explain what you plan to do and why if the matter remains unsettled.

Be persistent.

Keep a written record of all conversations and confirm your understanding in writing whenever you come to an agreement satisfactory to the project.

DON'T

Be provocative.

Make threats.

Be vague about what you want.

Involve third parties in the negotiation.

Argue over global issues.

Imply a lack of ethics to the other party.

Fail to listen to what the other party is saying.

Argue about who said what when there is no formal record or correspondence to which you can make reference.

Close all doors to further discussion.

Mediation and Appeal. These strategies come into play in situations where the project has not been satisfied with results of earlier efforts to negotiate a settlement. They involve the introduction of one or more third parties into the process. Most frequently this is a superior officer within the project, or in the host agency, or in the funding agency. "I'll talk to your boss about it," "Let me talk to the executive," "Talk to my supervisor," "I think you better discuss this with someone else" are the ways this involvement often begins.

When a third party becomes involved in a project-funder problem there are a number of things the project manager should do. These include making personal contact with the person so they know that you are "real people" and not some anonymous "project" out there. Send the person copies of the pertinent correspondence, reports, and the like. Outline the history of prior negotiations in a letter and reaffirm the project's position or request. Express openness to discuss and consider alternative solutions at the same time you convey that you are firm in the correctness of your request or position. Do not bad mouth the funder or host agency staff who have been previously involved. You are now dealing with their superior in the organization.

Don't be mislead by the fact that they will almost always express support for their staff. Even though they express support, they may decide to modify the decisions or positions at a later time.

An example of the involvement of a third party as a mediator took place in the case of a research project funded by a large city which had contracted with a private consulting research firm to survey social and economic conditions of tenants in an area designated for urban redevelopment. The city agency was responsible for submitting to the research firm the names of families to be interviewed each month. The contract called for 600 interviews a month, but the city housing agency was repeatedly late in providing names and had at times provided a lesser number than was required. After three months, only 1,200 families had been interviewed, and the city agency threatened to reduce the contract payment amount. The consulting firm offered to make up the additional interviews at the end of the study period, but the city agency contract manager would not accept this arrangement. The project director insisted that a meeting be held with the officials of the federal Department of Housing and Urban Development, since the money for the study had come to the city from that agency. HUD also was responsible for monitoring the entire city redevelopment program. The project director had a preliminary meeting with the federal staff. He explained the project's position. He provided them with the correspondence between the project and the city agency. The project's letters to the city had been carefully prepared and included descriptions of the problem and what had arisen. They had been prepared by the project director with an eye to the possibility of their being needed in future negotiations. The federal officials believed the project's position was legitimate and suggested to the city staff that they go along with the request. The city agreed and reversed its position but saved some face by requiring the contractor to keep more detailed records of the reasons why some tenants refused to be interviewed and of tenants who had moved but were still on the city's list of area residents.

In the case of many government funding agencies, there is a formal appeal mechanism that may be used. For example, the *Grants Policy Statement* of the Public Health Service of the Department of Health and Human Services states it has:

> . . . a policy of permitting grantees to appeal certain post-award adverse administrative decisions . . . the grantee must exhaust the PHS procedure before appealing to the Grants Appeal Board, Office of the Secretary. The following decisions may be appealed:
> •

1. Termination, in whole or in part, of a grant for failure of the grantee to conform with the grant terms and conditions.
2. A determination that an expenditure not allowable under the grant has been charged to the grant, or that the grantee has otherwise failed to discharge its obligation to account for grant funds.
3. The disapproval of a grantee's request for permission to incur an expenditure during the term of a grant.
4. A determination that a grant is void.
5. Establishment of indirect cost or patient care rates (except where the grantee has appealed to the Armed Services Board of Contract Appeals with respect to such determination under a contract with the Department).

As a first step in appealing an adverse decision, the grantee must submit a request for review to the appropriate PHS official, as designated in Chapter PHS: 1–520, following the procedures contained therein. Under the PHS procedure, a review committee, consisting of officials not involved in the adverse determination, will be appointed to consider the case. The committee will prepare a written decision based on its review for the signature of the committee chairman. If the decision is adverse to the grantee, the grantee has the option of submitting a request to the Department of Health and Human Services for a further review of the case by the Grant Appeals Board.

Additional details regarding the appeals procedures may be found in DHEW Grant Appeals Procedure: 45CFR16; PHS Grant Appeals Procedure: 42CFR50, Subpart D; and Indirect Cost Appeals: 45CFR75.

If one had to select the single most critical element in maintaining relationships with host agencies and funders, it certainly would be the ability to prepare effective written reports. Thus, the next chapter is devoted to this important aspect of project management.

Chapter 6

How to Manage an Effective Reporting Program

No matter how good your project's performance may be, it can be rendered useless unless you communicate your work to others. In the field of grant and project management most of this communication is carried out through the use of written material and reports. All projects invariably prepare one or more of the following kinds of reports: progress reports required by funders periodically (monthly or quarterly); reports to funders to support continuation of an award for an additional period of time; final reports required by funders; special reports requested by funders; periodic reports to funders and host agencies initiated by the project; interpretive reports to community and professional groups and key officials; internal reports to staff and participants; newsletters; annual reports; and financial reports (covered in chapter 9).

Most of these reports are submitted to funders and host agencies. Such reports are of critical importance because the continued payment of grant monies during the year may be contingent upon receipt of designated reports such as program progress reports and financial reports. This is always true in the case of contracts. It is somewhat common in the case of government grants, but much less common in the case of foundation grants. Almost all funders require at least a final report even though their funding is not contingent upon this report.

The range of foundation requirements is illustrated in these divergent positions stated by three national foundations.

As a Foundation which does not require nor want an endless stream of reporting, we encounter few problems with our grantees. Those problems that do arise are usually the result of carelessness in not following through on our request to "In due course please forward a report on the expenditure of these funds."

Where more than one payment is made, we require certain narrative and fiscal materials. They are outlined below. A set of the forms, recently simplified, for meeting some of these requirements is enclosed.

1. *Expense Plan* (Form E–1) outlining projected expenditures for the period of the grant. These are geared to our September 30 fiscal year. One sheet should be completed for each of our fiscal years for which expenditures are anticipated. This report is to be submitted *before the initial payment* is made on the grant.

2. *Activity Plan* (Form E–2) outlining a plan of work to be performed on the grant with an anticipated schedule for completion of each phase of it. This report, too, is to be submitted before the initial payment is made on the grant and should be revised annually or more often as needed.

3. *Expense Report and Payment Request* (Form E–3) detailing expenditures for the period since the last payment and projecting expenditures for the subsequent quarter. This report must be submitted each time an additional payment is requested.

4. *Quarterly Narrative Report* supplements E–2 and covers program progress and major activities, changes in program design, staff changes, primary problems encountered, and the objectives of the next quarter.

5. *Comprehensive final program report* reviewing the work undertaken and progress made toward the objectives of the grant, an assessment of the project's impact on its clients and other agencies, and a description of objectives yet to be reached. The report should be submitted within thirty days after completion of the grant.

6. *Final fiscal report* (Form E–2) within thirty days after the completion of the use of grant funds.

7. A copy of any *certified audit reports* concerning your organization during the term covered by the grant.

This foundation does not have any specific forms for grantees to use in following up on grant proposals. We do require substantive and financial reports on an annual basis, but we expend a considerable amount of time and energy obtaining these and very often find them inadequate to our purposes.

This chapter will review the principles that should guide effective report preparation; explain how to set up and manage a project report preparation system; and provide a checklist of techniques that increases the effectiveness of the reports you must prepare.

Principles for Effective Reports

These are four main principles of communication that apply to all reports: clarity, relevance and responsiveness, consistency, and interest and impact. The effectiveness of a report is largely dependent upon the extent to which these principles are reflected in the writing style, content, organization, and appearance of the report.

CLARITY

Reports must be written so that the language and organization of material can be easily followed and understood. Keep the style as simple as possible. Avoid long sentences, unnecessary verbiage, abstractions, and excessive cross referencing.

Use technical and professional terms when necessary; but, explain their meaning if you believe the funder is not thoroughly familiar with them. Organize the material in a logical sequence, using frequent headings and subheadings.

RELEVANCE/RESPONSIVENESS

Reports to funders and host agencies must be relevant to their interests. Information about the project that cannot be directly linked to the funded activities should not be included.

If the report is required by the funder, it should adhere to the funder's requirements as to content, length, and deadline dates. If the report is optional, it should still reflect the format (if any) that funders or host agencies use for project reports. The relevance of the report can be enhanced by the inclusion of information known to be of interest to the funder in terms of the objectives and/or philosophy of the granting agency. A simple example of this would be in reporting to a foundation that has an expressed interest in supporting projects in a particular geographic area. In this case your report should point out the activities you provide in this area and the number of people being served who come from the area.

CONSISTENCY

Obvious as it may seem that a report should not contain contradictory material, this is one of the most frequent problems that crops up in the reporting process. Each part of a report should be related to and consistent with the other parts. For example, one part may include a description of the number of staff people engaged in various activities, and in another section of the report there may be a listing and description of project activities. Be sure that the activities referred to in the two sections correspond.

Statistics used in one section should be exactly the same when used in another section. If they are not, this should be explained in the text or a footnote. Similarly, budget figures for items such as personnel, equipment, and the like should not vary in different sections of the report.

INTEREST AND IMPACT

Effective reports get attention and are regarded in a positive light by funders when the report's content and format are interesting and have substantive and visual impact. Brief case stories and examples are one way to do this. The use of graphs and charts is another way to do it. Use of headings and subheadings also contributes to a more interesting report, or using symbols such as bullets as substitutes for numbers as a way to set off listed items is another effective technique. Here is a typical example of this technique:

> "The program completed the following three major sets of activities during the past six months:
> • recruitment of training staff
> • organization of six groups of parents who enrolled in the single parent training program
> • completion of the first cycle of six-week training sessions"

Charts, graphs, and symbols also serve to reinforce particular points, and they make the report more interesting by periodically breaking up the text.

Reports and Freedom of Information

Project reports to federal agencies are subject to the provisions of both the Freedom of Information and the Privacy Act. This means that all grant-related reports to these agencies are available to the general public for inspection and copying. The exception is if the request is considered to be an "unwarranted invasion of personal privacy," which is unusual for such reports. This suggests that you need to always be careful that the content of your report is such that you would be willing for it to be public. To stamp the words "CONFIDENTIAL" on a project report to a funder is usually a meaningless act and you are only kidding yourself to believe it has any real effect.

How to Establish a Project Reporting System

"Where is the list of courses?" "Has anybody seen the last printout from accounting?" "Can you stay late to finish this report?" These are typical words of a project director the day before a progress report is due in Washington. Somehow, even though it is known ahead of time that particular reports must be ready on certain dates, most of us seem to wait until the last minute and then have to scurry around for much of the information we need.

One way to overcome this is to set up a system devoted specifically to the reporting activity. Such a system enables you to think ahead and to be prepared. It is easy to set up a reporting system by using the following step-by-step procedure.

STEP ONE: SET UP REPORT MATERIALS FILES

The initial step is to set up a central filing system so that the information needed for various reports is readily retrievable. Members of the project staff should be told to route any material that might be relevant to these files. Put one person in charge of this particular set of files.

Typical of the material that can go into individual file folders are: prior reports to funders and host agencies; the project proposal and grant award notice; information about the funding source such as the foundation annual report; information about the reporting requirements and forms, if any, utilized by the funder; and staffing information. Also the following may be included: correspondence and newsclips that refer to the project; articles, speeches, and papers given by project staff; program information on activities including descriptions of participants, services provided, memos from staff on their activities, and other information generated by the project activity reporting system (described in chapter 8); and financial information and reports generated by the project's own financial management system and/or by the financial management office of the host agency (described in chapter 9).

An alternative type of filing system is to establish a separate file folder for each report that the project is scheduled to prepare. If you decide to organize the filing system in this way, then project staff should be instructed to refer material to the file based on what particular report the material has the most relevance. This usually involves making copies of some material since it may be useful in the preparation of more than one report. Copies are then placed in each report file.

Files, of course, are to be used. Creating a set of files of resource material specifically for use in report preparation is an exercise in futility unless you and the project staff put helpful material in the files and then make use of them when writing the reports.

STEP TWO: PREPARE A MASTER SCHEDULE OF REPORTS

Most projects operate on a year-to-year, twelve-month calendar based on whatever fiscal year is being followed by the funding agency or host agency or beginning at the date specified in the grant award. During the year a number of different reports will need to be submitted. At the beginning of a project you should be aware of when most, if not all, of these reports will be due. Thus, the next step in the development of reporting system is to prepare a master timetable that lists each report, the number of copies needed, and when each is due. A sample of how to chart this information is shown in figure 6–1.

By preparing a chart along these lines, you can get a total picture of the reporting responsibilities of the project for the entire year. More often than not, project directors and other staff tend to underestimate the amount of work that goes into the preparation of reports. A chart like the one in figure 6–1, that is prepared in the early days of the project, helps to overcome this problem since it depicts the reality of the project's total reporting program over a one-year period.

STEP THREE: ESTABLISH A REPORT PREPARATION AND PRODUCTION SCHEDULE

Using the timetable from step two, the next thing to do is to estimate the amount of time needed to write and produce each report. Schedule these activities by expanding the timetable as shown in figure 6–2. Every report requires four activities: (1) preparation and writ-

FIGURE 6-1
Project Report Schedule

Month and Due Date

Report	JAN	FEB	MAR	APR	MAY	JUNE	JULY	AUG	SEPT	OCT	NOV	DEC
Quarterly Progress Reports: Report # 1 (15cc)				15								
Report # 2 (15 cc)							15					
Report # 3 (15 cc)										15		
Site Visit Report (20 cc)								31				
Special Report to University Provost (10 cc)									30			
Financial Reports to ABC Foundation Mid-Year (4 cc)							31					
Final (4 cc)												31
Final Report (50 cc)												31

ing; (2) review and editing; (3) final typing and duplication; and (4) submission. The starting date and amount of time needed for each of these activities should be shown on the chart.

Next to each report enter the due date from the Master Schedule using a symbol such as a square (□). Work backwards, figuring how many days you will need for actual production of the report including final typing, proofreading, duplicating, collating, and mailing. Enter this date using another symbol such as a circle (○). Then work backwards from this date and estimate the amount of time in days needed for editing and revisions. Enter this date using another symbol such as a hexagon (⬡). Still working backwards, estimate the time needed for gathering material and writing, allowing for one or more drafts. This will give you the starting date for preparation and writing. Enter it on the chart. You can use another symbol to represent writing such as (◗). Put the appropriate date of the month by or in each symbol. On the line connecting the symbol show the number of days estimated for each activity. Do not skip the editing and proofreading as many projects do! Sending a report with errors is one sure way to lose the confidence of funders.

Always be careful to allow enough time for the mail or delivery time between the completion of the report and the date it is due.

Show the number of copies needed for each report by entering this next to the report title in column one, as shown in figure 6-2. Show the legend that describes what each symbol stands for at the bottom of the chart.

Put the completed chart on a large sheet and display it in a prominent spot. As each step is completed, color in the symbol used to designate that step in order to show progress. Enter the completion date to show if it is done early, late, or on time.

STEP FOUR: ASSIGN PREPARATION RESPONSIBILITIES

It is surprising how often project staff members hear the phrase "these things don't get done by themselves." This usually reflects a lack of clarity about responsibility for various tasks among the project staff. The problem is easy to avoid. Using the Report Preparation Timetable from step three, assign specific individuals responsibility for each activity. Prepare a worksheet similar to figure 6-3 that indicates who is responsible for each activity for each report. Display this with the chart (figure 6-2) to keep all project staff aware of who has responsibility for what aspect of the reporting system.

FIGURE 6-2
Project Report Preparation Timetable

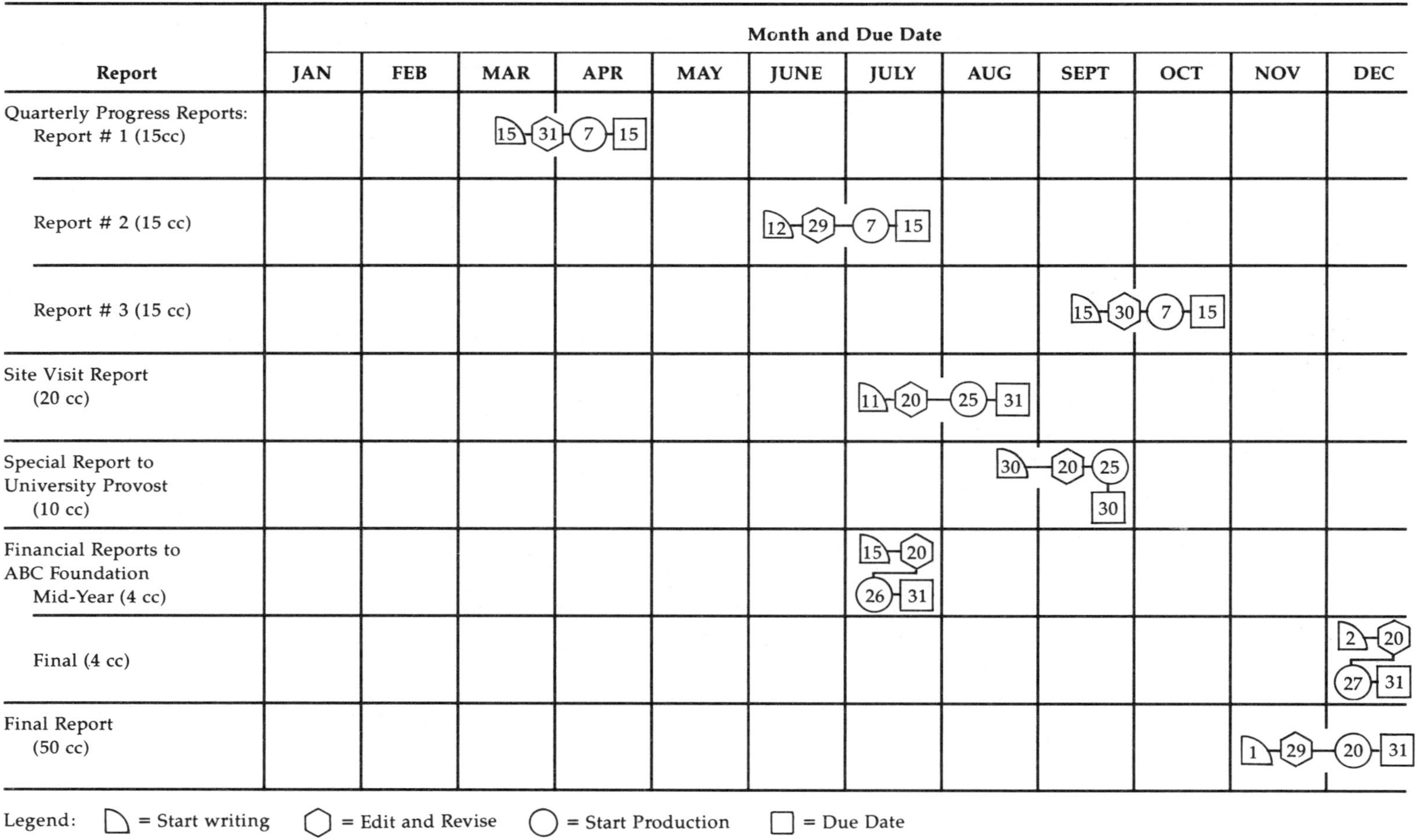

FIGURE 6–3

Project Report Responsibilities Form

Report	Activity		
	Preparation and Writing	**Editing and Revision**	**Final Production**
Progress Report # 1	Jones	Johnson	Harris
Progress Report # 2	Jones	Smith	Harris
Progress Report # 3	Jones	Smith	Harris
Site Visit Report	Johnson, Smith	Jones	Martin
Special Report	Johnson, Smith	Jones	Martin
Final Report	Jones, Johnson, Smith	Jones, Johnson	Harris

STEP FIVE: PREPARE REPORTS

The last step is to implement the system by writing, editing, duplicating, and submitting the report. Place a copy of each completed report in the files so that it is readily available for reference when the next report is to be worked on. This helps to assure consistency of material from one report to the next.

Report Appearance and Impact

The appearance of written material can be as important as its content. A sloppy report or one with typographical or grammatical errors reflects negatively on the credibility of the project. Such mistakes can destroy the confidence of funders and host agencies in a project that might otherwise be effectively carrying out its activities. Here are some tips on how to avoid common mistakes and to assure the attractiveness of the finished product.

Use a thesaurus. Many reports lose their effectiveness because the writers use the same words over and over again. This is easy to correct by using a thesaurus such as *Rogets** which provides extensive lists of synonyms, antonyms, and related words.

Double check all numbers. For some reason, numbers are anathema to many people. Simple numerical mistakes crop up in report after report. Check and double check the use of numbers in the text, in tables, in graphs and charts, and even page numbers.

Use a dictionary. A misspelled word or a word used incorrectly can make a reader wonder about the competence of a writer. If there is any question, check the dictionary. Some words most often misspelled or misused in reports that were reviewed in preparing this book are:

effect/affect	among/between
principle/principal	capital/capitol
there/their	imply/infer
criteria/criterion	literally/figuratively
fewer/less	irregardless/regardless
complement/compliment	respectfully/respectively
adapt/adopt	parameters/perimeter
deduce/induce	

Proofread. The vast majority of mistakes that creep into reports could be eliminated if reports were carefully proofread. The most effective way to do this is to have two people read—one reads from the final copy, the other follows it on the draft from which the final copy has been typed. This will not catch all mistakes since some will be in the draft and merely repeated on the final copy. But it will catch 90 percent or more of them.

Check sentence structure. In addition to misspelling and misuse of words, it is not uncommon for problems of sentence structure to appear in reports. The most frequent errors are either incomplete sentences or overly long and complex sentences. Reread your written material and watch for the incomplete sentence. More often, however, the problem is one of sentences that are so long and are almost impossible to follow. Try to fathom the meaning of this one adapted from a National Science Foundation funded project:

---

* *Roget's International Thesaurus,* Fourth Edition (New York: Harper & Row, 1979).

The instrument designed to measure the organizational items has some weak points since when we attempted to correlate the perception of adequate programmatic space with the general organizational profile we find that fifteen organizational items correlated at the .001 level of significance but the five items that are not correlated are sporadically mixed in different aspects such as the motivation item and the leadership item most likely due to the lack of clarity regarding the interpretation of these items.

How much more effective it would be to break this sentence up as follows:

The instrument designed to measure the organizational items has some weak points. This is shown when we attempt to correlate the perception of adequate program space with the general organizational profile. We find that 15 items correlate at the .001 level of significance. But, the five items that are not correlated are sporadically mixed in different aspects such as the motivation item and the leadership item. This is most likely due to the lack of clarity regarding the interpretation of these items.

Paragraph. Similar to the problem of overly long sentences, is that of paragraphs that are too long and go on for pages. Remember, readers need a rest. Paragraphing is one way to accomplish this and thus increase the clarity and comprehension with which a report is read. Whenever you have more than a page without a new paragraph go back over it and find a place to break it up. The basic principle in paragraphing is to identify spots in the narrative where there is a change of thought or a new idea or topic is introduced into the discussion.

Number pages. Numbering pages sounds so simple and obvious that you might wonder why it is included in this checklist. The reason is that reports are sometimes submitted with pages stapled together in their proper order but without page numbers. The easy solution is to always number pages.

Title pages. Any report that is more than three pages long will benefit from having a separate title page. The title page serves as a cover for the report and adds to its appearance and credibility. Report title pages should include: the title of the report; the name of the project and host agency; the name of the principal investigator or project director; the address of the project; the date of the report; the name of the funder; and the grant or contract number, if any. An example of a title page is shown in figure 6–4.

Include letter of transmittal. Send a brief cover letter with every report. This letter should state that you are attaching the report and re-

FIGURE 6-4
Sample Title Page

FINAL REPORT

A Qualitative Study of
Worker Alienation

June 1, 1983

Submitted by
Helen Typer, Principal Investigator
Department of Business
OJ University
Yourtown, Massachusetts

to
The Institute of Education
State Department of Human Services
Capitol City, Massachusetts

This is the final report of the work supported by the
Institute of Education under Grant Number 36012-82.

fer to the report title. In addition, you can use this letter to call attention to certain highlights or points in the report. The letter also provides you with a written record that documents the fact that the report has been submitted. If the report is being submitted in accordance with contract or grant requirements, this should also be mentioned. Figure 6-5 shows a typical letter.

Table of contents. Narrative reports that exceed five or six pages should have a table of contents on a separate page that follows the title page. List each major section and subsection of the report and show the page number on which each begins.

Use topic headings. One of the best ways to make reports more readable and to provide for clarity and emphasis is the use of topical headings. Each heading and subheading should be short (usually one to five words) phrases that are descriptive of the section of the narrative material that follows. This conveys to the reader the central concept or theme with which the material is concerned. Headings and subheadings must be carefully chosen. Many report writers do not pay enough attention to the development of adequate headings. When this happens, they can be more of a hindrance than a help since the reader's attention is focused on the wrong material or he or she is confused by the seeming lack of relationship between a heading and the accompa-

FIGURE 6–5
Sample Letter of Transmittal

RE: Six-Month Progress Report
Grant # H36054

Dear Mr. Reader:

We are pleased to submit the attached six-month progress report of the Project to Develop a Model Human Services Training Program on Work with Families Exposed to Environmental Hazards in accordance with the conditions stated in the letter of award.

As you will see from the report, we have completed all of the Phase One work related to surveying the literature and 100 universities to ascertain the state of the art and of existing programs in this field. A summary of the results of the survey is included in the Progress Report and shows that there are very few training programs in the universities surveyed.

We are now proceeding with Phase Two, Curriculum Development, and will report on the completion of this work in our final report. If you would like additional information, please let us know.

Sincerely yours,

Nora Cleanair
Project Director

NC/st
Enclosure

---

nying narrative. It is also desirable to give headings numbers and/or letters following outline style, using designations such as I, A, 1, a. It is also effective to vary type. Use all capitals for major headings. Use initial caps for other headings. Be consistent in the use of typeface throughout the report.

Covers and binders. A simple title page is a sufficient cover for most reports. Stapling is adequate for a binding; avoid the use of paper clips. Funders frown upon the use of funds for elaborate covers and binding for reports. As a matter of fact, it is not unusual for a government funder to formally prescribe that reports should not have elaborate art work and extensive illustrations or exhibits. When reports are quite long, it is desirable to use a heavy weight stock for a cover page.

Long reports may not staple well, and in such cases, it is a good idea to use one of the plastic binding devices that goes through punched holes. Whenever possible, however, you should use the simplest form of binding.

Use charts and graphs. A few simple charts and graphs will increase the effectiveness of any report. Bar charts, pie charts, line charts, flow charts, and organization charts are the most common types of charts. These can be prepared without requiring professional art work by following the instructions in one of the resource books listed in appendix A.

Form and Content

Projects funded by contracts often have certain standards for report content and format that are imposed on them by funders. An example of these standards is illustrated in the following rather elaborate description from a government Request for Proposal (RFP). This excerpt includes a number of helpful ideas that may pertain to any report.

VII. *Standards for Reports*—Final report and case studies will be announced and distributed through the National Technical Information Service of the U.S. Department of Commerce. The general principles outlined below concerning the content of research and study reports are standards for all major reports and case studies, whether final or interim, prepared under contract with the Office of Policy, Evaluation and Research.
  1. *Content*
     a. *Reports and case studies should address the objectives specified in the contract.* Important findings not related to particular objectives should be treated, of course. When the researchers have been unable to find pertinent data concerning a particular objective, this should be stated and explained.
     b. *Reports and case studies should be based on findings of the researchers.* The nature and extent of the information and data analyses on which these findings are based should be described in sufficient detail to enable the reader to draw conclusions about the validity of the findings. The integrity of the research and/or study design and methods should be reported. Findings or conclusions which are based on the pre-knowledge of the researchers, or on other research studies, or hearsay, should be clearly identified as such.
     c. *Personal opinion should be identified.* There is room for the personal opinions of the report writers, provided these opinions are based

on supporting information, do not merely reflect personal bias, and are clearly identified as personal opinions of the writers.

d. *Reports and case studies should be written clearly and succinctly.* Study findings and recommendations should be clearly identified. Advocacy of particular new policies or procedures should be supported by study findings and conclusions. All recommendations should be appropriately labelled and brought together at one point in the report, even though they may be scattered throughout the report.

e. *No pertinent topic is forbidden.* Researchers should bear in mind at all times that their findings may go beyond the specific study objectives, and that the validity or effectiveness of any policy, procedure, or program, may be questioned in a report, within the structure of objectivity and thorough analysis.

2. *Format*

a. *Abstract of highlights and recommendations.* The final report should be accompanied by a separately bound abstract of the highlights of the study. Contractors will be expected to furnish a draft abstract along with the draft final report. This document should not attempt to give a summary of the whole report, but should describe the report briefly and point out the most significant findings, conclusions, and recommendations. The abstract should be relatively short (1,000 to 5,000 words). The purpose of the abstract is to enable executives who do not wish to read the whole report to quickly know its purpose and results. The abstract should capture the tone and content of the principal findings and recommendations of the report. Report recommendations should naturally flow from the objectives and methodology and the specific study; however, all researchers should be particular about the back up information which supports findings and recommendations pointing to needed refinement or redirection of manpower policies and programs. Included among the recommendations should be suggestions for dissemination of the final report and plans for its utilization, as a means of enhancing the possibilities of application of the report's conclusion and recommendations. This concern with the ultimate utilization of the study results should guide the researcher from the point of writing the proposal though submission of the final report.

b. *Report identification and disclaimer.* All final and major interim reports and case studies will carry the following disclaimer on the title page:

"This study was conducted and this report was prepared under contract with the Office of Policy, Evaluation and Research of the Employment and Training Administration, U.S. Department of Labor. Organizations undertaking such projects under Government sponsorship are encouraged to express freely their professional judgment. Therefore, points of view or opinions stated in this document do not necessarily represent the official position or policy of the Department of Labor."

c. All final and major interim reports and case studies will carry the following identification page:

"This contract was awarded by the Office of Research and Development, OPER, at the request of the CETA R&D Committee, Employment and Training Administration."

Reporting and Public Relations

Continued success in obtaining grants is highly related to a successful track record in the use of prior grants. Such credibility can be furthered by maintaining good public relations about the project. Public relations efforts go beyond the reporting activities we have described earlier in this chapter. They also include: issuing press releases about the project to local newspapers and institutional newsletters; speaking to community and professional groups; conducting conferences and workshops related to the project's activities; issuing newsletters; placing articles in journals and other media; and speaking on radio talk-shows.

Some of the information for these public relations activities can come from the reports that the project prepares. But chances are you will need to develop a good deal of additional material. Most project directors have neither the skills nor the time to really implement all aspects of a public relations program. This is an activity in which you should make demands on the public relations or community relations departments that are available in most large host agencies. Get to know the people who work in these departments; talk with them about the project; send them copies of the reports you prepare for their information; and call them when you have something newsworthy going on.

Remember, things which you consider routine may often have news appeal. These may include: a visit to the project by a local state or national legislator; receipt of an additional grant, no matter how small; a visit from a professional from another community or project; or an appearance at a conference.

Sometimes you can arrange interesting public relations events. Invite the university president to visit the project and get coverage in the press by sending news releases with a picture and a positive quote. Do the same thing by inviting an official from the foundation or government program that is funding the project to visit it informally.

There are a number of good books on public relations for nonprofit and governmental agencies. These can help you become more aware of the public relations potential of your project and understand the elements of such a program. These books are listed in appendix A, on resources.

In the next chapter, we shall take up one of the major events in the proces of communication between projects and funders: the site visit.

Chapter 7

How to Plan For and Conduct Site Visits

One of the most difficult and critical events in the life of a project is the site visit from the foundation or government funding agency. "Anxiety," "worry," "uncertainty," "pressure," "who's coming," "when are they arriving," "are we ready," even "terror" are the typical words that describe pre-site visit feelings among the project staff. As one project head expressed the apprehension that often precedes the visit, "Of course we're worried. The team of people coming from NIMH hold the key of our future." And for good reason—the site visit can be the single most determining factor in a funder's decision making about the project and future funding. The program, budget, and personnel of the project can be vitally affected by the kind of report a site visit team gives to the funding agency.

In this chapter, we will discuss the various methods project directors can use to make site visits more successful. Every project person wants to achieve one thing from a site visit: they want the visitors to leave with a positive image of the project. They want the visitors to regard the project as effective and efficient, and they want the visitors to report this back to the funding agency with some documentation for this judgment.

Achieving this goal depends on the progress the project has made in carrying out its activities. It also depends on how well you plan for the visit, how you organize the visit, how you treat the visitors, how you present material, and the general climate that is established for the visit. There are many things related to site visits you cannot control, but following the methods outlined in this chapter will certainly increase your chances of success.*

What Is a Site Visit?

A site visit is the funder's review of a project and is conducted at the actual location of the project. It is a face-to-face meeting between project and grantor personnel. It is one of the few opportunities for you to show grantors what is really going on—who your staff is, what your program is, what your facilities are, how you actually operate, what you have achieved.

There are a number of different occasions upon which a funder will initiate a site visit. Sometimes the visit will be part of the negotiation prior to making a grant or awarding a contract. This is infrequent. More often the visit is a postaward site visit. The federal government's *Code of Federal Regulations* authorizes grant agencies to make site visits to grantees as "deemed necessary." Foundations also have the right to conduct site visits but do so much less seldom than government funders. Postaward site visits may be held for one or more of the following purposes: (1) to review, monitor, and assess the program accomplishments and progress of the project; (2) to review and assess project management, including financial controls and systems; (3) to provide technical assistance; (4) to examine and discuss a particular problem that has occurred; (5) to negotiate a change in the project's program or budget; (6) to make assessments in connection with refunding or continuation grants to the project; and (7) to receive and discuss final reports of the project.

Regardless of the specific purpose of the visit, there is always one theme that pervades all site visits—the element of evaluation. That is, the site visitors are there for the purpose of making some appraisal of the project: its personnel, its activities, its management. Most site visits are for one day. In the case of large-scale complex projects, they may sometimes be spread over two days.

---

* I am indebted to Lynne Soine, former assistant project director of the Training Program in Public and Community Service of the State University of New York at Stony Brook for permission to adapt portions of her paper on "Site Visits" for use in this chapter.

Occasionally, a project may ask for a visit in order to present the funder with first-hand, on-site information about the work being done. However, a project-initiated visit is a very infrequent occurrence, since funders seldom make themselves available for them. Nevertheless, it can be an effective tool for building support if a funder does have the time and interest to make the visit.

Who Are the Visitors?

A site visit may involve one person or a team of two or more persons from a funding agency. The site visitors are usually persons who are employed on a regular basis by the funding agency, such as their program managers, project managers, staff associates, unit chiefs (for example, director of research and evaluation, chief of the bureau of maternal and child health, training director).

They may also be people who are retained as consultants by the funding agency to carry out a particular site visit because they have some special competence in the program area in which the project is operating. They may be members of a government review panel who do not work for the funding agency since they have other full-time jobs. They may be members of the board of directors of a private foundation, or they may be managers from a large corporation who are responsible for managing corporate foundations or community relations programs.

Sometimes the visitors will be staff members of a private consulting or management firm engaged by the funder to conduct program evaluations, monitor projects, or provide technical assistance to funded projects. They may be government auditors who are conducting a review and assessment of government funded projects such as those often carried out by the federal government's General Accounting Office (GAO). This agency conducts administrative and program audits, as well as financial audits, and reports its results to the Congress and to the funding agency within the federal government.

The site visit team may include persons from other agencies who are knowledgeable in the field or who are in some way connected with the funding program. An example of this group would be a staff person from a state health department who accompanies a team of officials from the U.S. Public Health Service, or a person from a regional office of a federal agency who accompanies a team from Washington.

Know Your Site Visitors

The first thing you want to do in preparing for a site visit is to know your site visitors. What are their backgrounds and interests? Are they program people or financial people or both? How much do they know about the particular field in which you are operating and do they have professional backgrounds similar to those of the project staff? Do not hesitate to ask the program officer from the funding agency who is arranging the site visit these questions. You are entitled to this information. It will enable you to plan the presentation of material in a way that is geared to maximize understanding and that, of course, is in the interests of all parties involved. An example of what can happen when a project does not know the background of the visitors is illustrated in the case of one project staffed primarily by nurses. The project was visited by a team whose backgrounds were in the field of economics and social science. Halfway through the visit it became apparent that the language of nursing and that of economics were far apart since the site visitors began to ask a series of questions about the project that the project staff had already covered. One site visitor reported going through the entire visit in which the project people repeatedly referred to the "triage" approach but never explained the term and he never asked. Anticipating a problem of this kind enables the project presentation to provide plenty of opportunity for the visitors to ask questions early in the visit. It also suggests the importance of defining the terms that you are using and of always giving examples.

Project Staff and Site Visitor Roles

The site visit involves both project personnel and funding personnel in a rather complex set of roles and communication patterns. Funders come to a site visit having power over the project because funders, as noted earlier, control the money the project needs. However, they also recognize that funding agencies need projects to legitimize their own operations. In addition, site visitors are also as nervous as the project staff about what will take place during the visit. They want to be intelligent about the project's operations, ask perceptive questions, and submit a well-prepared report to the funding agency. They are in an unfamiliar situation with many unknowns. They have varying degrees of experience that may or may not prepare them to appear to be "experts" in the substantive field in which the project is operating. Finally, they need to quickly assess complicated programs and situations by eliciting the information they need in a very short period of time.

The visitors have usually been provided with written information about the project ahead of time, and they may have some familiarity with the original proposal and subsequent progress reports. They may have also been briefed by their superiors in the funding agency and been told to bring back the answers to certain specific questions.

Project personnel, on the other hand, are conditioned by other factors as they enter into the site visit process. Members of the project staff all want the project to be highly regarded, and they also feel pressure to perform well in the eyes of both the site visitors and the project director.

The burden is on the project director and the project staff to ensure a well-planned, well-managed visit. While it may seem as if the funding personnel should bear primary responsibility for organizing and shaping the details of the site visit (by virtue of their relative power in relation to the project), this is often not the case since they are usually geographically removed from the project site and cannot make these arrangements. Thus, primary responsibility for planning and managing a site visit rests with the project's administrative staff (the project director or principal investigator and the chief aides).

Planning for the Site Visit

Successful site visits are planned for well ahead of time. Planning for a site visit usually begins when the funding source announces that one is imminent, often on short notice. But, you can anticipate visits since many funding sources have general policies regarding the timing of site visits to projects. These policies may be formal or informal, so it is important for project directors to seek such information from the funder's program officer. In a three-year project, for example, a funding source might have a policy requiring a site visit by the middle of the second year. Or, a funding source might require a site visit prior to refunding a project. The earlier the project staff is aware of an impending site visit, the better prepared it can be.

A site visit may be announced by a funder with short notice or for an inconvenient time. If the funder announces a site visit for a time that would disrupt activities crucial to the project's operations rescheduling of the visit should be requested. The operational responsibilities of the project must be fulfilled as the first priority, regardless of the fact that the funder desires a site visit. Funding agencies are receptive to rescheduling if you clearly communicate the reasons for the request. The integrity of the project is maintained by the responsible fulfillment of its obligations as spelled out in its grant award, proposal, or contract.

In approaching the specific planning for a site visit, it is well to remember that the site visitors, in addition to representing the funding source, are human beings with normal needs which must be met during the course of the visit in order to insure a positive review.

A site visit must be planned for in connection with the three major components of every visit:

> Arrangements—assure the adequacy of all the logistical arrangements such as housing, travel, food, meeting rooms, and the like.

> Presentation—determine what to present, how to present it, and who will be responsible for presentation of material and other aspects of the visit.

> Structure—decide how to best structure the visit in terms of attendance, presentational methods, and the schedule or agenda of events, presentations, and discussions.

The following sections contain a series of methods to accomplish these three components of the site visit.

Arrangements for the Visit

The arrangements for the visit need to create a positive climate for the visit and to facilitate the work of the site visitors. This includes seeing that the visitors are comfortable, that the project recognizes their needs, and that their stay is marked by a sense of respect for their position and responsibilities.

How to Plan For and Conduct Site Visits

The following is a checklist of items that should be covered in connection with those arrangements.

Ascertain the travel plans and arrival times for each visitor. Send them maps and instructions on how to reach the project site and call them to be positive they received the instructions and understand them.

Reserve rooms in a comfortable hotel. Double check to be certain the reservations are confirmed and available. There is nothing worse than walking into a hotel and being told "we don't have a reservation for you," or "your room isn't ready."

Be sure there is parking at hotels and at the project site, for visitors who are driving.

Arrange to have visitors who are flying to be picked up at the airport and taken promptly to their accommodations; and don't forget to be just as careful with the travel arrangements for each visitor's departure.

Check that all visitors have transportation from the hotel to the project site.

Offer to have dinner with visitors who arrive the night before a visit.

Keep such dinners as informal as possible and avoid getting into the business of the visit itself.

If a visit begins first thing in the morning, make sure all the doors to the project site are unlocked. More than one site visitor who arrived early has been kept waiting until the doors were opened.

If it's raining, have a supply of umbrellas on hand. Airlines do it and so can you.

If possible, avoid starting and ending visits at times when the visitors will have to battle rush hour traffic.

Set aside office space with desk, telephone, and comfortable chairs for the use of the site visitors. Show the space to them at the beginning of the visit and give them an opportunity to settle in.

If you are located in a large building, provide the visitors with maps of the building if they will be moving from place to place. Mark where restrooms and eating areas are located.

Assign a member of your staff, if possible, to assist the visitors with administrative work, telephone messages, travel arrangements, and other details.

Reserve all of the rooms needed for the presentation of material and discussions well ahead of time; double check to be sure they are available; pick the most comfortable spaces available; have enough chairs on hand.

Make sure that all arrangements for coffee, meals, and social events are made and confirmed with caterers or whoever is to be responsible.

When using audiovisual equipment, confirm that it is reserved, in good working order, and that someone who knows how is going to operate the equipment. Check on whether charts and other displays are ready, and on the availability of easels, and the like.

Finally, distribute a written record to the project staff stating who has been assigned the responsibility for each item in this checklist.

Presentation of Material

Here are some guides to planning the presentation of material.

GEAR MATERIAL TO PROJECT OBJECTIVES

Deciding what to present is the most complicated part of pre-visit work. It includes establishing priorities for the presentation, as it is impossible to present everything about a project in a brief visit. Selection of material, of course, depends on the purpose of the visit. Is it a general review or is it directed toward some particular problem or component of the project? Assuming it is a general review, the place to start planning the presentation is with the objectives and activities of the project as spelled out in the grant proposal, notice of award, or contract. What are the major activities the project is responsible for carrying out, to meet what objectives, at what cost, and according to what timetable?

The material presented should describe the nature and the status of each of the activities and document the progress in meeting each objective. An example of this would be a project in the field of community development whose purpose is to increase the rehabilitation of buildings by residents. One objective is to provide assistance to residents on how to obtain low-interest loans in order to increase their ability to pay for rehabilitation. The site visit presentation should explain this objective and illustrate how the assistance is being provided to residents. This should include providing examples of the information that is being distributed to residents, documentation on how many people have received the information, how many low-interest loans have been obtained, and the number of buildings being rehabilitated.

One of the most frequent complaints from project staff people about site visitors is their apparent lack of understanding of the kind of work in which the project is engaged. Another is that visitors often fail to appreciate the philosophy or methodology of the project. Regardless of how accurate these observations may be, it is still incumbent upon the project to structure the presentation of material in a way that enhances understanding. Define terms and encourage questions and discussion to see if you are being understood. Use a mix of communication devices—verbal presentations and audiovisual aids add interest and clarity.

IDENTIFY STRENGTHS AND WEAKNESSES

It is important to identify the strengths of the project and gear most of the material to reflect these strengths. But it is also strategic to identify your own weaknesses and take the initiative in pointing them out. As part of this, explain why problems have developed and present your plans for overcoming them. Most experienced site visitors will identify these problems anyway, so anticipate these problem areas ahead of time and have your plans ready for dealing with them.

USE YOUR BUDGET CATEGORIES

A part of the presentation should include a report on the status of expenditures that reflect the project's major budget categories. These may be line-by-line categories such as personnel, equipment, conferences, contract services, and the like. In addition, you may have budget categories that are "functional" or "programmatic" such as interviewing, data analysis, administration, and training.* You can report on the budgeted amount for such items, how much has been expended and what you estimate expenditures for the remainder of the year to be. Show how any budget limitations are affecting your program.

ASSIGN RESPONSIBILITIES

Prior to the visit decide which project staff person will have primary responsibility to prepare and present particular material and to field questions. In larger projects that have administrative staffs, such as an administrative assistant or a financial officer, they (along with the

---

*The development of functional or program budgets is described in chapter 9.

project director) should handle only administrative material such as questions on expenditures and the budget. They should not respond to programmatic questions even if they are asked. Similarly, program staff should not deal with budget and management areas. Making these decisions ahead of time will help avoid presenting contradictory information and answers during the visit.

BE PREPARED FOR QUESTIONS

Decide ahead of time who will respond to inappropriate or highly problematic questions asked by the site visitors. Almost invariably it is best to instruct the staff to refer all of these to the project director for response. An example of such a question by one site visitor to a university-based research project was "tell me what the various factions are among the faculty in your department." The project director simply said "I really don't know" and ended the discussion.

PREPARE A PERSONALIZED FOLDER

A few days before the visit prepare a folder for each site visitor and give it to them upon their arrival. Use a regular manila folder, or better yet, the kind that includes pockets inside the front and back covers in which material may be inserted. Individualize the folders by typing the person's name on the outside cover or pasting on a name label.

The kinds of material to insert in the folder include:

> The agenda for the visit indicating each item, when it is scheduled to be covered, where, who will present the material.
>
> A list of the names and position titles of all the individuals participating in the site visit.
>
> Individual travel plans and arrangements, if any.
>
> A "floor plan" map of the building area where the site visit is to take place indicating meeting rooms, cafeteria, restrooms, and the office space that has been allocated to the visitors.
>
> "Orientation" material of useful basic information for the site visitors such as the telephone number at the project where they can be reached, a description of the project and program and financial data. If a map of the city or town where the visit is taking place has not been sent ahead of time, include this as well.

Structuring the Site Visit

Structure for the site visit includes scheduling the events, communication methods, the climate you establish, and who you involve.

PREPARE THE SITE VISIT AGENDA AND SCHEDULE

The final responsibility for formalizing the agenda for the visit almost always rests with the project staff. Usually the grantor will call and/or write to the project director to tell him or her that there will be a visit. In this communication, there may or may not be an indication of the specific items that will be discussed. The project should initiate follow-up discussion regarding the agenda and finalize it in consultation with the head of the site visiting team prior to the team's arrival.

The agenda should include each item to be covered, who will present the material, and the approximate time of the presentation (see figure 7–1).

Avoid the common mistake of overscheduling and trying to present too much material. As indicated earlier in this chapter, have at least one major presentation of material on the project's programmatic activities built around progress in achieving objectives. Also, include one major presentation on the administrative and financial aspects of the project.

In some cases, an actual visit to a "live" project activity such as a training session is requested by the visitors. Such visits cannot always be counted on to portray the project in its best light, however. Not every session of a fifteen-week training activity, for example, is terrific. Staff have "good" days and "bad" days. Thus, if not required by the funder, visits to ongoing, in-progress activities that have a chance of showing poorly should be avoided. Instead, use other means to convey the same basic message to the site visitors, such as presentation of a videotape, film, photographs of activites, presentation of case material, tours of the facility, and special meetings with selected participants in various activities.

PROVIDE A PROJECT FACT SHEET

One of the ways to be sure that the visitors get the message you want to communicate is to prepare a basic summary fact sheet highlighting the most salient information about the project. This can be

FIGURE 7–1
Sample Site Visit Agenda

COMMUNITY HEALTH MAINTENANCE PROJECT
Agenda

Monday, April 13, 1983

9:00 A.M. - 9:30 A.M.	Welcome: Site Visitors and Staff Coffee and Danish Lounge: Room 101
9:30 A.M. - 10:00 A.M.	Meeting: Site Visitors and Project Director Room 102
10:00 A.M. - 11:15 A.M.	Six-Month Progress Report on Program Room 103 (a) Overall Objectives and Activities Mary Smith, Project Director (b) Nutrition Component John Jones, Nutrition Coordinator (c) Hypertension Program Ellen Hampton, Hypertension Coordinator (d) Self-Care Program Thomas Wolf, M.D., Self-Care Coordinator (e) Accident Prevention Sara Sart, Accident Prevention Coordinator
11:15 A.M. - 12:00 Noon	Discussion of Reports Room 103
12:00 Noon - 1:00 P.M.	Lunch Lounge: Room 101
1:05 P.M. - 1:45 P.M.	Presentation of Family Health Maintenance Videotape—Helen Reed, Media Specialist Room 104
1:45 P.M. - 2:30 P.M.	Budget Report Mary Smith, Project Director and William Hart, Administrative Assistant Room 102
2:30 P.M. - 3:15 P.M.	Meeting with Community Advisory Board Room 103
3:15 P.M. - 3:30 P.M.	Coffee Break
3:30 P.M. - 4:00 P.M.	Discussion of Project Evaluation Mary Smith, Project Director and Dan Best, Evaluation Consultant Room 102
4:00 P.M. - 4:45 P.M.	Exit Meeting: Site Visitors and Project Director Room 102

---

provided to the visitors at the beginning of the visit. Be sure the information on the fact sheet is consistent with the verbal reports you will give them during the visit. Typical information to include in such a fact sheet would be: (1) when the project was initially funded, (2) the amount of current funding, (3) a summary of objectives and activities, (4) data on progress, and (5) a budget summary showing approved amounts for each item, expenditures to date and anticipated expenditures for the remainder of the project.

MEETINGS WITH PROJECT LEADERS

As part of site visit schedule, it is advisable to begin and end the visit with a meeting between the site visitors and senior project staff. The initial meeting sets the stage for the visit. At the initial meeting the visitors should be asked what basic questions they want covered in the visit. The schedule for the rest of the visit should be reviewed. The project director should use this meeting to briefly outline the material that will be presented and to gently emphasize those project elements which are the strongest. At the end of the visit, the site visitors usually have issues of concern and questions for clarification. These should be responded to by senior project staff at the final meeting. Also, the final meeting is often used by the site visitors to provide some feedback to the project staff as to the strengths and weaknesses that have been observed. It is difficult for site visitors to quickly assimilate the amount of information typically contained in a site visit, so the opportunity for final clarification of questions is essential. In addition, the final session can be used to determine additional information that the visitors may need that can be sent to them after the visit.

USE AUDIO AND VISUAL METHODS

Unquestionably, audio and visual aids can enhance and augment the presentation of material. While care should be taken to avoid overdoing audiovisual aids, the judicious use of these materials is well advised. Do not get too fancy however, since site visitors will wonder where the time and money came from for elaborate audiovisual aids used for the single purpose of the visit. Charts, graphs, films, videotape, slide shows, and tape recordings can be used to simplify and organize information in ways that make the visit more productive and easier for site visitors. The most frequently used and effective technique is the use of charts since they can be used to depict almost any aspect of the project in a well-organized, easily-understood manner. Charts can be completed in relatively short periods of time and can be impressive, at reasonable cost. An example of some charts used to describe both administrative and programmatic aspects of a project is shown in figures 7-2 and 7-3.

Other more expensive audiovisual aids such as videotapes or films should be used as part of a site visit only if they are developed in connection with the regular work of the project. Do not develop them exclusively for site visit purposes. If a new piece is to be produced and used initially for the site visit, care must be taken to insure that it can be completed in time and without interfering with ongoing project business. In appendix A, resources for preparation of such aids are listed.

PREPARE THE PROJECT STAFF

While it is primarily the senior staff person or persons who present material and determine the portrayal of the project, the entire project staff should be prepared for the site visit and involved in planning. Convening a meeting of all project staff as soon as a site visit is announced is effective in soliciting input and informing staff of the tasks to be addressed in the ensuing weeks. The professional, secretarial, and office personnel, for example, can judge the project's ability to produce certain material and identify the manner in which many arrangements can best be made. In addition, they have routine contact

FIGURE 7-2
Sample Site Visit Chart Presentation

FAMILY HEALTH MAINTENANCE PROJECT
Six-Month Program Budget Report

Program Component	12-Month Budget	6-Month Expenditure	Amount Over (−) or Under (+) Expended
General Administration	45,000	22,000	+ 500
Nutrition Education	15,000	7,000	+ 500
Hypertension	18,000	9,500	− 500
Self Care	18,000	10,000	− 1,000
Accident Prevention	12,000	5,500	+ 500
Materials Development	14,000	6,000	+ 1,000
Evaluation	10,000	1,000	+ 4,000
Total	132,000	61,000	+ 5,000

FIGURE 7–3
Sample Site Visit Chart

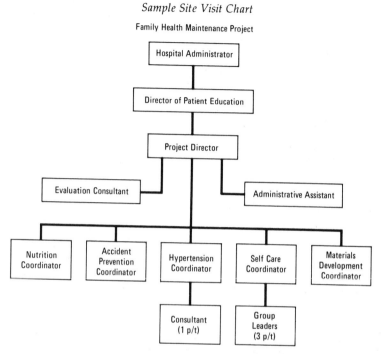

Family Health Maintenance Project

with the visitors, and the impression of your operation is often the result of their association with site visitors.

In larger projects, a "task force" may be established to coordinate and monitor the overall planning. As the date of the visit approaches, actual "dress rehearsals" may be scheduled to ensure staff preparedness. The list in figure 7–4 can be used to help check on your preparation for a site visit.

ENCOURAGE DISCUSSION

Site visitors need to participate in discussion since this is a way to help them understand and retain information about the project. There are several ways to help this happen. The most obvious is to make sure there is enough time for questions and discussion. Do not make the frequent error of having presentations run over their scheduled time. As project director, if you see this happening, signal the person making the presentation to finish up. Invite questions during a presentation. Include in your presentation of material some suggestions of the questions or issues that should be discussed further. Avoid answering every possible question in the presentation itself.

FIGURE 7–4

Site Visit Preparation Checklist

Preparation	Status	
	Yes	No
1. Has each staff member been briefed on the purpose of the visit?		
2. Has each staff member been briefed on the manner in which the project is to be portrayed?		
3. Does each person know his or her role and responsibilities?		
4. Does each person have a copy of the site visit schedule?		
5. Does each person have a copy of all project materials to be distributed to the site visitors?		
6. Has each staff member been informed about each site visitor's position, background, interests, etc.?		
7. Has each staff member been briefed as to project strengths and specific examples to demonstrate those strengths?		
8. Has each staff member been briefed as to perceived weaknesses in the project and explanations for such weaknesses?		
9. Does each staff member know what to do in the event of questions from a site visitor?		

INVITE HOST AGENCY PERSONNEL

The site visit can be enhanced by including some key persons from the host agency. Their presence will be regarded by the visitors as evidence that the host agency regards the project as an important activity. Inform these people beforehand if they are not familiar with the details of your operation. Arrange for them to give a brief welcome or present other material. Sometimes they may be regarded as "window dressing" but, if you don't overdo it, everybody likes a little special attention. The presence, for example, of a university president for the opening session of a site visit to a research project tells the site visitors you have the support and interest of your host agency. But be careful in this regard. Do not bring in a lot of "brass," or invite people who are not sufficiently knowledgeable regarding your activity and have nothing to say.

INCLUDE BOARD AND COMMITTEE MEMBERS

In the case of projects that have advisory boards, boards of directors, or other groups of persons with policy-making or advisory responsibilities, the chairperson and key members of these groups should be present for and have a role in the visit.

ESTABLISH THE CLIMATE

To the extent possible, the entire project staff should appear pleased and proud to welcome the site visitors. The success of the site visit is related to the subjective and personal experience of the site visitors as well as to their formal activities of information gathering and assessment. A conscious effort should be made by project personnel to communicate a message of confidence, capability, and credibility throughout the site visit.

FOLLOW UP ON THE VISIT

Within a few days after the site visit, letters should be sent to the site visitors expressing your pleasure in meeting them and thanking them for their efforts. These letters can also be used to document any changes that were made in the site visit schedule and/or other irregularities. For example, if a visitor arrived late and missed the first meeting, the letter might read: "We are sorry that you were unable to attend the morning meeting in which we introduced the new project proposal." The purpose of these follow-up letters is twofold: first, they continue to communicate a positive message to the site visitors, and second, they provide documentation of deviations during the site visit which may be important at a later date (especially if there are negative aspects of the assessments made by the site visitors). If promises were made to send additional information, this should be included. If negotiations and agreements regarding program, staff, or budget items took place during the visit, these should be confirmed in writing.

EVALUATE THE VISIT

You can learn a lot about your operations from a site visit and about how to improve on your site visit methods. Engage in an evaluation of a visit a few days after its completion, and include all the staff. Your office personnel may have seen things you did not know about. Ask the questions: what did we do well; what were our weaknesses; how can we do it better next time in terms of arrangements, planning, presentation, and structure?

A Final Word

Experience shows that there are three categories of things that influence site visitors' responses. The first has to do with the substantive programmatic and financial material that you present. Is it clear, complete, interesting, and relevant? The second has to do with the process and relationships. Are arrangements adequate, are questions welcomed, is there discussion back and forth, is the climate one of mutual respect? And, the third has to do with the impression of project management. Are roles among project staff clear, does the projet director demonstrate leadership, is the operation orderly and efficient, is information available?

There is no way you can "fake" good managerial practice in a site visit. In the next two chapters we shall discuss methods for effectively managing project personnel, program activities, and finances.

Chapter 8

How to Manage Project Staff and Program Activities

Project directors spend most of their time on the day-to-day management of the project's research, program, training, or staff activities. This aspect of project administration includes the following components:

STAFF MANAGEMENT

    Adopting a leadership style
    Recruitment and selection of project staff
    Orientation of project staff
    Assignment of staff responsibility
    Delegation of authority
    Organization and deployment of staff
    Establishment of chain of command, span of control, and lines of communication
    Supervision of staff activities and evaluation of staff

PROGRAM DIRECTION

    Focusing program direction
    Using objectives as a basis for program direction

Refining project objectives
Refining project activities
Relating objectives and activities
Assigning responsibility
Using timetables as a management tool
Using performance reporting techniques
Managing crises

EVALUATION MANAGEMENT

Understanding evaluation
Selecting evaluation personnel
Deciding on evaluation design
Relating to evaluation activities
Reviewing evaluation reports

COMMITTEE MANAGEMENT

Selecting committee members
Orienting committees
Keeping committee records
Establishing committee procedures

In the following sections, we shall examine the nature of each of these aspects of managing the project's staff and activities and set forth a number of principles, methods, and managerial tools that have proven useful to control, supervise, and give direction to project activities.

Staff Management

ADOPTING A LEADERSHIP STYLE

A vexing issue for project managers has to do with the type of leadership they want to adopt as they work with the project staff. Managerial style can range along a continuum from a leader-centered style in which the manager exerts a high degree of authority to a very permissive style that gives the staff considerable freedom in decision making and task implementation.* Project managers are subjected to a number

---

*Paul Pigors and Charles A. Myers, *Personnel Administration*, 7th ed. (New York: McGraw Hill, 1973), p. 19.

of contradictory pressures that influence their leadership style. They must keep the project operating in line with its timetable and preconceived objectives, which requires central direction and assertiveness with respect to staff activities and productivity. Each staff person must accomplish the assigned tasks. But, managers also, are dependent on the staff who have the skills in scientific, technical, and methodological areas, and the expertise to help solve project problems. The staff members often have work values that stress individual freedom to exercise professional judgment. Project managers must also be concerned with the personal and professional interests of each staff member to obtain job satisfaction and advancement.

Thus, project managers must do a balancing act. They must exercise their own authority at certain times and must maximize staff participation at other times. As one project director states "I try to find a middle ground by making my own decisions in order to assure project efficiency, but I always try to at least consult with the staff before finalizing important decisions that affect them." Or, as another manager states "sometimes I'm a Theory X person; other times I'm a Theory Y person."*

Managing the project staff may require a project director to suspend some traditional administrative concepts. For example, a distinction is often made in public and business administration between line and staff functions in the organization of personnel. However, in most projects this distinction is seldom very clear cut. Project staff members often carry out direct programmatic responsibilities (a line function) and also may be consulting with other project personnel (a staff function). Similarly, a project director may have administrative responsibility for budget control (a staff function) and may also run one of the project's self-help groups for the visually handicapped (a line function). This attribute of project work has some real advantages to project directors in relation to the management of staff since the director and staff members share more similar work experiences than in large ongoing organizations.

In summary, project managers are subject to what Weiner has called "irreconcilable value tensions" as they decide upon leadership strategies. These are basically the tensions of democracy versus dominance;

---

*Theory X refers to the work of Douglas McGregor, *The Human Side of Enterprise* (New York: McGraw Hill, 1960). Theory X stresses the need for authoritarian hierarchical direction. Theory Y is an alternative concept of management that stresses the need for management to establish conditions for worker participation in the achievement of objectives.

of efficient calculation and being instrumental in dealing with staff versus maintaining positive relationships and allowing staff to realize their potential.*

As one considers the various administrative techniques described in this chapter, these tensions must be dealt with as you decide on what approach to take at any given time. There are many ways to get to the same objective and seldom is there any universal "right" way.

STAFF RECRUITMENT AND SELECTION

Projects seldom begin with a full-blown staff. One of the early major activities of most project directors is the recruitment and selection of the project staff. This involves: (1) preparing job descriptions; (2) integrating project personnel requirements into those of the host agency; (3) preparing and implementing recruitment plans; and (4) screening, interviewing, and selecting staff.

Job descriptions should include: the job title; a description of the responsibilities and duties of the job; the educational, experiential, and skill qualifications; the salary range; and the classification of the job, if any. In preparing job descriptions you need to decide whether to maximize or minimize the duties, qualifications, and salary level. Some project directors try to minimize these factors and thus reduce the salary budget. Others do just the opposite; they maximize the factors to get the highest qualified person within the budgeted amount.

One way that project managers try to save money is by hiring some persons who would usually be considered as regular staff as consultants. When this is done, it is not necessary to pay any fringe benefits including social security and paid vacations. Some project directors see this as a way to stretch dollars as far as possible. Others, however, view this practice as a form of denying adequate compensation to an employee and will try to maximize salaries and benefits as far as possible.

It is the project director's responsibility to determine and adhere to the recruitment policies and procedures of the host agency and the funding agency. These will include procedures for assuring equal opportunity and affirmative action in the recruitment plan. In large host agencies, particularly public agencies, you will go about recruiting for the job and submit your selections to an affirmative action committee

---

*Myron E. Weiner, *Human Services Management: Analysis and Applications* (Homewood, Ill.: The Dorsey Press, 1982), pp. 553–589.

or officer for approval. Many agencies have procedures for requesting waivers in special cases where, for example, there is no time for a thorough search or where there is a need for short-term, specialized appointments. Find out who the affirmative action officer and/or committee chairperson is and solicit their help in explaining the rules and procedures and in preparing your recruitment plans.

In many host agencies you will also have to complete a report on the selection process, including how many people applied, how many were interviewed, their ethnic, sex, and age characteristics, and the basis for selection.

There are many other details that project directors must handle in terms of recruiting and selecting staff such as preparing advertisements, contacting sources for potential employees, reading résumés, getting letters of recommendation, and interviewing candidates. The most frequent problems that project directors run into are difficulties in finding the right person and delays in getting that person appointed. The way to help overcome this is to start immediately with job recruitment. Follow the affirmative action procedures to the letter and consult the affirmative action staff and/or committee chairperson.

Most projects are located within host agencies that have personnel systems to which the project must conform. These systems include policies and procedures for selection and appointment of staff, rank, job titles, salary schedules, staff benefits (for example, insurance, vacation), general personnel practices and policies, and, in some cases, union agreements. In addition, nonprofit organizations and all governmental agencies have developed job classification systems over long periods of time that outline the duties, qualifications, titles, salary ranges, and other characteristics of each position. Projects must also classify their jobs, but usually do not have the benefit of years of trial and error and revision. Some jobs in a project may be routine and fit into the regular classification. Other jobs may be unusual but will still have to be defined in a way to fit into the host agency's classification system. Project directors, therefore, should study the host agency classification system in order to describe jobs in a way that will be most advantageous to the project when they are slotted into the routine system.

Project managers should conform to the language of the host agency in devising such materials whenever possible. But be careful! Don't define project jobs in a manner that is consistent with routine jobs if the salary level, rank, or title you are seeking for a given position is different from that normally associated with the routine position description. For example, a county department of social services may have a caseworker I and caseworker II classification. If the project wants to maximize the qualification level and salary level for a nutrition counselor, it should define this job in a way that will make it clear it is consistent with the higher caseworker II classification. This job classification may require three years of counseling experience. Stretch as far as possible the interpretation of the experience of the person you want to appoint.

Sometimes it is difficult to define project jobs in ways that fit in with host agency classifications because of the special needs of the project. For example, a project may require a research associate at a high level of experience and commensurate salary but finds the host agency personnel system has rather low salaries for persons with this job title. Find another title such as assistant director and stretch your definitions to fit these requirements.

Project personnel requirements must be interpreted to host agency personnel administrators. Call on them in person. Explain what the project is all about, outline your needs, and enlist their help. Find the right titles, grades, and ranks for personnel that fit your needs the best.

There are, of course, substantial benefits to projects in the personnel area that derive from host agency personnel systems that offset the kinds of problems previously discussed. There are many aspects of personnel administration with which project directors in large host agencies do not have to be concerned. These include, for example, the routine (and not so routine) aspects of administering employee benefits, maintaining personnel files and records, handling union relationships, managing sick leave and vacation time records, to say nothing of the administration of salaries. (In free-standing projects, of course, the project administrator must be concerned with all of these matters since, in effect, the free-standing project is a new nonprofit organization.)

ORGANIZING THE STAFF AND PROJECT STRUCTURE

Once the staff has been selected, it must be organized into units to carry out the project's activities. The work of a project is carried out through a structure in which staff members are assigned specific duties and activities. These formal organizational arrangements define not only the functions of staff but also their relationships. At the same time, all projects also develop informal relationships among staff that usually do not conform to the formal structure. Project managers must identify these arrangements and relate to them in ways that will foster cooperation and enable staff to work together to promote achievement of the project's objectives.

There are a few major models that are followed organizing a project staff. Most projects organize their staff on a functional basis. That is, the unit is organized around particular functions such as administration, training, interviewing, data analysis, research, intake, service, community relations, and counseling. The larger the project, the more the staff tend to be specialized. A given staff person will work full time at a single function such as interviewing, programming, bookkeeping, counseling, or training. In smaller projects, however, there is less specialization and the same staff persons may have to perform a number of these functions.

Another model is to organize staff on the basis of target populations such as youth services, neighborhood services, services to adults. Staff may also be organized according to professional skills such as a nursing unit, a social work unit, and so forth. The extent to which the project staff is organized into formal units or departments is largely a matter of size. Projects of six or more people generally have some formal units as part of their structure.

Another model of staff organization is one of geographic decentralization. This is appropriate for projects that are carrying out activities in more than one location. For example, a training program may have units in three different communities; a research project may be conducted in a number of different cities; a drug abuse prevention project for adolescents may have units in a number of different schools.

In addition to function and geography, one of the other factors to consider in devising the organizational structure is that of assuring adequate control, supervision, and communication. This involves what is often referred to as "span of control" and "chain of command." Span of control has to do with the number of different people or activities that are supervised by any one person. Because projects must move quickly in carrying out their activities, they generally should keep the span of control as small as possible, since this enables more intensive control and direction of program. Certainly no more than six persons should be supervised by one person in most cases.

The chain of command reflects the formal lines of responsibility and communication among the staff. An example of this is shown in figure 8-1 in which the lines of responsibility and communication are depicted. Projects are usually well advised to be as flexible as possible in this regard. Project directors need communication to be as open and infor-

FIGURE 8–1
Sample Organization Chart

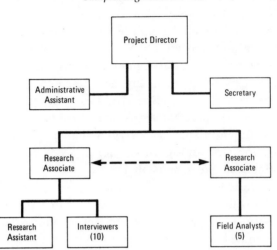

mal as possible in order to keep informed as to what is going on. In addition, open communication contributes to team building and development of shared commitment among the staff to the project's mission and program.

Once you decide how to organize the staff, it is helpful to prepare an organization chart such as the one depicted in figure 8–1. Distribute copies to the staff, to host agency officials, and to funders. Display the chart in a prominent place in the project headquarters and make reference to the chart from time to time during staff meetings to reinforce the staff's understanding of the project structure and their own roles.

STAFF MEETINGS

Project staff meetings are one of the principal means by which project managers formally communicate with the staff. Weekly or biweekly meetings are the usual pattern. These meetings may be used for a number of purposes. Foremost, is the opportunity to identify progress and problems in achieving project objectives and carrying out the activities and tasks associated with those objectives. The development of plans to overcome problems and barriers to task achievement can often be devised in staff meetings. In addition, the staff meeting can be used to communicate administrative information regarding all sorts of items ranging from salary information to scheduling the use of duplicating equipment.

Staff meetings also have a more subtle purpose. They are important arenas in which relationships may be either strengthened or weakened among the staff and between the staff and project head. Wise project directors are sensitive to these relationships, and they pay close attention to what each person has to say. They provide verbal rewards for work well done; are sympathetic to problems; and, provide concrete evidence that they are advocating for the project staff and trying to overcome any problems in their working conditions.

TASK-ORIENTED SUPERVISION

A main task of a project manager (and his or her chief assistants in large projects) is the direct one-to-one supervision of individual staff members. Projects vary with respect to how this task is structured. Some projects have formal arrangements in which a weekly conference between each staff member and his or her supervisor or the project director is scheduled. In other projects, individual supervision is less formal, and supervising personnel or the project director meets with staff members as needed for planning and implementing their specific work activities.

In either case, supervision in the project setting should be a highly task-oriented process. It is always in the context of the project's need to implement its activities quickly and achieve its substantive objectives. Thus, individual supervision will include such things as a principal investigator meeting with a research assistant to discuss the best kind of statistical test to use in analyzing data; or a supervisor of interviewers in a research survey project meeting weekly with each interviewer to go over the results of the interviews they have completed and the adequacy of the research forms they have completed; or a project director meeting weekly with a counselor to review progress in working with a group of teenagers. The task orientation of supervisory activities can be used by project heads as a way to keep aware of the progress being made in carrying out objectives, identifying problems, and devising individual solutions and work plans to facilitate the project's program.

Program Direction

FOCUSING PROGRAM DIRECTION

Project directors always assign priorities to how they use their time and energy with respect to managing program activities. These priorities need to be as conscious as possible and not, as is so often the case, dictated solely by the need to pay attention to crises and other demands on the manager's time. The basis for developing program management priorities in the case of a project should be related to its characteristic of needing to implement and achieve certain activities and results within a given time period. Project managers should guard against being diverted from this central task by "interesting matters" or pressures of staff or requests for nonproject-related services.

Managers must, therefore, focus their attention on the following four key questions:

1. What must be accomplished (specific objectives)
2. How are they to be accomplished (specific activities)
3. By whom are they to be accomplished (staff and organizational units)
4. What needs to be done when (timing of project implementation)

To do this the project director must have information related to each of these four questions. This raises the issue of how closely the project manager should monitor or supervise staff performance. In the case of ongoing organizations, many administrators believe that "management by exception" is a desirable form of program control in which managerial control is exercized only when there is evidence of problems. In the case of projects, however, with their pressure on goal achievement and a time-limited period for implementation, it is usually necessary to exercise more systematic control.

The following are some ways that project managers are able to organize program management, gain the information they need, and to give more effective direction to program activities.

USING OBJECTIVES AS A BASIS FOR PROGRAM MANAGEMENT

The acid test of successful project managment is the extent to which the project achieves its objectives. Is the study completed? Were the requisite number of interviews conducted? Did the teenage alcohol abuse counseling project reach its target population? Did high school students receive the educational information and help that was to be provided? In order to meet this test, the successful project manager institutes procedures that are aimed at controlling project activities in a way that gears them to the achievement of the specific objectives of a given project.

There is, of course, a formal system for managing in relation to objectives called MBO (Management By Objectives). At times, the use of this system may be appropriate for projects, but more often, it is necessary to adapt the MBO system to make it fit the time-limited nature of the special project. MBO in its purest form is a rational approach to management that calls for intensive involvement of all relevant organizational interests (that is, staff and units of the organization) in the process of setting organizational objectives and assessing progress is meeting them. But projects seldom have sufficient time for such a process-intensive approach. Furthermore, projects almost always have their objectives predefined in one way or another since the objectives have usually been set forth in the proposal on the basis of which the project has been funded and approved by funders and/or host agencies.

Finally, it should be recognized that although objectives are extremely important, the effective and smooth operation of a project involves more than organizing program management around a set of hierarchical objectives. Nevertheless, project managers can help assure a project's success by instituting a number of actions aimed at exercising control of program activities in order to bring them into as close alignment as possible with the project's objectives. The methods that follow reflect the manner in which project directors can adapt the MBO approach for use in project management.

REFINING THE PROJECT OBJECTIVES

A first step in the use of objectives as a basis for program direction is to take the project's objectives as stated in the proposal for the project and refine the way they are expressed in order to make them as specific and measurable as possible. (Naturally, if the proposal did not list objectives, it will be necessary to first develop them before they can be refined.) Objectives must be written. To use them for management purposes, they are best stated in behavioral terms (that is, subject to observation) and in measurable terms (subject to measurement). Remember that projects have two kinds of objectives: process objectives and outcome objectives.

Process objectives are those that relate to achieving activity goals such as "completing 1,000 interviews" or "training 500 teenagers." Outcome objectives are those related to accomplishing some behavioral change such as "improving communication among family members," "decreasing the rate of school dropouts"; or a final achievement such as "determining the factors that contribute to school truancy," "ascertaining the incidence and prevalance of upper respiratory illness among hospital employees." Every project has both process and outcome objectives, and project managers must be sure that both are expressed in terms that are subject to close monitoring and some quantifyable measurement of achievement.

An example of how to refine objectives that are stated rather broadly would be a case of a project aimed at providing assistance to children and families in which there has been a report of sexual abuse. The proposal for this project includes as one of its six objectives "to reduce the trauma of abuse for child victims." This objective can be further broken down into two subobjectives: (1) to increase opportunities for children to discuss this experience in an understanding and supportive environment and (b) to increase the security the child has in relation to further contact with the abuser. Figure 8–2 shows a format for breaking down objectives into subobjectives and assigning them identifying numbers and letters.

REFINING PROJECT ACTIVITIES

It is also necessary to refine the manner in which project activities are defined in order to express them in measurable or observable tasks. The major project activities are usually outlined in the project proposal in rather general terms. For example, a proposal for a re-

FIGURE 8–2
Format for Objectives and Subobjectives

OBJECTIVE # I:	Reduce Student Alienation
Subobjectives	
I–a	Increase Meaningful Community Service Roles for Students
I–b	Decrease Negative Labeling in Schools
I–c	Increase Student Decision Making in Schools
I–d	Promote Greater Community Awareness of Student Achievements

search project may have as one of the activities "to conduct interviews with a sample of 500 graduate students" and may go on to explain the manner in which the interviews will be conducted. This description needs to be further reduced to a set of specific tasks that, when taken together, represent an interview. For purposes of program management, this activity can be defined as comprising seven tasks of subactivities.

1. Letter Contact—sending a letter to each interviewee explaining the purpose of the interview and asking them to return a card indicating if they will or will not participate.
2. Phone Follow Up—calling up each interviewee who has not returned a card to see if they will participate.
3. Phone Appointments—telephoning each interviewee to make an appointment for the interview.
4. Interview Sessions—conducting the actual interview.
5. Follow Up on Broken Appointments—contacting each interviewee who did not keep an appointment to reschedule the interview.
6. Completion of Interview Guide—filling out the interview guide following the interview.
7. Submission of Interview Guide—providing the completed guide to the study director.

Similarly, a service project proposal might include an activity such as "reception and intake" at a neighborhood health center and explain something of the intake process. For purposes of management, the activity "reception and intake" can be broken down into the following eight tasks:

1. Determine Patient Status—is the person a new patient or seen previously?
2. Determine Patient Condition—is the patient's condition possibly an emergency or not?
3. Refer Emergencies—if an emergency, sending patient to examining nurse.
4. Determine Appointment Status—does patient have an appointment or not?
5. Make appointment for Patient—for those patients without prior appointment.
6. Refer Nonemergencies with Appointments—to nurse and inform record room.
7. Complete Patient Data Form—for new patients.
8. Refer New Patients to Nurse—and submit data form to record room.

Figure 8–3 shows a format for breaking activities down and assigning them identifying numbers and letters.

FIGURE 8–3

Format for Activities and Subactivities (action steps)

ACTIVITY # 1:	Develop Youth Volunteer Program
Subactivities	
1–a	Recruit Volunteer Coordinator
1–b	Hire Volunteer Coordinator
1–c	Prepare Volunteer Job Description
1–d	Distribute Description to Schools
1–e	Interview Volunteer Applicants
1–f	Select Thirty Volunteers
1–g	Prepare Volunteer Training Guide
1–h	Train Volunteers
1–i	Assign Volunteers

RELATING OBJECTIVES AND ACTIVITIES

Once the project's objectives and activities have been listed, the next step is to specify the relationship between the activities and the objectives. This is accomplished by developing an objectives/activities matrix as shown in figure 8–4. The project's objectives are listed across the top and the project's activities are listed down the side. Each activity is checked off in the appropriate box under the objective that the activity is intended to achieve. Figure 8–5 is a more detailed format for showing these connections. This is particularly useful in cases where a group of activities are related to a single objective. Often, however, this is not the case, and a particular activity may serve to implement more than one objective. In these cases the matrix in Figure 8–4 is the more useful device.

ACTIVITY RESPONSIBILITY ASSIGNMENTS

"Project activities only get done if someone does them," said one project director. Obvious as this may be, it reveals the necessity for eliminating any fuzziness about who is to do what. This can be accomplished by devising a responsibility chart that lists each activity down the left side and the project staff across the top. Then check off the box under the staff members responsible for each activity, as in figure 8-6.

Project directors can use this particular program management tool as the basis for supervision of staff and the control of activity implemen-

FIGURE 8–4

Relating Objectives and Activities

Activities	Objectives				
	I	II	III	IV	V
1.					
2.					
3.					
4.					
5.					
6.					
7.					
8.					
9.					
10.					
11.					
12.					

tation. It pinpoints exactly where problems are occurring, who is responsible, and eliminates ambiguity about the staff member's accountability.

USING TIMETABLES AS A MANAGEMENT TOOL

As pointed out in chapter 2, one of the main features of a project, as compared to an ongoing organization, is that projects are time limited. Most projects are funded for a one-, two-, or three-year period. They are expected to complete a certain piece of work during that time. And, if they are seeking refunding or a continuation of funding, receiving it will be highly dependent on their record of accomplishment. Therefore, project directors need to institute measures to assure that the project operates on a timetable. Like "keeping the trains operating on time," it is the effective manager who keeps his or her project on the track and running on time.

The simplest and most frequently used method for managing the

FIGURE 8–5

Objectives/Activities Form

Objective:	I-a Increase Meaningful Roles		
	Activity 1: Develop Youth Volunteer Program		

Objective/ Activity	Action Step	Completion Date	Staff Responsible
I–a–1–a			
I–a–1–b			
I–a–1–c			
I–a–1–d			
I–a–1–e			
I–a–1–f			
I–a–1–g			
I–a–1–h			
I–a–1–i			

project's activities in relation to a timetable is the Gantt chart (named after the industrial engineer who developed this technique). The Gantt chart approach, like other time-management approaches, is a method to enable managers to exercise control over project activities and give direction to the work. This is done by keeping account of the progress being made in implementing and completing every major task that must be performed. It also enables project managers to coordinate these activities. The steps necessary to design and use this method are as follows:

Step One: Activity Listing. The first step in preparing a time chart is to make a list of every activity that must be carried out from the beginning to the completion of the project. This is identical to the activity listing described earlier.

Step Two: List Major Activity Phases. After listing all activities, the next step is to group them together into major activity categories or phases. For example, the initial activities involved in the first three months of setting up and operating a health education center project in a hospital might fall under four categories such as:

FIGURE 8–6
*Monthly Responsibility Chart**

Activities Month _____	Staff Responsibility					
	Jones	Smith	Jackson	James	Powers	Grant

*Based on Myron Weiner, *Human Services Management: Analysis and Applications* (Homewood, Ill.: The Dorsey Press, 1982), p. 394.

Phase I: Staffing

Define staff positions
Classify positions
Prepare recruitment plan and submit to Affirmative Action Committee
Advertise for staff
Screen applications
Interview applicants
Select staff
Process staff appointments
Plan staff orientation
Conduct staff orientation

Phase II: Site Acquisition

Prepare space requirements
Negotiate space with administrator
Prepare space utilization plan
Occupy space

Phase III: Develop Materials

Conduct computer search of literature
Acquire health education material
Review health education material
Decide on materials to use

Phase IV: Promotion

Prepare brochure on program
Prepare and distribute newspaper release
Prepare and mail announcements to community agencies

Step Three: Assign Time Estimates. After completing the list of all project activities, the next step is to decide upon (1) the amount of time available for the phase and (2) the amount of time required for each activity. For most projects that operate on a one-year basis, the use of the time-measurement unit of a week will usually work best for this purpose. Prepare a worksheet on which the time estimates are entered. Using the foregoing example for Phase I, such a worksheet would start like this:

Phase I: Staffing Activities

	Time Estimate 2 Months
Define staff positions and classify positions	1 week
Prepare recruitment plan and submit to Affirmative Action Committee	1 week
Advertise for staff	3 weeks
Screen applications	1 week
Interview candidates	3 days
Select staff	1 day
Process staff appointments	2 weeks
Plan staff orientation	4 days
Conduct staff orientation	2 days

You will note that the time required for all activities adds up to more than the two months available for the entire phase. This means that a number of activities must be implemented at the same time. This is accounted for in the next step.

Step Four: Estimate Start and Completion Dates. The key to planning an effective timetable is to be able to coordinate activities in a way that assures their completion within a deadline. This is done by charting the activities using the format illustrated in figure 8-7, which is a sample of a timetable for a research study.

This example uses months as the unit of count. Obviously, you can use any other appropriate unit of time. For each activity, a line is entered to represent the starting point, how long the activity will go on, and the completion point for each activity.

In the process of estimating these times, you will often find it necessary to make changes in order to assure that various events fit within the time available and are coordinated.

Use the chart to keep track of how well the project is keeping on its timetable. Any slippage needs immediate attention from the project director. As part of using this management tool, you will need to develop formal or informal systems to obtain information from staff on the progress of the work they are doing. Some of this can be obtained by using or adapting some of the reporting forms shown in figures 8-10 and 8-11. Other information can just as easily be obtained from observation and regular contact with the staff. The progress in completing a brochure, for example, does not require the use of a staff reporting form. The extent to which a targeted number of counseling

147

FIGURE 8-7
Sample Timetable Chart

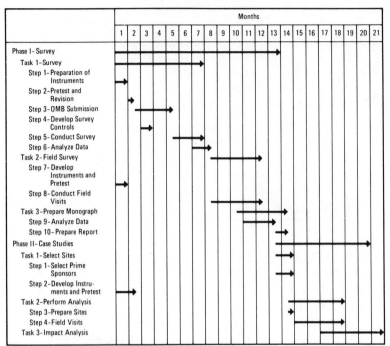

		Months																			
	1	2	3	4	5	6	7	8	9	10	11	12	13	14	15	16	17	18	19	20	21

Phase I- Survey
Task 1- Survey
Step 1- Preparation of Instruments
Step 2- Pretest and Revision
Step 3- OMB Submission
Step 4- Develop Survey Controls
Step 5- Conduct Survey
Step 6- Analyze Data
Task 2- Field Survey
Step 7- Develop Instruments and Pretest
Step 8- Conduct Field Visits
Task 3- Prepare Monograph
Step 9- Analyze Data
Step 10- Prepare Report
Phase II- Case Studies
Task 1- Select Sites
Step 1- Select Prime Sponsors
Step 2- Develop Instruments and Pretest
Task 2- Perform Analysis
Step 3- Prepare Sites
Step 4- Field Visits
Task 3- Impact Analysis

sessions per week is being achieved, on the other hand, does lend itself to use of formal reporting forms.

Another time-oriented management tool is the Program Evaluation Review Technique (PERT) originally developed in connection with large-scale defense construction projects. This device allows for a recognition of the dependency of one activity on another. For example, an activity such as staff training cannot start until you complete the prior activity of staff selection. A simplified format for how a PERT chart is developed is seen in figure 8–8.

In a PERT chart, the numbered circles represent a sequence of events, such as (1) approval of grant; (2) approval of job descriptions; (3) hiring of staff; (4) training of staff; and (5) beginning of program. The numbers in the event circles do not represent time; they are used simply to identify events.

The arrowed lines represent the necessary activities that connect these events. The events represent the start or completion of the activity. The numbers on the lines represent the time period (number of days) to progress from one event to the next.*

One of the things you can do if you adopt the PERT approach to

* Harry Evarts, *Introduction to PERT* (Boston: Allyn and Bacon), 1964.

FIGURE 8–8
Sample PERT Chart

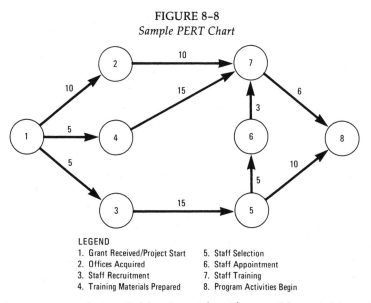

LEGEND

1. Grant Received/Project Start
2. Offices Acquired
3. Staff Recruitment
4. Training Materials Prepared

5. Staff Selection
6. Staff Appointment
7. Staff Training
8. Program Activities Begin

chart out your project activities is to identify possible activities where you can reduce the amount of time to be taken. Technically, this is a method known as Critical Path Method (CPM) which is used in construction projects to "crash" the time between certain events. CPM is a highly technical method requiring the use of the computer and is not appropriate to the kinds of projects covered in this book. However, the general principle of reducing time for selected activities is certainly something that project directors should adhere to whenever possible.

USING FLOW CHARTS

Another technique that can be useful in the control and direction of project activities is the use of flow charts to depict the steps in operations, or decisions that are required in carrying out a series of activities. An example of such a chart is seen in figure 8–9 which shows the flow of activities for a neighborhood health center.

The value of this technique is that it can help you identify the interdependence of activities and/or decisions in a much simpler form than the typical PERT system.

USING PERFORMANCE REPORTING TECHNIQUES

Performance reporting is a form of program control that enables managers to go beyond the "start-completion" structure of the Gantt chart and to assess progress in the actual production of the project's

FIGURE 8–9
Sample Flow Chart *

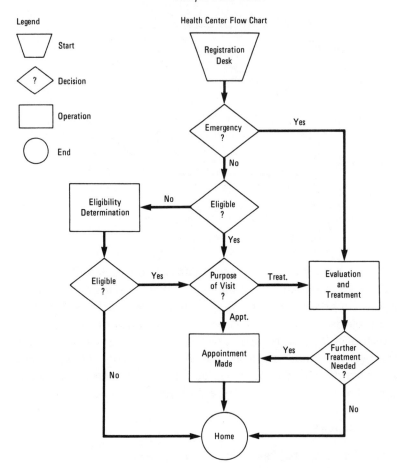

* Reprinted with permission from Robert Lefferts, *How to Prepare Charts and Graphs for Effective Reports* (New York: Harper & Row, 1981), p. 126.

activities by the responsible staff members. Performance reporting intergrates the use of selected management tools described earlier in this section. Productivity may be measured in terms of process such as the number of hours spent in counseling, as training, or interviewing. Productivity may also be measured in terms of outputs such as number of interviews completed, workers trained, patients discharged, or youth referred to other agencies. Or, it may include both process and output measures.

Performance reporting can be amplified to include the use of program timetables by setting process or output targets for a time period (for example, weekly, monthly, or quarterly). The work actually accomplished is then matched against these productivity targets.

In order to utilize such performance measures, it is critical that information be supplied to managers by the project staff members who are actually doing the work. This requires the development and use of some type of reporting system in which workers keep track of particular information on standardized forms. Two samples of forms developed for this purpose are seen in figures 8-10 and 8-11. Figure 8-10 measures productivity against targeted objectives. Figure 8-11 measures the nature and extent of various activities. These activities are related to the achievement of one or more objectives as described earlier in this section. Thus, one can use this information to (1) identify the progress being made in accomplishing program objectives, (2) document the project's achievements, and (3) provide data for purposes of evaluation.

MANAGING CRISES

Projects are often faced with two kinds of crises: those that arise from internal problems and those that are generated by outside forces, usually funders or host agencies. It should be no surprise that projects experience frequent crises since they are developing organizations with little history or experience in dealing with operating problems. In addition, they are often engaged in innovative activities. And, they are always vulnerable to the requirements and pressures of funders and host agencies. More often than not project crises are the result of

FIGURE 8-10
Sample of Performance Report Form

PROJECT FOR FAMILY LIVING
Worker Name _____ Month _____

Activity	Services Performed	
	Targeted Objective	Actual Performance
Home Interview	100	110
Counseling Sessions	66	60
Group Sessions	22	22
School Consultants	10	18

FIGURE 8–11
Sample of Performance Report Form

PROJECT FOR FAMILY LIVING

Worker Name _____

Week of _____ to _____

Activity	Day						
	Mon	Tues	Wed	Thurs	Fri	Sat	Total
Home Interviews Number of Interviews							
Number of Hours Interviewing							
Counseling Number of Clients Counseled							
Number of Counseling Sessions							
Number of Hours Counseling							
Group Sessions Number of Group Meetings							
Total Attendance							
Number of Hours							

Consultation
    Number of Consultation
        Sessions with Schools							

Number of Hours							

these factors rather than inefficiency and incompetence. Crises can paralyze a project by diverting attention and energy away from the project's program. Project managers must, therefore, devise tactics to resolve crises as quickly as possible. While there is a school of thought that, in the case of ongoing organizations, suggests managers should let some crises fester and resolve themselves, this is not a tactic that projects can affort to adopt.

Successful crises resolution requires that the manager first identify the type of crises that he or she is faced with. Most crises fall into five categories:

152

1. Those that are primarily rooted in interpersonal relationships
2. Those that involve equipment or supply breakdowns
3. Those related to meeting funder or host agency requirements
4. Those related to conflict over power, rules, policies, responsibilities, authority, or competence
5. Those related to conflicts with other units and organizations over boundaries, roles, power, values, and resources

Crises can be resolved by the use of a variety of tactics available to managers. The goal of crises resolution is to get the project back on track and functioning at optimal efficiency.

Managers may select from a number of actions in their efforts to resolve crises. These include:

Technical resolutions to expedite the solution to breakdowns in equipment and supplies

Interpersonal resolutions to mediate crises that are rooted in personal conflicts

Authority resolutions in which the manager asserts his or her decision-making authority in a take-it-or-leave-it style

Cooperative resolutions in which the problem is left to the parties involved to work out

Communicative resolutions in which the problem is resolved simply by providing necessary information or facilitating information flow among affected parties

Compliance resolutions in which the manager decides to comply with the demands or requirements of the agency or person generating the problem

The chart in figure 8–12 includes a checklist of how these methods are most frequently utilized in relation to different types of crises.

Evaluation Management

UNDERSTANDING EVALUATION

Project evaluation includes a range of activities from assessments made during a site visit or included in project program reports, to appraisals made by auditors and formal internal or external research-oriented evaluations. In this section, we are concerned with the role of project directors in connection with the latter area of formal evalua-

FIGURE 8–12

*Relationship of Crises Management Methods
Employed for Different Types of Crises*

Crises Management Resolution Methods	Type of Crises				
	Inter-personal	Equipment	Requirement Compliance	Policy/ Responsibility	Inter-organization
Technical		X	X	X	
Interpersonal	X			X	X
Authority	X			X	X
Cooperative	X			X	X
Communicative	X		X		X
Compliance			X		

tion activities that are conducted either by the project or by an outside organization.

Funders often require that there be an evaluation of project activities since they seek documentation of the effects of the grants that they make. Thus, in addition to directing program activities, many project directors must also be responsible for the management of some type of formal evaluation of the project's activities. It is necessary, therefore, that a project director who does not have a background in evaluation research acquaint themselves with this area of activity. Some resources for this purpose are described in appendix A. It is important to recognize that there are different types of evaluation in which projects may be involved and different levels of information and analysis that may be required. The three major types of evaluation are:

1. Internal evaluation in which the evaluation process is carried out entirely by the project staff which may include specialized evaluation staff who are either full-time or part-time members of the regular staff.
2. External evaluation which is conducted by evaluators who are hired by the project as consultants and who may or may not collaborate with project staff in the evaluation design and analysis of the evaluation data.
3. External evaluation which is carried out by an independent third party (usually a university or consulting firm) hired by the grantor to conduct

the evaluation, or the evaluation is carried out by staff of the grantor who are assigned for this purpose.

The evaluation process also varies in terms of the kind and amount of data to be used for the evaluation and the focus or purpose of the evaluation. Some evaluations are based solely on monitoring information that is collected by the project and is focused primarily on documenting the project's implementation. Information of this kind is primarily descriptive in that it focuses on questions like: Was the staff hired? Did activities start on time? How many people were served or involved and what were their demographic characteristics? Analysis in this type of evaluation focuses on determining how consistent these numbers and characteristics are with what was originally proposed and funded.

Other evaluation designs require more depth of analysis and focus more on determining the project's impact or outcomes, the extent to which its objectives are realized, and on identifying the strengths and weaknesses in the project's performance (for example, its staff, its methods, its organization).

Project evaluations have varied purposes. Sometimes these evaluations are required by the legislation that establishes a particular grant program, or they may be to provide the project with ongoing feedback about its activities so that it can identify problems in implementation and institute changes in order to increase effectiveness. Evaluations may be primarily to assist the grantor such as a foundation to assess its grant-making activities and evaluate its own goals and priorities. An evaluation may be for the purpose of appraising a project's effectiveness in order to provide information for use in considering refunding the project, or it may also be used for the purpose of identifying the effectiveness of a particular service methodology or of a certain approach to a particular problem in order to disseminate this information in the hope of changing practice in a field or promoting more widespread adoption of a program.

Evaluations also vary according to the degree of sophistication of the research design and according to the resources made available for purposes of evaluation. A $100,000 mental health counseling project that has $3,000 in its budget for evaluation is not going to have the resources to mount a very complex research design that calls for control groups, sampling, assembling large amounts of data, interviewing clients, using computers to analyze data, or engaging in multivarient data analysis. And, even if sufficient resources are available, there is a remaining question of the state of the art including the difficulty of identifying what variables really influence the outcomes of project activities and the complexities and difficulties involved in definitively measuring social and behavioral phenomena.

Given the multiplicity of purposes, the variety of possible approaches to evaluation, and the methodological complexities involved in assessing social programs, it is no wonder that most project directors shudder at the thought of evaluation. Regardless of how benign the purpose of an evaluation may be stated, everyone knows the evaluation may affect future funding as well as the professional status of project personnel. Thus, evaluation is anxiety provoking regardless of whether it be an internal evaluation or one conducted for the funder by an outside research or management organization or university. There is often a good deal of resistance expressed by project staff to evaluators and evaluation activities. Nevertheless, it is an area of activity that must be managed, and project directors have a variety of tasks they must carry out which are discussed in the following sections.

SELECTING EVALUATION PERSONNEL

Finding a competent evaluator, whether it be an evaluation consultant hired by the project for ten days or a management consulting firm to be given a $500,000 contract to evaluate a national federal program, is never an easy task. The majority of evaluations are conducted by projects that have funds included in their grants to hire their own full-time or part-time evaluation staff. Project directors must decide on what the qualifications should be for such a person or persons. The major problem regarding qualifications for evaluators usually revolves around questions of how to weigh the importance of their technical training and experience versus the extent of their understanding of and orientation to the project's philosophy and program versus the extent to which they have personal qualities and skills such as being able to work cooperatively with people, being insightful, and possessing good communication and writing ability.

Professional research skills are, of course, important. But given their presence, they are not the only or even primary consideration. According to Marvin Alkin of the UCLA Center for the Study of Evaluation:

> Apparently, the menu of individual skill content areas which ought to be part of the evaluator's repertoire include statistics, research design, interviewing, questionnaires, ratings, survey methods, psychometrics and measurement, observation techniques, goal-setting, cost effectiveness proce-

dures, etc. Personally, I am chary about using such lists as the basis for selecting evaluators. While I would subscribe to the necessity of the evaluator having some measure of expertise in these areas, they hardly seem like the primary bases for evaluator selection. Unfortunately, I have little to offer in the way of discrete, easily measured evaluator characteristics. I have found, however, were I drawing up a Christmas shopping list, that I more likely would use such expressions as sensitivity, intelligence, insightfulness, and the ability to integrate data in logical ways. Moreover, the evaluator should have interpersonal skills, writing abilities, be credible, and most importantly, have a service orientation.

From my own research on evaluator effectiveness, I have become particularly attuned to the importance of evaluators' orientation to service. If evaluators view their role as one oriented to user's information needs, then greater likelihood exists that the evaluation will be effective and have an impact on the decision-making.

Orientation towards service encompasses a number of the other characteristics as well—communication and interpersonal skills, understanding of political constraints, and development of increased credibility. I have found, for example, that credibility is in large measure acquirable during the course of the conduct of the evaluation. If evaluators are viewed as performing relevant functions related to real user needs, credibility can easily be enhanced.*

Projects that have funds to retain an outside consulting firm to conduct a third-party evaluation are faced with the problem of selecting the most appropriate company or organization. Shall we use a university, a profit-making firm, or a nonprofit organization are the typical questions that must be faced. Experience does not suggest that any one group is necessarily better than the other. The same principles noted previously for selecting a staff person may be applied in seeking an outside organization. But some additional factors are of importance here. What is the organization's track record? What other evaluations has it conducted? Did they finish on time? Did they do all the work that was promised? What were the results? How was the project affected by the evaluation? Get copies of other evaluation reports they have completed and ask projects that were evaluated to provide references.

DECIDING ON EVALUATION DESIGN

Most project evaluations are designed to focus on the achievement of the project's objectives. To use objectives as the basis for evaluation

---

*Reprinted with permission from: *Conducting Evaluations: Three Perspectives.* Published by The Foundation Center, 888 Seventh Avenue, New York, NY 10106.

involves a number of steps. First, the project's objectives must be specified in detail along the lines described earlier in this chapter. Second, the design must include clear statements of what information will be used as the basis for measurement. Third, the design must set forth how the measurement information will be collected. Fourth, the design must describe how this information, once collected, will be assembled and analyzed. And, as part of this fourth step, the criteria that will be used for making an evaluative judgment of the data need to be outlined.

An example, using just one objective to illustrate this approach to evaluation, is a project that brought together adults and youth in intergenerational discussion groups. The topic of discussion was the social and sexual activities of high school students. The project had the following objective.

PROJECT OBJECTIVE ONE: To increase intergenerational communication.

Measurements:
(a) Frequency of contacts between adolescents and adults.
(b) Frequency of participation in the same activity by adolescents and adults together.
(c) Perception of adolescents of change in the extent of communication they have with adults.
(d) Perception of adults of change in the extent of communication they have with adolescents.

Data Collection Methods:
(a) Tabulation of communication pattern and interaction forms kept by leaders of intergenerational workshop groups.
(b) Tabulation of activity participation forms kept by leaders of intergenerational workshop groups.
(c) Interviews with adolescent participants in workshop groups during first month of project and during eleventh month.
(d) Interviews with adult participants in workshop during first month of project and during eleventh month.

Evaluation designs may also focus on issues of quality, impact, and/or efficiency. These designs may include conducting cost analyses, cost-benefit studies, cost-effectiveness studies, or assessing the extent to which project activities adhere to accepted standards.

Project managers need to be involved in the evaluation design whether or not they are research or evaluation specialists. The primary interest of the project manager is to assure that the design is:

1. Appropriate to the project's activity
2. Consistent with the available staff, financial, and technical resources
3. Fair to the project
4. Able to generate the information that a funder requires
5. Feasible and can be completed in the available time
6. Not going to require evaluation activities that will interfere with the smooth operation of the project's programmatic and administrative functions
7. Consistent with the state of the art with respect to the research problem of adequately identifying the variables that influence performance and developing adequate measurements of their effects.

RELATING TO EVALUATION ACTIVITIES

There are a number of different responsibilities that project managers have in relation to evaluation in addition to selecting evaluation staff and assessing the evaluation design. The project director should facilitate the evaluation process by being sure that the project staff is oriented to the purpose of the evaluation and the research procedures that will be used. The importance of the staff's cooperation in the evaluation needs to be stressed. A certain amount of staff resistance to evaluation can always be anticipated since it may be viewed as a threat to, or as an additional burden on, the staff, since they usually will need to provide information, fill out forms, and be interviewed. Staff may resent "outsiders" examining their work and may often feel the evaluators do not sufficiently understand the philosophy or methods that they are using. Staff may believe the evaluation is poorly timed because it comes too soon in the life of the project and the results of the project's activities cannot yet be seen. While most of the responsibility for overcoming these problems lies with the evaluators, project managers share this responsibility. They are the ones who set the tone for how the evaluation is to be regarded. Through frequent meetings with staff they can help assuage their fears and promote their participation.

Every evaluation depends on information that must be provided by the project from existing records, which are kept in the course of the project's regular operations as well as from special information gathered through interviews, questionnaires, and observations done specifically for purposes of evaluation. Project directors are responsible for assuring that project records and information are made accessible to the evaluators and are up to date and in suitable form.

159

Sometimes evaluators make unreasonable demands on the time of project staff or request information that may be inappropriate or considered confidential. The project director should be sure that any situations of this kind are immediately called to his or her attention, and meetings with evaluators should be initiated by the project director to resolve these difficulties. When it is clear that the evaluation is pursuing inappropriate procedures, the project director has every right to object to such procedures. When this happens the usual result is to work out some sort of compromise that meets the needs of the evaluation but still protects the project's integrity.

REVIEWING EVALUATION REPORTS

The final set of responsibilities of the project director is in connection with the review of the final evaluation report prior to submission to the funder or host agency. Most evaluators prefer to submit a draft report to the project before it is made final since this permits correction of any errors of fact. If they do not initiate this procedure, you should insist on it. Project directors should review these reports very carefully and examine them not only for factual correctness, but in terms of the kinds of assessments, analysis, and conclusions that are reached. There is usually a good deal of judgment that goes into any evaluation of social programs. These judgments reflect not only data but their interpretation based on values and political perspectives regarding what is desirable and "worthwhile." While it would be inappropriate to try to change a report simply to have the project look better, there is no reason why your disagreement with any aspect of the report should not be expressed to the evaluators. Meet with them, point out their errors or biases, if any, and provide additional information and documentation. And, if you disagree with the evaluators and you are sure you are right and have solid data to back up your position, you should communicate this to the funder.

In cases of internal evaluation, the project director is usually the person who submits the final report to the funder. Project directors, in these cases, should use the material and reports prepared by their evaluation staff and rewrite or at least edit the report so that it reflects the broadest possible perspective on the project. As part of this process, put the evaluation data in the context of the total project. Point out the constraints under which the project operates, such as limitations of time, difficulty in locating qualified staff, or budgetary limitations. Do not make this sound like a set of excuses, but rather, set forth this information as statements of fact. Explain the reasons why certain things were not done. Admit to shortcomings since no operating program is ever perfect. And, most importantly, do not hesitate to highlight the real accomplishments of the project.

Committee Management

Many projects include one or more advisory boards or committees as part of their operations. For example, a research study conducted by a university group to evaluate an experimental day-care program has an advisory committee composed of people working in the day-care field; a counseling and education program on teenage alcohol abuse has a committee of school administrators and faculty to approve the overall operating policies; a training program for child-care workers has an advisory board of people from fifteen different child-care agencies in the community. Projects also have administrative committees comprised of project staff, such as a committee to review and recommend the procedures to be used for a household survey to locate persons with health problems to come to a screening program on hypertension; or a committee of staff members to devise a plan to publicize an energy conservation recycling program; or a staff committee to decide on the schedule of productions for a community street theater project.

Project directors have the responsibility to see that such boards and committees are properly organized and managed. The nature of these groups may have been described in the project proposal, or they may be initiated by the project director based on a need. Boards and committees of this type may sometimes be permanent for the life of the project, or, other times, they are ad hoc groups that are set up for a time-limited period to accomplish a specific task. Service projects lodged in nonprofit agencies and governmental agencies will usually have some sort of overall advisory board. Research projects have such groups much less frequently.

Managing project committees and boards can be improved by following a number of guidelines that are described in the following sections in connection with membership, orientation, records, and procedures.

SELECTING COMMITTEE MEMBERS

Keep membership as small as possible. The more members a group has, the more time is required to discuss and reach agreement on items. Project timetables do not usually allow for long drawn out deliberations. At the same time, it is essential to include representation of all major interests on these groups, but, if there is any doubt, limit the membership as far as possible.

Members who come from outside the project should receive a written invitation from the project director or the head of the host agency. Tell people in the invitation what the purpose of the board or committee is; when and how often it will meet; why they are being asked to serve; and who else will serve. Follow up in two or three days with a phone call to pin down their membership. A sample of a letter of invitation is shown in figure 8-13.

When deciding on the characteristics of the people being selected as members, you will often need to balance a number of factors that may be in conflict. For example, you can expect a grant agency site visit team to want to meet with a project advisory board, so you want members who are articulate and supportive of the project. But you may also need an advisory board to be representative of the community, or of cooperating agencies, or of various professional or technical viewpoints. Some of these people may not always be as supportive as others, but they play an important role in legitimizing the project.

Thank all members in writing after they complete their service. Everyone likes recognition, and you may need them again and want them to feel positive about their experience.

ORIENTATING COMMITTEES

One of the key ingredients in the management of committees is the orientation of members. At a minimum, this includes supplying the members with (1) a description of the project's objectives and program, (2) the responsibilities of the committee, and (3) where it fits into the project. Project directors should take the time to provide this orientation at the first meeting of the committee. If a committee is important enough to have, it is important enough to warrant the director's personal attention. Some project directors make it a practice to give each member a written fact-sheet that explains this same material.

FIGURE 8–13
Sample Letter of Invitation

FAMILY ARTS CENTER
ADULT THEATRE PROJECT
111 Your Street
Hometown, New York   11717

April 1, 1983

Ms. Mary Understanding
11 Oval Drive
Hertown, New York 11770

Dear Ms. Understanding:

The Adult Theatre Project, supported by the XYZ Foundation, is forming an advisory board to review the project's policies and program. We would like to invite you to be one of the twelve members of this board of which Ms. Adele Smith has agreed to serve as Chair. The board will meet monthly.

The Adult Theatre is a three-year project to demonstrate the ways in which theatre arts can contribute to the social well-being of mature adults whose talents in this field have never been developed. The XYZ Foundation grant of $100,000 supports activities which range from running ticket offices to performing in musical and dramatic productions. The role of the advisory committee is to provide the project staff with guidance regarding these activities, deciding what productions should be offered to the community, and to participate in the final evaluation of the program.

Ms. Smith will call you in a few days to discuss this further. Because of your leadership in the field of the arts, we believe your participation will be of great value. We trust you will accept.

Sincerely yours,

John Curtain
Project Director

JC/st

KEEPING COMMITTEE RECORDS

Because projets are, in effect, temporary organizations, there is a tendency for project managers to overlook the necessity for keeping written records of the meetings of advisory boards and project committees. This can result in problems when a site visit team, for example, asks for minutes or records of meetings, or when you need to go back and check on a particular decision made by a committee. Trusting to memory is dangerous inasmuch as different participants will recall different things even though they were present at the same meeting (sometimes it may even seem that they were at different meetings). So take the time to keep minutes of meetings and to have a file for each project committee. Minutes do not need to be long detailed accounts of what went on at the meeting, but can be limited to showing (1) the date and attendance; (2) the items covered in the discussion; (3) the decisions or agreements that are reached; and (4) when needed, an explanation of the major factors that were considered in making the decision. A sample of brief minutes is shown in figure 8–14. Note that in the margin is shown the names of committee members responsible to follow up or implement the decisions. Distribute the minutes to all members as soon as possible after the meeting, since they will rely upon them for confirmation of their assignments and the meeting will still be fresh in their minds.

FIGURE 8–14
Sample of Responsibility-Based Minutes

ABC Juvenile Delinquency Prevention Project

Minutes

March 10, 1983

Attendance: Edwards, Hart, Johnson, Jones, Keeler, Main, Smith, Wells, Wheeler.

Follow-Up Responsibility	Planning tasks for the coming month were discussed as follows:
Wells	*Advisory Boards.* Two neighborhood advisory boards remain to be set up in the next thirty days and agencies need to be contacted, names assembled, and letters of appointment sent out.
Keeler	*Court Diversion.* Many problems have developed in the procedures for courts referring youth to the project and these need to be corrected through a new agreement with Judge Henry.
Edwards	*Emergency Shelter.* With acquisition of the building at 101 Main Street on March 1, the next step is to prepare specifications for renovating bedrooms and kitchen facilities by April 1.
	Etc.

ESTABLISHING COMMITTEE PROCEDURES

Some procedural tips for achieving more efficient meetings include:

Written agendas should be distributed to members before the meeting listing each item that will be discussed. Some project directors like to put the time to be allotted to each item on the agenda. Others think this inhibits free discussion.

Short meetings accomplish more than long meetings. Members who know ahead of time that a meeting will last from 10 a.m. to 11 a.m. will be motivated to keep to the agenda and accomplish the committee's work.

Assign and delegate responsibility to members during the meeting for tasks they are to carry out following the meeting.

Note these in the committee minutes as suggested earlier.

Matching Management Systems to Needs

The last fifteen to twenty years have witnessed a tremendous growth in the development of so-called "management systems." These systems have largely been associated with the growth of the fields of organization development and business administration. Endless forms and procedures, all promising to improve managerial functioning, have been generated. Without getting into an assessment of the effectiveness of various systems such as Management By Objectives, Matrix Organization, or Quality Circles, it is apparent that project managers need to be very cautious in the adoption of such systems, because the processes involved in all these systems all require a period of "installation," a process of staff orientation and training in their use, and a period of time for trial and error and "debugging."

Projects do not have the luxury of sufficient time to allow for these processes to occur. Thus, even the most effective system can become useless because of the lack of time a project can devote to properly instituting the necessary procedures and processes. In addition, many projects are relatively small (six persons or under) and do not require paper-oriented systems for control and supervision. Many management systems were developed for use in large-scale, ongoing organizations with a high degree of routine operations. As pointed out earlier, these are not the attributes of projects and thus many of these management systems and tools are not only diversionary to the project's mission but are inappropriate and irrelevant for purposes of project management. So the final word in connection with program management is to keep paperwork and developmental processes to a minimum. If you adopt them, always assess their usefulness and discard any procedures that do not clearly facilitate the work of the project.

Closely related to program management is the management of the project's financial and business operations, which will be discussed in the next chapter.

Chapter 9

Financial Management: How to Manage the Project Budget

The effectiveness of a project's fiscal operations can make or break a project regardless of how good its program may be in practice. Effective financial management means much more than bookkeeping or accounting. It involves using financial data as a tool in decision making regarding the allocation and use of resources. As such, it is clearly not something to be considered unimportant. Yet, some project directors tend to pay as little attention as possible to this aspect of project management, and they invariably pay a high price for this in many different ways. Their credibility with host and granting agencies suffers, they run into audit problems, and are faced with unresolvable cash flow difficulties, and must scurry around at the last minute to complete financial reports required by funders.

Financial management includes three main components: financial accounting, financial control, and financial reporting. These components, discussed in this chapter, include the need to gain an understanding of the agencies, units, and people that are involved in fiscal matters and of the details of the project budget; how to deal with the problems of accounting and establish an "audit trail"; and ways to exercise control over the project budget by controlling underexpenditures, overexpenditures, cost-sharing arrangements, and allowable costs. The ability to do this depends upon a sound system of internal financial reporting so that the project director knows exactly where he or she stands in relation to expenditures and can make informed decisions regarding what expenditures to approve and to also request changes in the project budget when necessary. This ability is enhanced by including as part of the financial reporting system a method for forecasting what the future expenses will be and assuring an adequate flow of cash. Another key aspect of financial management is to be able to control purchasing by an effective system for ordering supplies, equipment, and materials. The final aspect of a sound financial management system is to provide funding agencies with accurate up-to-date financial information to meet their requirements.

The Importance of Financial Management

The project budget is the instrument through which the project's activities, plans, priorities, and organization are expressed. Management of the budget is the major means by which a project director can maintain control over the project's operations. In addition, management of the budget is a primary tool in insuring accountability to funders and host agencies for the use of funds allocated to the project.

One of the main characteristics of a project budget is its relative lack of flexibility. Funders have granted a certain amount of money to the project on the basis of a line-by-line budget estimate submitted as part of a grant proposal. Such a budget estimate typically itemizes costs for personnel (including a list of each staff person and their salaries), fringe benefits, equipment, travel, telephone, supplies, and the like. Most government granting agencies expect that the project will adhere to these items and that any proposed change will be submitted to the funder for approval prior to the change being made. A number of foundations also require prior approval of changes. In addition, all funders expect periodic reports on financial expenditures, ranging from monthly financial reports to some government funding agencies to only a final financial report to some foundations.

The most frequent concerns expressed by both funders and project directors alike regarding project direction are in relation to problems of financial management. This is true among projects of all sizes and types. It is even more critical in the case of a project with multiple funding from different foundations and government funders. And, as the availability of financial support from grants becomes more restricted as the result of government cutbacks and depressed economic conditions, more and more projects are compelled to rely on multiple funding to maintain their activities. When a project simultaneously has three or four foundation grants and one or two government grants, the problem of financial management becomes more complicated since the project must manage five or six separate accounts and also find ways to integrate these separate accounts into an overall management system.

What are the first things that a project director should do in connection with organizing the project's financial management system? Experienced and new project directors alike have the same advice for projects located in larger host agencies. As one director said, "find out what the larger system is all about and what you must do." In the case of free-standing projects, one comptroller advises, "make arrangements to handle finances so you get a complete financial report as often as possible and a balance sheet." A head of a multiple-funded project advises "visit organizations with similar financing and find out how they do it."

Know the Financial Management Environment

Before you worry about balance sheets or other elements of financial management, the first thing project directors need to do is concern themselves with the organizational structure and arrangements related to financial and business matters; the people who are involved; and the policies and procedures that the director is expected to follow. The way to get started here is to first identify the organizational structure that deals with matters that impinge upon financial management. These may include:

A central grants management office in the host agency—sometimes more than one office is involved in large agencies or universities. One for program-related matters and another for financial matters.

A chief host agency staff person(s) or officer(s) who have the overall responsibility for fiscal affairs—these may go by a wide variety of titles such as a vice-president for administration, a budget director, an associate director for fiscal affairs or administration, or the executive director.

The units and chief persons responsible for central services in areas such as purchasing, personnel, maintenance of equipment and facilities, travel, supplies, and computer services where these exist.

The financial person in the funding agency may be a grants manager or financial analyst whose only responsibility is financial, or the person may be a program officer who handles financial as well as program issues.

The key financial person within the project who will keep the financial records—in a small project, this may be the project director or principal investigator. In larger projects, it may be an administrative assistant, bookkeeper, secretary, graduate assistant, or comptroller.

The next step is the need to take the initiative in establishing relationships with the people in these various positions. It is surprising how many university project directors, for example, admit they never met the grants administrator, or purchasing director, or personnel officer in their host agency. There is only one way to do this and that is to go and meet with these people. Ask them for the policies and procedures they follow that will affect your financial management. Solicit their advice and follow it to the extent possible, because it will smooth the way when you need to get someone on the payroll in a hurry, or need a ream of paper, or a quick air ticket, or need an ally when trying to get a federal grant manager to agree to a change in your budget.

Know Your Budget

The project budget is the key element in managing finances. You should get to know it in detail. There are two types of budgets that a project may have: a line-by-line budget and a program or functional budget.

LINE-BY-LINE BUDGET

Practically every grant proposal of any size is funded on the basis of a line-by-line budget approved by the funder. A typical line-by-line budget includes what are known as direct expenses and indirect expenses. Direct expenses are comprised of the following items of expenditures: (1) Personnel—salaries (listing each position), fringe benefits, consultants (listing each consultant), and stipends; (2) Other Direct Expenses such as—travel (local mileage, air fares), subsistence (a per diem amount for lodging and meals), equipment, office supplies, rent, postage, printing and duplicating, telephone, books and publications, and computer services.

Direct expenses are all the costs of the project that will be paid directly to personnel or a vendor and are clearly assignable to a project activity. They are discretionary in the sense that the project director can decide whether or not to incur the cost by hiring a person, renting an office, buying paper, authorizing travel, and the like. Sometimes a foundation will receive a grant application with a line-by-line budget that totals a certain amount (let's say, $40,000), but it will approve a grant of $25,000. If this has happened or if there has been any renegotiation of the original budget, you should prepare a new line-by-line expenditure budget. It should come out to exactly the amount of the grant or to the grant plus whatever other income your project has from fees, contributions, fund-raising events, and the like.

Indirect costs appear as a single separate item in the budget. This item represents the total costs to the host organization that are estimated as being in support of the project but cannot be directly attributed to a project activity. This includes a portion of the organization's overall administration, such as central purchasing, personnel, payroll, building maintenance, and maintenance of libraries. Indirect costs are generally computed as a rate (a percentage) of the project's personnel budget or total direct expenditure budget. These funds are, in effect, never seen by the project, and the project director has no discretion over their use.

Some funders will not pay any indirect costs, while others may limit the amount. Still others routinely question the item. Many project directors express concern over indirect costs, because they do not have any power over their use; the amount is dictated by host agency policies (which have usually been negotiated with government auditors); and the indirect costs are included in the total grant request budget for the project and may make the request less competitive with other applications. A university with an indirect cost rate of 33 percent against direct expenses of $100,000 for a project will be submitting a budget request of $133,000. Another organization that has no indirect costs can submit a total budget of $100,000 to perform exactly the same activities.

There is not much a project director can do about this except at the time of submitting a request for a new or renewed grant. Many large institutions have indirect costs rates that vary in terms of different types of projects. A different rate may apply to training projects as compared to research projects or to on-campus versus off-campus activities for a university-based project. Determining these policies and defining the type of work you are doing in a way that fits into a lower indirect cost rate is a management skill that can make the difference in obtaining an additional grant.

In figure 9–1 a typical budget for a foundation supported project is shown. In figure 9–2 a sample of the standard federal budget forms in use in 1982 is shown.

PROGRAM BUDGET

A program or functional budget is one that allocates the line items in the total project budget to various program categories. These categories represent the project's major activities or functions, such as administration, intake, training, counseling, hot line, evaluation, referral.

FIGURE 9–1

Typical Project Line Item Budget

Personnel		
Salaries:		
Project Director—12 p/m @ $30,000 per annum	$ 30,000	
Research Associate—12 p/m @ $20,000 per annum	20,000	
Senior Counselor—12 p/m @ $20,000 per annum	20,000	
Counselor—12 p/m @ $18,000 per annum	18,000	
Research Assistant—6 p/m @ $16,000 per annum	8,000	
Senior Stenographer—12 p/m @ $12,000 per annum	12,000	
Total Salaries:	$108,000	
Fringe Benefits @ 30% of salaries	32,400	
Education Consultant—10 days @ $200/day	2,000	
Total Personnel		$142,400
Other Direct Expense		
Travel		
2 r/t air fares (NY/D.C.) @ $150 = $300		
Mileage 1,000 miles @ $.23/mi = $200	$ 500	
Subsistence 5 days @ $50/day	250	
Office Supplies	2,000	
Telephone	2,200	
Postage	1,000	
Printing	600	
Total, Other Direct		$ 6,550
Indirect Expense @ 40% of salaries		$ 43,200
TOTAL EXPENSE		$192,150

FIGURE 9–2
Sample of Federal Budget Form

GMS NO. 00-M0104

PART III – BUDGET INFORMATION

SECTION A – BUDGET SUMMARY

Grant Program, Function or Activity (a)	Federal Catalog No. (b)	Estimated Unobligated Funds		New or Revised Budget		
		Federal (c)	Non-Federal (d)	Federal (e)	Non-Federal (f)	Total (g)
1.		$	$	$	$	$
2.						
3.						
4.						
5. TOTALS		$	$	$	$	$

SECTION B – BUDGET CATEGORIES

6. Object Class Categories	Grant Program, Function or Activity				Total (5)
	(1)	(2)	(3)	(4)	
a. Personnel	$	$	$	$	$
b. Fringe Benefits					
c. Travel					
d. Equipment					
e. Supplies					
f. Contractual					
g. Construction					
h. Other					
i. Total Direct Charges					
j. Indirect Charges					
k. TOTALS	$	$	$	$	$
7. Program Income	$	$	$	$	$

SECTION C – NON-FEDERAL RESOURCES

(a) Grant Program	(b) APPLICANT	(c) STATE	(d) OTHER SOURCES	(e) TOTALS
8.	$	$	$	$
9.				
10.				
11.				
12. TOTALS	$	$	$	$

SECTION D – FORECASTED CASH NEEDS

	Total for 1st Year	1st Quarter	2nd Quarter	3rd Quarter	4th Quarter
13. Federal	$	$	$	$	$
14. Non-Federal					
15. TOTAL	$	$	$	$	$

FIGURE 9-2 *(continued)*

SECTION E – BUDGET ESTIMATES OF FEDERAL FUNDS NEEDED FOR BALANCE OF THE PROJECT				
	FUTURE FUNDING PERIODS (YEARS)			
(a) Grant Program	**(b) FIRST**	**(c) SECOND**	**(d) THIRD**	**(e) FOURTH**
16.	$	$	$	$
17.				
18.				
19.				
20. TOTALS	$	$	$	$

SECTION F – OTHER BUDGET INFORMATION (Attach additional Sheets If Necessary)
21. Direct Charges:
22. Indirect Charges:
23. Remarks:

PART IV PROGRAM NARRATIVE (Attach per instruction)

These may also represent functional organizational units in large projects that are departmentalized.

To prepare a program budget, an estimate is made of the proportion of each line item that goes toward each activity. For example, an assistant project director whose annual salary is $25,000 may spend two-fifths time on administration, one-fifth on the project evaluation, one-fifth supervising the training program, and one-fifth supervising the counseling activities. Thus, this person's salary would be allocated as follows:

$2/5 \times \$25,000 = \$10,000$ administration
$1/5 \times \$25,000 = 5,000$ evaluation
$1/5 \times \$25,000 = 5,000$ training
$1/5 \times \$25,000 = 5,000$ counseling

This allocating is done for every item in the budget. Then the expenditures for each program category are added up and a budget like the one in figure 9-3 is prepared.

Effective project direction of multifunction projects requires that you have both kinds of budgets in order to make informed decisions on expenditures and in order to use fiscal management to facilitate program activities and the achievement of program objectives.

FIGURE 9–3
Typical Program Budget

Alcoholism Project

Program Budget

Program Component	Cost
Administration	$ 20,000
Intake	13,000
Counseling	18,000
Training	22,000
Hotline	9,000
Information and Referral	7,000
Evaluation	11,000
TOTAL	$ 99,000

AUDIT TRAILS

Government auditing of projects may take two forms. One is a straight forward financial audit that accounts for accuracy and compliance with funder regulations and accepted accounting procedures in the use of money and in the keeping of financial records. A second form of auditing goes beyond this and covers the extent to which resources are being used efficiently and the extent to which programmatic results are being achieved. The "Yellow Book" issued by the U.S. General Accounting Office, for example, emphasizes that a "complete" audit should include all of these components.

While many projects are never audited by funders, you never know when your project may be the one selected for an audit. Therefore, every project should manage its fiscal affairs on the assumption that there will be an audit. This means having a written record that permits reconstruction of all the financial transactions of the project in a way that is consistent with the funder's rules and regulations regarding such expenditures. The record-keeping system must be able to provide answers to the following questions:

1. What was the project's budget?
2. What was actually spent?
3. Where did the money come from?
4. Were all of the expenditures eligible under the grant?

5. What is the proof that the expenditures were made and that the work was actually done and the material received?

Financial management systems must be able to provide documented answers to these questions if the project is to be regarded as being fiscally responsible. Such responsibility is built upon following what are known as Generally Accepted Accounting Principles (GAAP). The principles and practices that apply to nonprofit organizations have been set forth by the American Institute of Certified Public Accountants (AICPA) in various audit guides for nonprofit organizations, such as its *Standards of Accounting and Financial Reporting for Voluntary Health and Welfare Organizations* and reports of the Financial Accounting Standards Board. These and other resource materials are listed in appendix A.

While a project director does not need to be an accountant, an understanding of some of the language and principles of accounting is helpful in understanding the financial statements that must be reviewed and in assuming adequate fiscal management of the project's funds.

Fund Accounting and Ledgers

Financial management systems are all built upon information that is compiled to be consistent with the two basic general financial record keeping devices: the journal and the ledger. A journal is used to keep daily entries of the expenditures (costs and debits) and of funds received (credits). A ledger is used to keep monthly records that are compiled from journal entries and are usually kept for separate accounts. The monthly records provide the information needed for the two elements of financial control, cost control, and budget control. Cost control is the amount that has been spent for each line item; budget control is how much of the budget for that item has been used and what is left. Cost and budget control may be applied to line-by-line budgets and to program budgets. There are a number of different formats for journals and ledgers which an accountant can adapt to your organization. An example of one format for a daily journal and a monthly ledger is shown in figures 9–4 and 9–5.

The daily journal record also includes the date of purchase requisi-

FIGURE 9–4

Sample Format for a Daily Journal

Month _____

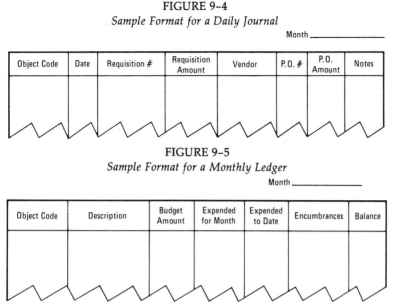

Object Code	Date	Requisition #	Requisition Amount	Vendor	P.O. #	P.O. Amount	Notes

FIGURE 9–5

Sample Format for a Monthly Ledger

Month _____

Object Code	Description	Budget Amount	Expended for Month	Expended to Date	Encumbrances	Balance

tions and purchase orders, their numbers, the amount, who the payee is, and the amount actually paid. In addition, each line item, such as salaries or supplies, has an identifying budget code number or line number. The journal record should be backed up by the documentation in files of purchase orders, invoices, and the like; and, of course, by the record of checks written to pay all salaries, taxes, and bills to vendors.

Project directors in large institutions will have a good deal of this done for them by central offices but many of them still need to keep similar records at the project level. In smaller organizations, the project director may need to keep all these records. For a detailed example of how a project within a large state university manages its financial record-keeping, see appendix C.

CASH AND ACCRUAL

Accountants like to see financial reporting kept on an accrual basis; that is, they believe the records should show the expenses that have been incurred even though the actual payment has not been made. Thus, if in June a project purchases $1,000 worth of supplies but has not yet paid the office supply store, this billing should be recorded. This helps to avoid over expenditures of a budget item at a later time.

177

On the other hand, pure accrual accounting would also record the full $50,000 foundation grant at the time it is awarded even though half of it might not be paid until six months later.

Cash accounting only records the actual disbursements or receipt of cash at the time the actual cash transaction takes place, that is, a check is written or received.

Obviously, it is a great help to financial control and planning to know what unpaid expenses and unreceived income can be expected. Therefore, the general trend in financial management among projects in the voluntary nonprofit and governmental field is to use a modified version of the accrual method. This approach is reflected in the examples given in the next section.

Managing the Budget

A FINANCIAL REPORTING SYSTEM

Managing the project budget means controlling expenditures and income in order to avoid under- or overexpenditure of the total grant. This can only be accomplished by controlling the expenditures for each line item, and such control can only be exercized if you have up-to-date information that lets you know (1) how much you have to spend; (2) how much you have spent; (3) how much you are already obligated to spend in the future; and (4) how much is left to spend. With this information, you can make efficient decisions regarding the approval of expenditures. It also can help you to ascertain whether you need to revise your budget by shifting expenditures from one item to another and request funder approval for budget changes.

Accounting systems for free-standing projects can be readily adopted from the recommended systems in the various books on accounting for nonprofit organizations mentioned in appendix A or set up by the certified public accountants who do your annual audit. Projects in host organizations will generally have to conform to the system that is in place in the host organization. It will help you to know what is going on if you understand some of the main elements of these systems.

Figure 9–6 illustrates a copy of a monthly financial report for a project. The first column is the code number assigned each budget category. In this example, a four-digit code is used to designate each major item of revenue and expenditure. The second column lists what the

FIGURE 9-6
Sample Expenditure Report

Account No.: 431-10026

THE ABC PROJECT
ACCOUNT EXPENDITURE REPORT

Month Ending: 6/30/83
Page No. 1

(1)	(2)	(3)	(4)	(5)	(6)	(7)	(8)	(9)
Budget Code	Item	Annual Budget	Expended This Month	Expended Year to Date	Total Encumbered	Total Committed	Uncommitted Balance	Percentage Expended or Variance

particular items are, for example, salaries, fringe benefits, postage. The third column lists the amount that is in the project's approved budget for the year for each item. Column four shows the amount spent during the month and column five shows the total amount spent for the year to the date of the report.

This is the minimum amount of information that there should be on a monthly basis. However, it is not sufficient to enable you to really plan your expenditures and guard against overexpenditures or underexpenditures. To do this, you need the kind of information shown in the remaining columns. For example, column six shows the encumbrances for each item. An encumbrance is the amount that is committed to be spent for an item for the entire year. It is in addition to the amount actually expended for the item that is reported in column five which is the total expended for the year to date. An example of an encumbrance would be in the salary item. An assistant project director at a salary of $20,000 is included in the approved budget. If the person is hired at the beginning of the year, there would be an encumbrance of $20,000 against this item. In a sixth month report, you would see a spent-to-date amount of $10,000 (in column five) and the remaining amount of $10,000 in the encumbrance column. Another example would be for a fixed expenditure such as rent. The entire amount of the rent for the whole year is committed to be spent and therefore is shown as an encumbrance even though only one-half has been spent at the end of six months. Column seven, total committed, is the amount committed for the entire year. This is the amount spent to date (column five) plus the encumbered amount (column six). Take the case of a counselor who is in the budget for a salary of $18,000 for a twelve-month period but is not hired until the beginning of the third month. At the end of the sixth month only three months salary has been paid, which is $4,500, and is shown in the total expended column. Six months salary, $9,000, remains to be paid and is shown in the encumbrance column. In all, $13,500 ($4,500 + $9,000) will be spent and is shown in the total committed column. This leaves an amount of $4,500 ($18,000 − $13,500) in this item. This is an uncommitted balance and is shown in column eight. Using this approach, you can forecast where you will end up at the end of the year and plan accordingly. In this example, you might request a transfer of money from the salary budget, where you will save $4,500, to the printing item and supply item which will most likely be overspent due to increased costs. This information also enables you to increase or decrease controllable expenses. When you see an annual postage budget item of $3,000 that has a balance of $500 at the end of the sixth month, you know you must be very cautious about approving activities that involve any large mailings.

In some reporting systems, a percentage of the amount spent or remaining in an item is shown as in column nine. Other systems show the percentage of variance which is the percentage overexpended (−) or underexpended (+) for each item.

WHAT TO DO IF YOU ARE UNDERSPENDING

If you find that you are underspending in a particular item and your projections indicate that you will underspend for the entire year, there are three alternatives open. You can continue to underspend and not use all of the grant monies. You can ask that the money from the underspent item be transferred. Or, you can request that the money be carried over to the next year if the project has been approved for more than one year. If it is a one-year project, you can ask to extend the project for another month or whatever time period could be covered by the unexpended amount. This is called a no-cost extension.

In requesting transfer carryover or extension, you should write the grantor explaining the reason for the underexpenditure. For example, you may have hired a staff person at $2,000 less than budgeted. Or you may have not been able to find someone to hire until the third month of the project even though the salary was budgeted for a full twelve month period. You should also justify the need for the transfer or carryover. In effect, the transferring of money from one item to another results in a revision in the budget. When requesting transfers, you should indicate to the funder how this will effect the budget as in the sample letter (figure 9–7) in addition to the submission of a revised budget proposal (figure 9–8).

WHAT TO DO IF YOU ARE OVERSPENDING

Sometimes you may find that you are overexpending a particular item in the budget and your projections indicate it will be overspent for the entire year. When this occurs, there are three alternatives. First, you can take steps to reduce the rate of expenditure (cut down on travel, do less duplicating, restrict the use of the telephones). Second, when the overexpenditure will result in overspending the total budget, you can explain the reasons for the overexpenditures to the grantor and request supplemental funds to cover this amount. This may be successful, but usually such requests are not met and, in addition, they can reflect poorly on the efficiency of your financial management. Third, if another item is being underspent, you can request transfer of

FIGURE 9-7
Sample Letter Requesting Budget Changes

YOUTH ADVOCACY PROJECT
Central Organization
Midtown, Indiana

August 1, 1983

Mr. Jerome Nice
Project Officer
Office for Youth Programs
50 Lane Street
Washington, D.C. 20000   Ref: OYP-1133-1-0
                                          Office of Youth Programs 401-1133D

Dear Mr. Nice:

Pursuant to our telephone conversation on July 15, 1983, we are writing to request the following changes in the approved budget of the above-referred grant for the year 7/1/83 to 6/30/84.

The purposes of these changes are to utilize savings that will result from reductions of our indirect cost rate and travel budget in order to increase staff time and educational activities in our high school program component. This will be accomplished by:

1. Increasing the time of our high school counselor, Harvey Howe, from three-fourths time to full time so that we can serve an additional twenty students per month. This will change his annual salary to $17,000 and will add $3,500 to our salary budget for the last nine months of this year;

2. Increasing the printing item from $500 to $2,200 in order to print and distribute a brochure to teachers on the school's responsibility to establish special programs to prevent drop-outs.

The accompanying revised budget reflects the proposed changes that we would like to implement on September 1, 1983. So that we may effect these changes, please send us your written approval at your earliest convenience.

Sincerely yours,

Janet Hopeful
Project Director

JH/st
Attachment

FIGURE 9–8

Youth Advocacy Project Revised Budget

Budget Category	Current Approved Budget	Requested Change	Revised Budget
Salaries	$ 60,000	$ +3,500	$ 63,500
Fringe Benefits @ 30%	18,000	+1,050	19,050
Consultants	10,000		10,000
Travel	3,000	−2,000	1,000
Supplies	2,000		2,000
Telephone	1,500		1,500
Postage	500		500
Printing	500	+1,700	2,200
TOTAL DIRECT COST	$ 95,500	$ +4,250	$ 99,750
Indirect Cost	36,000[a]	−4,250	31,750[b]
TOTAL BUDGET	$131,500	—	$131,500

[a] @ 60%/salaries

[b] @ 50%/salaries

money from that item to cover the overexpended item. You must make a convincing case to the funder that the overexpenditure is not controllable and that the underspending will continue that way to the end of the year.

Unit of Service Reimbursement

There is a trend in some government programs to control the payment of monies on the basis of the amount of service you provide. This is more usual in the case of projects funded by contracts than by grants. An example of this would be in the case of a mental health project which has an approved line-by-line budget of $100,000 under a contract with a state department of mental health to provide life-skills competency training to deinstitutionalized mental hospital patients. The grantor includes in the contract that its payments will be contingent upon the provision of a certain number of units of service per quarter. One unit might be counted for each person who participates in a three-hour meeting of a training group of twenty persons. The project may be given a target of 1,000 units a quarter. If it only reaches 500 units, its money would be reduced by 50 percent.

There are certain strategies a project director can use to protect against the possible loss of monies under unit reimbursement contracts. The most obvious, of course, is to keep close track on a weekly basis of the units of service being provided by adopting forms such as those shown in chapter 8, figures 8–10 and 8–11. If there is slippage in the "production" of units, this must be caught early and additional services offered. A second strategy is to attempt to negotiate a waiver from the grantor's standard on the basis of a special situation the project faces. In the preceding example, this might be the need to have smaller groups since the participants have characteristics that require small group experience. A third strategy is to try to reclassify the work being done to a more favorable category. Using the same example, this might be from a category called "competency training" to a category called "counseling" in which the unit requirements are more favorable.

Cost Sharing

Often a government granting agency has a policy that requires a grantee to share in the cost of a project. Very few foundations have such requirements, however, There are two ways that projects share costs. One way, which is most frequently used, is to donate a portion of the time of regular host agency staff members, and also supplies, office facilities, telephone service, and the like. This is called in-kind cost sharing. It is the most preferred method used to share in project costs. The other way is to share in certain costs by providing actual cash from the regular budget, funding raising events, or other sources of income. This is done less frequently. Cost sharing is always shown so that it applies to a particular line item in the project budget. For example, a YMCA may provide office space for one of its projects and the value of this space is shown as an in-kind contribution against the rent item in the budget. The nature and extent of cost-sharing arrangements is generally set forth in the proposal budget or budget negotiation at the time the project was funded. The project director's responsibility is to manage the project in a manner that assures the project abides by its cost-sharing commitments. This requires that you must be able to document that the shared contributions have actually been made.

Large host agencies have forms, such as those shown in figures 9–9 and 9–10, that are used for the purpose of certifying the time of employees, for example, who are to work on a project as part of the cost-sharing agreement. Projects supported by HHS agencies that require cost sharing must agree to bear a certain percentage of cost (see form shown in figure 9–4) included in the indirect expense (overhead) item in the project budget. If they are, they should not be considered part of the host agency's in-kind contribution, and the project director has no responsibility for documenting the provision of the item. For example, the same YMCA-based project mentioned earlier may have an indirect cost item of $10,000 which includes, among other things, the provision of space. In such a case, there would not be a rent item in the budget against which to show matching funds.

In keeping track of the share of any costs that are contributed by the project itself, you should be careful not to claim certain types of costs. Federal grants cannot be matched by funds from another federal grant or by the time of personnel who are 100 percent supported on another grant. At the same time, it may be possible to use any money received as part of federal-state-local revenue sharing for this purpose. Any personnel who are included as part of your contribution cannot be spending over 100 percent of their time. Thus, a staff person cannot be counted as giving 50 percent time to your project if he or she is in a second grant for 40 percent and a third grant for 20 percent.

Mismanaging cost-sharing arrangements can and have proved costly at the time of federal audits. More than one project has been penalized in this regard.

One allowable item that can be used as part of your matching share is the value of the services of volunteers. Their value is computed by identifying the going rate of pay for employees doing similar work. For example, a qualified person who volunteers to lead a discussion group of teenagers in your project one day a week for thirty weeks may be counted as representing a value of $3,000 if it is your policy to pay group leaders $100 a day. Any cost-sharing items must be justified in terms of achieving the project's stated objectives and activities.

The main rules and conditions are included in federal regulations set forth in OMB circulars listed in appendix D.

FIGURE 9–9
*Cost-Sharing Agreement for
HHS-Supported Projects*

PROJECT BY
PROJECT COST-SHARING
AGREEMENT FOR HEW RESEARCH AWARDS

Note: This form is used only when the applicant does *not* have an institutional cost-sharing agreement with HEW. Questions about the form should be directed to the HEW awarding office's grants management office.

NAME OF HEW AWARDING OFFICE _____

APPLICATION OR AWARD NUMBER (*if known*) _____

NAME AND ADDRESS OF APPLICANT ORGANIZATION _____

PROPOSED PROJECT PERIOD: from _____ to _____

TITLE OF PROJECT _____

AGREEMENT: In order to satisfy HEW cost-sharing requirements, _____

_____ (name of applicant organization)

agrees to bear at least _____ percent of the total cost of the above project.

Total project cost is the sum of the total allowable direct and indirect cost incurred by the recipient and sub-recipients or cost-type contractors, plus the value of any third party in-kind contributions which benefit the project. These amounts will be calculated according to the rules in HEW grant administration regulations at 45 CFR Part 74.

If the project period consists of more than one budget period, the agreed-upon rate will apply to the project period as a whole, including any non-competitive extensions, but not necessarily to each individual budget period.

If HEW stops funding this project prior to the close of the originally agreed-upon project period, the rate will apply to the actual period of support.

If the project period is extended competitively, another cost-sharing agreement will be negotiated.

SIGNATURE AND TITLE OF AUTHORIZED APPLICANT OFFICIAL _____

_____

DATE _____

HEW FORM 490 (Jan. 1980)

FIGURE 9–10
Sample Form for Reporting Time of
Cost-Sharing Personnel

PERSONNEL ACTIVITY REPORT
F 35-3-680

NAME: _____ SOC. SEC. NO. _____ LINE ITEM: _____
DEPT: _____ TITLE: _____
REPORTING PERIOD:ACADEMIC _____ INTERIM PERIOD _____ TO _____

SPONSORED PROJECTS ADMINISTERED THROUGH THE RESEARCH FOUNDATION				DISTRIBUTION OF EFFORT	
ACCOUNT NO.	AWARD PERIOD	APPOINTMENT PERIOD	SOURCE	REPORTED OR EST'D.	ACTUAL EFFORT
			TOTAL SPONSORED PROJECTS EFFORT		%

INSTRUCTION AND DEPARTMENTAL RESEARCH _____

DEPARTMENTAL ADMINISTRATION (DOCUMENTATION REQUIRED) _____

ORGANIZED RESEARCH—STATE FUNDED _____

OTHER INSTITUTIONAL ACTIVITIES _____

     ORGANIZED ACTIVITIES _____

     EXTENSION AND PUBLIC SERVICE _____

     PATIENT CARE _____

     SPECIALIZED SERVICE FACILITIES _____

     OTHER _____

INDIRECT COST ACTIVITIES

     SPONSORED PROJECTS ADMINISTRATION _____

     GENERAL ADMINISTRATION _____

     MAINTENANCE AND OPERATIONS _____

     LIBRARY _____

GRAND TOTAL EFFORT 100%

CERTIFICATION OF EMPLOYEE:	CERTIFICATION OF PERSON HAVING FIRST HAND KNOWLEDGE:
I CONFIRM THE ABOVE DISTRIBUTION REFLECTS A REASONABLE ESTIMATE OF ALL EFFORT BY ME DURING THE STATED PERIOD.	I CONFIRM THE ABOVE DISTRIBUTION REFLECTS A REASONABLE ESTIMATE OF ALL EFFORT DURING THE STATED PERIOD.
_____ _____ SIGNATURE DATE	_____ _____ SIGNATURE DATE

NOTE: This form is used by the Research Foundation of the State University of New York.

Allowable Costs

If you do not want to lose part of your federal grant, you must manage your expenditures in a way to avoid any expenditures for items that are not allowed by federal policies that govern this aspect of financial affairs. These allowable and unallowable costs vary among different granting agencies. While it can be assumed that the major issues regarding these costs have been ironed out at the time the project budget and grant were approved, it is still necessary to be aware of what is unallowable and allowable in order to avoid permitting unallowable items to creep back into the budget. Some of the major costs that are usually clearly not allowed as direct costs are items such as reserved funds, entertainment, cost of preparing proposals, and fund raising. Other costs are allowable under certain conditions which the funding agency specifies and which are outlined for federal grants in the various OMB circulars.

All costs must meet federal criteria of being of a reasonable amount, related to the project's objectives, consistent with the way items are charged within the host institution, and consistent with conditions of the grant award. Thus, if a grant award specifies that a particular staff person is to be on a one-half time basis and you apply them on a full-time basis, you can expect one-half that salary to be declared unallowable by the government grant or program manager and by government auditors.

Federally-sponsored projects can be affected by presidential decisions. During the Reagan administration, there was a renewal of the prohibition on flying to any destination on a plane that was not a U.S. flag carrier (except if a U.S. plane did not go to the place). Unaware of this, a number of trips by project personnel were disallowed or had to be explained to auditors.

The cost principles that govern the allowability of costs are set forth in various OMB circulars (listed in appendix D) and are codified in the *Code of Federal Regulations*. Each program has the responsibility to inform a grantee of the rules it follows in connection with allowable costs. For example, the National Science Foundations states:

1. ALLOWABLE COSTS

a. The allowability of costs and cost allocation methods for work performed under this grant, up to the amount specified in the grant letter, shall be determined in accordance with the applicable Federal Cost Principles in effect on the effective date of the grant and the terms of the grant.

b. The Federal Cost Principles applicable to specific types of grantees are as follows:

(1) Institutions of Higher Education. OMB Circular A-21 is applicable to both public and private institutions of higher education is codified in 34 CFR 254, and reproduced in 41 CFR Subparts 1-15.3 and 1-15.8.

(2) Other Nonprofit Organizations. OMB Circular A-122, 6/27/80, "Cost Principles for Nonprofit Organizations," HHS publication *Guide for Hospitals*, OSAC-3, or Subpart 1-15.2 of the FPR (41 CFR Subpart 1-15.2) as appropriate.

(3) Commercial Firms. Subpart 1-15.2 of the FPR (41 CFR Subpart 1-15.2)

(4) State and Local Governments. OMB Circular A-87 is codified in the Code of Federal Regulations as 34 CFR Part 255. It also is reproduced as 41 CFR Subpart 1-15.7.

Requisitions and Purchasing

Project budgets are used to purchase services and materials. The problem for project directors is how to get the services and materials as quickly as possible and at the best price. At the same time, project directors need to control purchasing so that it is in line with budgeted amounts for various items such as equipment, supplies, consultants, or travel.

Large host agencies will generally have a written statement of policies and procedures that govern the purchasing process. You can assume these are designed to conform to accepted business practices and to allow for purchases to be reviewed so that they will conform to the requirements of the granting agency. One of the jobs of a project director in host agencies without such established procedures will be to set up a purchasing system, including the necessary forms and written procedures. This is best done by asking agencies that have such systems in place for copies of their materials. A sample of a typical purchase order is shown in figure 9–11.

In large agencies, the ordering of supplies and equipment is a two-step process. The project's initial responsibility is to complete a requisition, or a request for purchase, or purchase order request, as it is sometimes called. This goes to a purchasing department (sometimes being first approved by a central grant management office or research

FIGURE 9–11
Sample Purchase Order

		PURCHASE ORDER			
		Project Name			
		Address			

TO: _____   SHIP TO: _____

_____   _____

_____   _____

Date	Delivery Date	Ship Via	F.O.B.	Terms	Purchase Order #

QUANTITY	DESCRIPTION	Unit Price	Total

Tax Number _____   Purchasing Agent _____

Account or
Grant # _____   Project Director _____

foundation). The formal purchase order is prepared by one of these other units and a copy returned to the project.

To expedite purchasing, whether through a centralized system or directly by the project, the project director should: ascertain that the items to be purchased are allowable under the terms of the grant or contract; check to be sure that enough money is available in the budget item that covers the purchase; try to order as far in advance as possible; and assure that purchase orders are filled out completely and accurately.

Getting the most out of your purchasing dollars is another responsibility of the project director. The most traditional way this is done is by getting bids from different vendors, bargaining with them for the best price, and creating competition among vendors. One project that is engaged in rehabilitation of run-down buildings keeps an account with two different lumber yards. They give their business to one, but then switch to the other until the first one brings its prices down. Asking for stores to contribute material can be a costly activity, but can pay off if you are seeking an expensive piece of equipment. Explore government surplus availability by calling the regional office of the U.S. General Services Administration that covers your community. Mailing rates keep changing and it pays to cultivate someone at your local post office to advise you on the cheapest way to send mailings. Frequently, there is more than one phone system or company you can use and these prices can vary considerably. Always ask vendors if they give discounts to nonprofit organizations. Many projects are paying full price to vendors whose policy is to give a 10 percent discount, but the project never asked about the possibility.

Occasionally, a particular discrete project activity can be performed by faculty and students in specialized university programs as part of their work. One project had, for example, a group of graduate students do a marketing study in connection with the project's economic development program.

Always check out the relative costs of purchasing versus leasing of equipment. Leasing is expensive, but not if you are leasing from your own host organization. Contracts for maintenance of equipment can be a good investment. The middle price range contracts are often the best.

There are some cost-saving devices that can easily backfire and should be cautiously approached. While there is no question that the use of volunteers can be worthwhile, some projects have found this to be costly in terms of both supervision and time. Using the computer facilities of another agency or of a granting agency that may be willing to make them available has often proved unsatisfactory to research projects. The other agencies often do not give priority to your work and may not be familiar with the kind of data you have.

Financial Reports to Funders

Every funder requires that a project submit some kind of financial report, and it is the project director's responsibility to see that this requirement is met. Reports may be required monthly or only a final report. The first task for the project director in this regard is to ascertain from the funder how frequently reports are to be submitted and what the format is to be for the report. Federally-funded grant projects usually use the Federal Form 269, *"The Annual Financial Status Report"* for this purpose (see figure 9–12). It is usually due within ninety days following the close of the grant budget period. A sample of the instructions for this form is shown in figure 9–12. State and local governmental funding agencies have similar requirements. Projects funded by contracts are usually required to submit similar reports on a monthly basis.

Foundations vary greatly in their financial accounting requirements. Some require no report, while others require quarterly, semi-annual, or, most frequently, a final report at the end of the grant period. Most foundations do not have prescribed forms for this purpose. An example of the kind of financial report required by one foundation is shown in figure 9–13.

Financial reports for projects in large host agencies with central grants management offices are usually prepared by the central office and submitted to funders and copies sent to project directors. In other agencies, however, the report must be prepared and submitted by the project itself. Some guidelines for preparing these reports based on problems that project directors have run into include:

Start preparing the report early!

Be sure your financial record-keeping system is geared to providing the information needed to meet the funder's format and budget categories.

Assign responsibility for preparation of the initial financial report.

Never let a report go to a funder without your review as project director.

This is one piece of paper you should never sign without a careful reading.

Check your financial report against your program progress reports to make certain that all figures match and that fiscal and programmatic material is consistent.

FIGURE 9-12

Sample of Federal Financial Report and Instructions

| FINANCIAL STATUS REPORT
(follow instructions on the back) | 1. FEDERAL AGENCY AND ORGANIZATIONAL ELEMENT TO WHICH REPORT IS SUBMITTED | 2. FEDERAL GRANT OR OTHER IDENTIFYING NUMBER | OMB Approved
No. 80-R0180 | PAGE
1 | OF
2 | PAGES |

3. RECIPIENT ORGANIZATION *(Name and complete address, including ZIP code)*

| 4. EMPLOYER IDENTIFICATION NUMBER | 5. RECIPIENT ACCOUNT NUMBER OR IDENTIFYING NUMBER | 6. FINAL REPORT
☐ YES ☐ NO | 7. BASIS
☐ CASH ☐ ACCRUAL |

8. PROJECT/GRANT PERIOD *(See instructions)*	9. PERIOD COVERED BY THIS REPORT
FROM (Month, day, year)	TO (Month, day, year)	FROM (Month, day, year)	TO (Month, day, year)

10.

PROGRAMS/FUNCTIONS/ACTIVITIES ▶	STATUS OF FUNDS						
	(a) S & W	(b) BENEFITS	(c) SUPPLIES	(d) TRAVEL	(e) OTHER	(f) INDIRECT COSTS	(g) TOTAL
a. Net outlays previously reported	$	$	$	$	$	$	$
b. Total outlays this report period							
c. *Less:* Program Income credits							
d. Net outlays this report period *(Line b minus line c)*							
e. Net outlays to date *(Line a plus line d)*							
f. *Less:* Non-Federal share of outlays							
g. Total Federal share of outlays *(Line e minus line f)*							
h. Total unliquidated obligations							
i. *Less:* Non-Federal share of unliquidated obligations shown on line h							
j. Federal share of unliquidated obligations							
k. Total Federal share of outlays and unliquidated obligations							
l. Total cumulative amount of Federal funds authorized							
m. Unobligated balance of Federal funds							

11. INDIRECT EXPENSE	a. TYPE OF RATE *(Place "X" in appropriate box)*	☐ PROVISIONAL	☐ PREDETERMINED	☐ FINAL	☐ FIXED
	b. RATE	c. BASE	d. TOTAL AMOUNT	e. FEDERAL SHARE	

12. REMARKS: *Attach any explanations deemed necessary or information required by Federal spending agency in compliance with governing legislation.*

13. CERTIFICATION I certify to the best of my knowledge and belief that this report is correct and complete and that all outlays and unliquidated obligations are for the purposes set forth in the award documents.	SIGNATURE OF AUTHORIZED CERTIFYING OFFICIAL	DATE REPORT SUBMITTED
	TYPED OR PRINTED NAME AND TITLE	TELEPHONE *(Area code, number and extension)*

269-102

STANDARD FORM 269 (7-76)
Prescribed by Office of Management and Budget
Cir. No. A-110

FIGURE 9–12 *(continued)*

INSTRUCTIONS

Please type or print legibly. Items 1, 2, 3, 6, 7, 9, 10d, 10e, 10g, 10i, 10l, 11a, and 12 are self-explanatory, specific instructions for other items are as follows:

Item	*Entry*
4	Enter the employer identification number assigned by the U.S. Internal Revenue Service or FICE (institution) code, if required by the Federal sponsoring agency.
5	This space is reserved for an account number or other identifying numbers that may be assigned by the recipient.
8	Enter the month, day, and year of the beginning and ending of this project period. For formula grants that are not awarded on a project basis, show the grant period.
10	The purpose of vertical columns (a) through (f) is to provide financial data for each program, function, and activity in the budget as approved by the Federal sponsoring agency. If additional columns are needed, use as many additional forms as needed and indicate page number in space provided in upper right; however, the totals of all programs, functions or activities should be shown in column (g) of the first page. For agreements pertaining to several Catalog of Federal Domestic Assistance programs that do not require a further functional or activity classification breakdown, enter under columns (a) through (f) the title of the program. For grants or other assistance agreements containing multiple programs where one or more programs require a further breakdown by function or activity, use a separate form for each program showing the applicable functions or activities in the separate columns. For grants or other assistance agreements containing several functions or activities which are funded from several programs, prepare a separate form for each activity or function when requested by the Federal sponsoring agency.
10a	Enter the net outlay. This amount should be the same as the amount reported in Line 10e of the last report. If

there has been an adjustment to the amount shown previously, please attach explanation. Show zero if this is the initial report.

Item	*Entry*
10b	Enter the total gross program outlays (less rebates, refunds, and other discounts) for this report period, including disbursements of cash realized as program income. For reports that are prepared on a cash basis, outlays are the sum of actual cash disbursements for goods and services, the amount of indirect expense charged, the value of in-kind contributions applied, and the amount of cash advances and payments made to contractors and subgrantees. For reports prepared on an accrued expenditure basis, outlays are the sum of actual cash disbursements, the amount of indirect expense incurred, the value of in-kind contributions applied, and the net increase (or decrease) in the amounts owed by the recipient for goods and other property received and for services performed by employees, contractors, subgrantees, and other payees.
10c	Enter the amount of all program income realized in this period that is required by the terms and conditions of the Federal award to be deducted from total project costs. For reports prepared on a cash basis, enter the amount of cash income received during the reporting period. For reports prepared on an accrual basis, enter the amount of income earned since the beginning of the reporting period. When the terms or conditions allow program income to be added to the total award, explain in remarks, the source, amount and disposition of the income.
10f	Enter amount pertaining to the non-Federal share of program outlays included in the amount on line e.
10h	Enter total amount of unliquidated obligations for this project or program, including unliquidated obligations to

FIGURE 9-12 *(continued)*

INSTRUCTIONS

Please type or print legibly. Items 1, 2, 3, 6, 7, 9, 10d, 10e, 10g, 10i, 10l, 11a, and 12 are self-explanatory, specific instructions for other items are as follows:

Item	*Entry*
	subgrantees and contractors. Unliquidated obligations are:
	Cash basis—obligations incurred but not paid;
	Accrued expenditure basis—obligations incurred but for which an outlay has not been recorded.
	Do not include any amounts that have been included on lines a through g. On the final report, line h should have a zero balance.
10j	Enter the Federal share of unliquidated obligations shown on line h. The amount shown on this line should be the difference between the amounts on lines h and i.
10k	Enter the sum of the amounts shown on lines g and j. If the report is final the report should not contain any unliquidated obligations.
10m	Enter the unobligated balance of Fed-

Item	*Entry*
	eral funds. This amount should be the difference between lines k and l.
11b	Enter rate in effect during the reporting period.
11c	Enter amount of the base to which the rate was applied.
11d	Enter total amount of indirect cost charged during the report period.
11e	Enter amount of the Federal share charged during the report period.
	If more than one rate was applied during the project period, include a separate schedule showing bases against which the indirect cost rates were applied, the respective indirect rates the month, day, and year the indirect rates were in effect, amounts of indirect expense charged to the project, and the Federal share of indirect expense charged to the project to date.

Cash Flow

Cash flow refers to always having enough money on hand or available to pay the project's bills, salaries, and taxes. For projects located in large institutions, such as a public university, this is an infrequent problem for the project director since the institution generally has financial systems in place to assure its ability to cover its obligations, regardless of whether the grant for your project has been received or not. However, for many projects this has been a serious problem. This sometimes has been the result of a lack of adequate information. A project financial reporting system should include regular reports that reveal the cash flow situation. The format in figure 9-14 is one way to do this.

FIGURE 9–13
Sample of Foundation Financial Report Form

The Edna McConnell Clark Foundation

EXPENSE REPORT AND PAYMENT REQUEST

ORGANIZATION: _____

DATE: _____ PREPARED BY: _____ FOUNDATION GRANT # _____

	Actual Expenditure for Latest Quarter (*) From _____ To _____	Estimated Expense for Next Quarter From _____ To _____
PERSONNEL COSTS Project Leader Professional and Administrative Staff Clerical Fringe Benefits Outside Consultants		
1. TOTAL PERSONNEL COSTS		
PROGRAM COSTS Travel Equipment Miscellaneous		
2. TOTAL PROGRAM COSTS		
ADMINISTRATIVE COSTS Rent and Utilities Office Costs (Supplies, phone, postage, reproduction, etc.) Miscellaneous		
3. TOTAL ADMINISTRATIVE COSTS		

The most critical factor you must deal with is the arrangement with the funding agency regarding how often, in what amounts, and under what conditions the project will receive its grant monies. While cash management is a technical and complex aspect of business administration, there are a number of techniques that project directors can use with funding agencies as they manage the project budget. Foundations are the easiest group to work with since most of them will advance at least three months of the grant at the outset or will often send a check

FIGURE 9–14
Sample Cash Flow Analysis Chart

	Month			
	January		February	
Cash Flow Item	Expected	Actual	Expected	Actual
Beginning Balance	—	—	7,500	6,000
Grant Receipts	15,000	14,000	7,500	7,500
Cash on Hand	15,000	14,000	15,000	13,500
Monthly Expense	7,500	8,000	10,000	11,000
Ending Balance	7,500	6,000	5,000	2,500

for six months or the whole twelve-month period right at the beginning of your grant period. But even under these circumstances, it could be a few weeks before you receive the check and you have salaries due for the first two weeks of the project. Anticipating this possibility, you need to call the foundation and get them to send the check as soon as possible. Explain the anticipated problem and offer to pick it up, if possible.

With government funders, the problem can sometimes be harder to solve. You should be aware that most government agencies have a procedure and standard form (No. 270 for federal agencies is shown in figure 9–15) that permits you to request an advance against your grant or contract. In addition, federal granting agencies use a letter of credit technique for grantees that have a continuing relationship with the government and where (in most cases) the grant is over $120,000 or $125,000. Lesser grants are generally eligible for advances. A letter of credit allows you to draw funds from the banks as needed for immediate disbursement. Each agency has a somewhat different procedure, and you should discuss the various payment options with your grant officer in the granting agency to determine the payment procedure to be followed with your project.

Other ways to reduce the cash flow problem is to slow down the paying of bills from vendors. Do not pay bills as they come in but set a regular payment date and tell the vendor. Short-term bank loans, which usually have high interest rates, are the least desirable way to

FIGURE 9–15
Sample Federal Advance Request Form

REQUEST FOR ADVANCE OR REIMBURSEMENT *(See instructions on back)*	Approved by Office of Management and Budget, No. 80–R0183		PAGE OF PAGES
	1. TYPE OF PAYMENT REQUESTED	*a. "X" one, or both boxes* □ ADVANCE □ REIMBURSE-MENT *b. "X" the applicable box* □ FINAL □ PARTIAL	2. BASIS OF REQUEST □ CASH □ ACCRUAL

3. FEDERAL SPONSORING AGENCY AND ORGANIZATIONAL ELEMENT TO WHICH THIS REPORT IS SUBMITTED	4. FEDERAL GRANT OR OTHER IDENTIFYING NUMBER ASSIGNED BY FEDERAL AGENCY	5. PARTIAL PAYMENT REQUEST NUMBER FOR THIS REQUEST

6. EMPLOYER IDENTIFICATION NUMBER	7. RECIPIENTS ACCOUNT NUMBER OR IDENTIFYING NUMBER	8. PERIOD COVERED BY THIS REQUEST	
		FROM *(month, day, year)*	TO *(month, day, year)*

9. RECIPIENT ORGANIZATION	10. PAYEE *(Where check is to be sent if different than item 9)*
Name :	Name :
Number and Street :	Number and Street :
City, State and ZIP Code:	City, State and ZIP Code:

11. COMPUTATION OF AMOUNT OF REIMBURSEMENTS/ADVANCES REQUESTED

PROGRAMS/FUNCTIONS/ACTIVITIES ▶	*(a)*	*(b)*	*(c)*	TOTAL
a. Total program outlays to date *(As of date)*	$	$	$	$
b. *Less:* Cumulative program income				
c. Net program outlays *(Line a minus line b)*				
d. Estimated net cash outlays for advance period				
e. Total *(Sum of lines c & d)*				
f. Non-Federal share of amount on line e				
g. Federal share of amount on line e				
h. Federal payments previously requested				
i. Federal share now requested *(Line g minus line h)*				
j. Advances required by month, when requested by Federal grantor agency for use in making pre-scheduled advances 1st month				
2nd month				
3rd month				

12. ALTERNATE COMPUTATION FOR ADVANCES ONLY

a. Estimated Federal cash outlays that will be made during period covered by the advance	$
b. *Less:* Estimated balance of Federal cash on hand as of beginning of advance period	
c. Amount requested *(Line a minus line b)*	$

13. CERTIFICATION

I certify that to the best of my knowledge and belief the data above are correct and that all outlays were made in accordance with the grant conditions or other agreement and that payment is due and has not been previously requested.	SIGNATURE OF AUTHORIZED CERTIFYING OFFICIAL	DATE REQUEST SUBMITTED
	TYPED OR PRINTED NAME AND TITLE	
	TELEPHONE *Area Code* *Number* *Extension*	

FIGURE 9–15 *(continued)*

INSTRUCTIONS

Please type or print legibly. Items 1, 3, 5, 9, 10, 11c, 11e, 11f, 11g, 11i, 12, and 13 are self-explanatory; specific instructions for other items are as follows:

Item	*Entry*
2	Indicate whether request is prepared on cash or accrued expenditure basis. All requests for advances shall be prepared on a cash basis.
4	Enter the Federal grant number, or other identifying number assigned by the Federal sponsoring agency. If the advance or reimbursement is for more than one grant or other agreement, insert N/A; then, show the aggregate amounts. On a separate sheet, list each grant or agreement number and the Federal share of outlays made against the grant or agreement.
6	Enter the employer identification number assigned by the U.S. Internal Revenue Service, or the FICE (institution) code if requested by the Federal agency.
7	This space is reserved for an account number or other identifying number that may be assigned by the recipient.
8	Enter the month, day, and year for the beginning and ending of the period covered in this request. If the request is for an advance or for both an advance and reimbursement, show the period that the advance will cover. If the request is for reimbursement, show the period for which the reimbursement is requested.
Note:	The Federal sponsoring agencies have the option of requiring recipients to complete items 11 or 12, but not both. Item 12 should be used when only a minimum amount of information is needed to make an advance and outlay information contained in item 11 can be obtained in a timely manner from other reports.
11	The purpose of the vertical columns (a), (b), and (c), is to provide space for separate cost breakdowns when a project has been planned and budgeted by program, function, or activity. If additional columns are needed, use as many additional forms as needed and indicate page number in space provided in upper right; however, the summary totals of all programs, functions, or activities should be shown in the "total" column on the first page.
11a	Enter in "as of date", the month, day, and year of the ending of the accounting period to which this amount applies. Enter program outlays to date (net of refunds, rebates, and discounts), in the appropriate columns. For requests prepared on a cash basis, outlays are the sum of actual cash disbursements for goods and services, the amount of indirect expenses charged, the value of in-kind contributions applied, and the amount of cash advances and payments made to subcontractors and subrecipients. For requests prepared on an accrued expenditure basis, outlays are the sum of the actual cash disbursements; the amount of indirect expenses incurred, and the net increase (or decrease) in the amounts owed by the recipient for goods and other property received and for services performed by employees, contracts, subgrantees and other payees.
11b	Enter the cumulative cash income received to date, if requests are prepared on a cash basis. For requests prepared on an accrued expenditure basis, enter the cumulative income earned to date. Under either basis, enter only the amount applicable to program income that was required to be used for the project or program by the terms of the grant or other agreement.
11d	Only when making requests for advance payments, enter the total estimated amount of cash outlays that will be made during the period covered by the advance.
13	Complete the certification before submitting this request.

THE BASIC HANDBOOK OF GRANTS MANAGEMENT

meet the cash flow problem, and many banks will not make such loans unless you can secure them adequately. A few communities have an organization or fund that maintains revolving funds for organizations with cash flow problems. Check to see if there is one in your area. For example, the Fund for the City of New York does this for New York agencies.

Changing the Budget

A project budget is an estimate of expenses and income that is made at the time a grant or contract proposal is submitted and negotiated. When a project swings into operation, it often turns out that the original budget estimates that were approved for personnel, travel, equipment, supplies, and the like need to be changed. There are two typical types of budget changes that project directors may wish to make. Most frequent are changes in the line items within the approved total grant amount: reducing one or more items and increasing others. Second, are efforts to increase the total grant amount.

The latter type of change seldom meets with success during a current grant period since most funders do not have the flexibility or inclination to permit this. However, asking for a budget supplement should not be regarded as out of the question, particularly with funders that have a good working knowledge of your project. A request for supplemental funding should be well documented and should be submitted to the funder not as an emergency measure to bail you out of an overexpenditure but as the result of replanning the project's work or expanding the scope of work. Supplemental requests should be made on a line item basis even though they will increase the total budget. An example of this approach is to request a supplement of $1,000 to a $5,000 equipment budget based on the need for one more typewriter for an office worker whose duties have changed from filing to include typing because of the pressure to develop a newsletter and information service that was not originally proposed as a major activity. Explain why this activity should be carried out and why other activities cannot be given up to handle the problem by transferring money within the budget. Show how the entire original item of $5,000 is already committed to other necessary expenditures. Supplemental requests within a grant period must always be in writing, usually by letter, but some government funders require completion of new budget forms.

Also, in connection with getting additional funds, you should keep in mind the fact that funders want to spend their money. Sometimes, toward the end of the fiscal year, a funder has excess money in their grant program. Thus, if your request is initially turned down, ask the funder to keep it active for reconsideration at a later date.

Changes between budget items that do not change the total budget amount are much more frequently approved than supplemental awards. Many foundations do not even have a formal requirement that you submit such transfers for prior approval. But, it is always a good idea to write and tell them what you plan to do. A sample of such a request is shown earlier in figure 9-7. Some foundations and most government funders have policies limiting the extent of changes and requiring prior approval, but these policies are not at all uniform. Various funders, for example, will allow a percentage of variation between items that may be overspent and underspent by 10 percent or so. Other funders do not permit any changes without some kind of clearance or approval. Large host agencies that have many different projects, such as universities, may have an internal approval system, which is sanctioned by funders such as the Public Health Service and the National Science Foundation and permit a committee internal to the institution to approve changes as long as the funds have not yet been spent.

How can a project director approach such a maze of possible different policies? In the words of one grant manager the thing to do is "to pay attention to guidelines of your particular award and ask questions of the funder and the institution's grants management office before you shift money and overspend an item. If this is done, you will often find that there is a lot more latitude than you thought."

A Final Word

The grants director of a large university has this advice for project directors:

Pay attention to the guidelines that accompany your particular award. Ask questions of the funder and grants management office of your organization before making any expenditures about which there may be any question.

The project director or principal investigator must retain final control of financial management. You can't farm financial control out to a graduate assistant or secretary. Everything you do must be beyond reproach. Never take the position that any aspect of financial management even if it is only filling out forms is unimportant. Anticipate your needs and plan your expenditures, staff appointments and purchasing as far ahead of time as possible. Finally, project directors and principal investigators need to understand that the base of support for their work is not as strong as they might think. Since it can be easily affected by public sentiment and political considerations, effective fiscal and business management can be more important in building support than any other aspect of a project's work.

Glossary of Terms Commonly Used in Project and Grant Administration

Account Number. The number assigned to an individual grant as part of a financial management system in order to identify and allocate all of the costs and revenues associated with each grant. It is also sometimes used to designate a particular cost such as the salary account, postage account, and so forth. However, such items are better designated as line numbers or object codes. (See *Object Class Categories.*)

Accounts Receivable. These are funds scheduled to be received from a grantor and other sources of project income.

Accounting System. The method of recording the costs and income of a project, either on a cash, accrual, or modified accrual basis.

Accrual Accounting. An accounting method whereby costs and income are recorded in relation to the specific time that they were incurred or obligated regardless of whether actual payment has been made or received.

Advance. An amount of a grant or contract that is made available to a grantee prior to the expenditure of funds or prior to a scheduled grant payment.

Affirmative Action. The development and implementation of a plan to assure that steps are taken in the recruitment of employees to seek out applicants from "protected groups" (women, minorities, disabled) and that selection will provide for a reflection of their representation among those eligible for a particular position.

Allowable Costs. The specific items of cost for which a grantee may be reimbursed as described in the requirements and/or statement of cost principles of a funding agency. In the case of federal agencies, these costs are set forth in various OMB circulars and federal management circulars that apply to different types of grantee organizations. Allowable costs in federal grants must be reasonable, necessary (allocable), consistent, and must conform to any terms of the grant award or agreement (also see *Disallowance*).

Appeal. Refers to requesting a reversal or modification of a postaward administrative decision made by an official of the granting agency through the formal channels established to consider such cases.

Assets. The value of an organization's property, equipment, cash, investments, and accounts receivable.

Assurances. The formal agreements made by a grantee that it will comply with specified rules, regulations, laws, and requirements designated by the funding agency. These are also referred to as "assurance of compliance." In federal programs, a grantee must complete forms to indicate compliance with sections of the Civil Rights Act, various OMB circulars, the Hatch Act, and all requirements imposed by the federal sponsoring agency.

Audit. When applied to projects, an audit involves an examination of financial operations by outside auditors (authorized by the funding agency or part of that agency) of the financial status and procedures of the project, including its adherence to sound and systematic accounting practices and to funding agency rules, regulations, cost principles, terms, and conditions. Project audits may also involve an examination of the effectiveness and efficiency of management practices and of the nature and extent of program activities.

Award. A grant amount set forth in a notice of award, awarding letter, contract, or other written notification from a grantor.

Awarding Agency. The particular agency that awards a grant (see *Grantor*).

Balance Sheet. A periodic financial statement which shows the financial status or position of an organization based on the value of assets, liabilities, and fund balances (also called net worth or equity). A balance sheet is not a statement of income and expenditures, which reveals financial activity (money spent and received).

Block Grant. A grant from a government agency to a class of political subdivisions such as states, counties, or cities and which is made to all recipients in that class on the basis of some formula to cover a relatively broad group of programs with a minimum of control over its utilization. Block grants are contrasted with categorical grants which are for a narrower purpose and have tighter restrictions as to their use.

Glossary of Terms

Boiler Plate. The standardized, routine, uniform provisions that apply to all grants and contracts awarded by a particular funder as contrasted to special provisions that apply only to the individual grant or contract.

Budget. The list of itemized expenditures and income for a project for a special period of time (usually twelve months).

Budget Code. The identifying number assigned in an accounting system to designate different accounts and line items of expenditure, such as rent, postage, supplies, salaries, fringe benefits.

Budget Period. The interval (usually twelve months) from the beginning to the end of the time when costs may be incurred against a grant or contract.

Budget Revision. Changes made from the planned expenditures included in the budget originally submitted to and approved by the funding agency.

Business Officer. See *Grants Management Officer.*

Contract Services. The budget category that includes the amount of all subcontracts, consultant services, and subgrants made by a project for goods and services.

Capital Support. Funds made available for acquisition or construction of buildings, major equipment, and renovations in facilities.

Capitation. A grant awarded according to the number of persons to be served or trained in which the funds are provided on a per capita (an amount per person) basis.

Carry Over. Funds that remain at the end of a grant period which are applied to the following grant period.

Cash Accounting. An accounting procedure in which expenditures and income are recorded on the basis of the time when they are actually made or received.

Cash Flow. The amount of money that is required to meet the expenses which a project is obligated to pay at any given time in relation to the amount of money on hand to meet those expenses.

Catalog of Federal Domestic Assistance Programs. A federal publication of the Office of Management and Budget that lists and describes federal grant programs.

Certifications. Written assurances that the grantee will or has met requirements specified by a funding agency (e.g., certifying that the grantee has nonprofit status approved by the Internal Revenue Service; certifying the grantee will comply with Section VI of the Civil Rights Act, and so forth).

Certified Public Accountant (CPA). An independent professional accountant certified to practice by a state agency.

Code of Federal Regulations (CFR). The multivolume publication of the federal government that incorporates and codifies all of the federal rules and regulations which apply to federal grants.

Cognizant Audit Agency. The federal agency designated to carry out the audits of federally-sponsored projects. The audit agency for most federal nondefense projects is the Department of Health and Human Services Audit Agency.

Commerce Business Daily. A daily publication of the federal government which lists the announcement of all contracts that will be made available by federal agencies and lists contract awards (published by the Department of Commerce).

Compliance. Refers to adherence to the rules, regulations, requirements, and guidelines of a funder that apply to the project grant (see *Assurances*).

Conditions. See *Terms and Conditions.*

Continuation Grant. The amount granted to support a project that has been approved for more than one year (usually three) after its initial grant period(s), as distinguished from a new grant or a renewal grant which requires a new application. Continuation grants are noncompetitive but the funder is not obligated to automatically continue the grant.

Contract. A legally-enforceable document that provides for the rights and duties of the grantee and grantor, including provisions regarding the services or goods to be provided, work to be performed, terms and conditions, amount of the contract, basis for payment, time period, schedule of reports, and the like.

Contract Officer. The agency official who has the authority to develop, negotiate, and enter into contracts.

Contractor. This term is used variably to refer to the organization under contract to a funder to perform a specific work or service; or to refer to the agency that awards the contract.

Cooperative Agreement. An instrument used by federal agencies that lies between a grant and a contract when the services to be provided by the project are not for the direct benefit of the government (as in a contract) but will involve substantial involvement between the project and the government (which is not true of a grant).

Cost Overrun. The amount of additional costs that are incurred beyond those that were originally estimated and approved in the budget in a proposal or contract.

Glossary of Terms

Cost-Plus Contract. A contract that provides for payment to the contractor on the basis of allowable costs that are incurred within an approved budget, plus a fixed fee or profit usually expressed as a percentage of the total budget paid upon successful completion of the prescribed work.

Cost Principles. Federal regulations that establish principles for determining direct and indirect costs, for determining allowable and unallowable project costs, and for determining reimbursement rates.

Cost Reimbursable Contract. A contractual arrangement in which the payments to the contractor are on the basis of the actual approved or allowable expenditures made in the course of carrying out the scheduled work.

Cost Sharing. That portion of the project costs which are contributed by the grantee from its own resources or other nongrant sources in the form of cash or in-kind contributions or both.

Debits. In an accounting system, a debit is an entry on the left side of an account in a ledger. An item of project expenditure is considered a debit.

Demonstration Project. A project whose purpose is to demonstrate or test a method to provide a particular service, activity, or technique. Demonstration projects are sometimes called pilot projects.

Direct Assistance. A grant of goods or services made by a grantor in lieu of cash, such as equipment, personnel, computer service, or supplies.

Direct Costs. Items of expense that can be specifically attributed to project objectives and activities, such as expenditures for salaries, fringe benefits, travel, supplies, rent, equipment, postage, telephone, printing.

Disallowance. An expenditure made by the project that is not approved by the grantor or by an auditor since the expenditure was not allowable or intended under the terms of the grant (see *Allowable Costs*).

Disclaimers. Refers to the inclusion of any written document of a direct statement that the work does not represent the opinions, position, or endorsement of the funding agency and/or that responsibility cannot be ascribed to the funding agency.

Discretionary Funds. Funds which may or may not be spent that are allocated for a particular purpose according to the discretion of a funding agency in awarding grants or a project director in managing a project budget.

Encumbrance. An obligated cost that has not yet actually been expended, usually on the basis of purchase orders, contracts, or other obligatory forms that must be paid at the time the material or the services are delivered or performed.

Excess Government Property. See *Surplus Property.*

Equal Opportunity. The certifications that a grantee will not discriminate in employment and other activities on the basis of sex, age, ethnicity, race, or handicap in accordance with provisions of legislation and executive orders (also see *Assurances and Affirmative Action*).

Federal Assistance Program Retrieval System (FAPRS). A federal government computerized system of information from the *Catalog of Domestic Assistance Programs* and other sources to identify federal grant programs in various fields.

Federal Financial Participation (FFP). Refers to those items of cost or proportion of costs of a grantee that are eligible for reimbursement from a federal funding agency.

Federal Management Circulars (FMC). Federal government publications that establish principles, requirements, and procedures that apply to grantees. These are similar to OMB circulars and in some cases are being replaced by OMB circulars.

Federal Register. A daily publication of the federal government that sets forth proposed and approved rules and regulations that apply to federal grant programs (published by the Government Printing Office).

Fellowship. A grant or budget item to support individual training, study, or research in a particular field.

Financial Analyst. See *Grants Management Officer.*

Financial Officer. See *Grants Management Officer.*

Fiscal Year (FY). A twelve-month period that designates the beginning and end of the allocations and financial affairs of an organization or unit of government. The federal fiscal year runs from October 1 to September 30. Most states and local governments and agencies are on a different fiscal year. Many nonprofit agencies follow a fiscal year that corresponds to the calendar year.

Fixed Price Contract. A contract in which the work to be performed is carried out for a set amount of money which is paid the contractor upon satisfactory completion regardless of the total costs actually incurred.

Flow Through. Funds that are granted to a project which are then provided to another organization as a subcontractor or subgrantee.

Formula Grant. A grant made on the basis of a specific formula such as population characteristics or unemployment rates for a particular state or area (also see *Capitation*, which is a specific type of formula grant).

Glossary of Terms

Foundations. Nonprofit organizations that provide funds from an established source to support social, charitable, educational, scientific, cultural, religious, and similar activities. Foundations are either independent, privately endowed, or are community foundations (or trusts) that focus on a particular geographic area, or are corporate foundations that disburse grants on behalf of a private corporation.

Freedom of Information Act. A federal act requiring federal agencies to release information in their possession regarding grants (and other matters) requested by any member of the public except for certain nondiscloseable information that invades the privacy or rights of grantees and others.

Fringe Benefits. The budget category that includes costs to the grantee associated with project personnel beyond their salaries, such as health insurance, social security taxes, pension plans, unemployment, and disability payments, and are paid by the grantee. Fringe benefits are usually included in a budget on the basis of a percentage of the salary item.

Full-Effort Reporting. A reporting system used to account for 100 percent of the time of an employee in various activities regardless of whether or not the person is full time on a project. Such reporting is required of federally-funded projects in educational institutions by OMB Circular A–21.

Gantt Chart. A timetable that shows in chart form the starting and ending time for each activity or task involved in a project.

General Accounting Office (GAO). An independent agency which reports directly to Congress by monitoring and studying the efficiency and effectiveness of government-sponsored programs. The GAO seldom carries out grant financial audits but does examine the auditing work of other federal agencies and establishes audit standards. It makes recommendations to Congress and agencies regarding program improvements.

General Provisions. See *Boiler Plate.*

General Support. A grant (usually from a foundation) intended to support the regular ongoing operations of an organization as contrasted to grants restricted to special purposes.

Generally Accepted Accounting Principles (GAAP). These are the principles that have been agreed upon by accountants as the preferred methods for dealing with financial data. In the field of nonprofit accounting, these principles have been changing and are still developing, in large part through the work of the American Institute of Certified Public Accountants (AICPA) and others.

Grant. An award made by a funding agency to a grantee to support a project or other work that has usually been sought by the grantee in a proposal or application.

Grants-in-Aid. The term applied to cover the wide range of programs that comprise the system of intergovernmental transfer of funds.

Grant-Supported Activity. Those activities that a grantor has approved in awarding a grant, as set forth in the project proposal, a notice of award, an award letter, contract, or agreement.

Grantee. The individual or organization to which grant monies are actually paid and which is technically responsible for their use. In the case of most projects, the grantee is the larger organization (host organization) in which the project is located.

Grantor. The government agency or foundation that awards a grant (also known as awarding agency or as sponsoring agency).

Grants Management Officer. The person designated by a funding agency to be responsible for the financial and business aspects of a particular grant and liaison with projects in relation to financial policies and practices and budgets. Also known as grant officer, financial officer, financial analyst, business officer. Persons with similar titles and responsibilities are also part of the structure of most grantee organizations. The activities of grants management officers are usually restricted to finance and business. Other persons are responsible for programmatic aspects of the grants management process (see *Program Officer*).

Guidelines. A set of general standards, principles, and policies established by a funder to which a project is expected to conform.

Host Organization. The larger organization within which a grant or contract-supported project is located and which is the technical grantee.

Human Subjects, Protection of. Requirement of the federal government that federal grantees establish procedures whereby any research plan involving human subjects is reviewed by an Institutional Review Board (see IRB) prior to carrying out the research in order to assure that the rights and welfare of persons are safeguarded.

Indirect Costs. Costs that are incurred by the organization within which a project is located which cannot be directly attributed to specific project objectives and activities since they are related to the general operation of the organization but are necessary to the maintenance of the project, such as provision of office space, payroll services, building maintenance, libraries, personnel services, and general administration. Indirect costs are usually computed on the basis of a percentage of the project's total salaries or total direct expenses.

Institutional Review Board (IRB). The group established to review the adequacy of project procedures with respect to the protection of human subjects.

Glossary of Terms

In-Kind Contribution. The value of the services of personnel, equipment, facilities, supplies, and the like that a grantee contributes as its share of project costs (see *Cost Sharing*).

Journal. In an accounting system, the journal is known as the book of original entry in which the daily transactions of expense (debits) and income (credits) are entered.

Ledger. In an accounting system, the ledger is the record book in which accounts are kept based on transferring (posting) information from the daily journal and shown on a monthly (or other period) basis.

Letter of Credit. An optional method of payment by federal agencies for grants for at least one year and exceeding $120,000 by which a letter is prepared and certified by a federal official authorizing the grantee to draw funds from the U.S. Treasury or through the Federal Reserve Bank that go either to the grantee's commercial bank or directly to the grantee.

Level of Effort. A measurement of the total amount of staff time to be expended by a project, usually expressed in person-years, person-months, person-weeks, or person-days.

Liabilities. An accounting term that refers to debts such as bills that are owed, rent, salaries, utilities, and interest.

Maintenance of Effort. The requirement of a grantor that a grantee maintain its activities at a particular level of expenditures or services in order to avoid using grant monies to replace the cost of already existing programs.

Man-Years. See *Level of Effort.*

Management by Objectives (MBO). A managerial technique in which managers and other workers participate in a process to identify and implement goals and responsibilities of managers and units of an organization. These include the results that are expected which are then used as a basis for monitoring and evaluating performance of persons and units.

Matching Funds. That portion of the project costs which are provided by the grantee in the form of cash or the value of in-kind contributions. These may be stipulated by the grantor or may be voluntarily included by the grantee.

Milestones. Refers to the completion of particular activities or events as part of a project timetable (also see *Gantt Chart*).

Modified Accural Accounting. A method of accounting in which most items are recorded on a cash basis except unpaid bills and other obligations which are recorded on an accrual basis (see *Cash Accounting and Accrual Accounting*).

No-Cost Extension. An extension of the project's period of time beyond the original grant period (usually a year) without requiring any additional funds beyond those already approved or incurring costs greater than those in the original approved or revised budget.

Notice of Award. A formal written notification used by federal granting agencies and others indicating approval of a grant, its amount, time period, and conditions and terms.

Object Class Categories. Budget items of particular kind, such as salaries, rent, office supplies, designated by different code numbers known as object codes.

Organizational Prior Approval System (OPAS). Delegates the right to grantee organizations to establish a system to provide review and approval of changes in certain grant budget items prior to any actual expenditure. Appropriate officials other than project directors or principal investigators may constitute the OPAS.

OMB Circular A–21. Establishes financial and administrative requirements governing allowable and unallowable costs and the determination of direct and indirect costs for grants to educational institutions.

OMB Circular A–95. Establishes requirements for organizations which are seeking certain types of federal grants to notify and gain approval of authorized regional planning groups that are designated as part of the Project Notification and Review System.

OMB Circular A–102. Establishes uniform financial and administrative requirements for federal grants in aid to state and local governments.

OMB Circular A–110. Establishes uniform financial and administrative requirements for federal grants and agreements with institutions of higher education, hospitals, and other nonprofit organizations.

OMB Circular A–122. Establishes financial and administrative requirements governing allowable and unallowable costs and the determination of direct and indirect costs for nonprofit organizations.

Person-Years. See *Level of Effort.*

Planning Project. A project whose purposes are to design a particular program or methodology in which implementation is limited to testing the feasibility of the design.

Principal Investigator. See *Project Director.*

Prior Approval. Requirement of a granting agency to obtain its permission to

212

spend funds, change budget items, and perform or modify certain services before the expenditures or activities are actually undertaken.

Privacy Act. Federal legislation that prohibits the release of information by federal agencies that would invade the privacy of individuals.

Project Cost. The direct and indirect costs that are attributable to a grant-supported activity. Some funders limit these costs to those included in the budget it approved when the grant was made (also see *Allowable Costs*).

Program Evaluation Review Technique (PERT). A management system to plan and control project activities (and their related costs) by scheduling the timing of all events and activities in a way that recognizes their interdependence and enables their completion in the shortest possible time.

Program Manager. See *Program Officer*.

Program Officer. The official in a governmental or foundation funding agency who is responsible for the liaison between the grantor and grantee and for supervision of any technical or programmatic conditions imposed by the granting agency on the project. These persons may also be called project officers, program managers, program analysts, contract officers. In some cases, they may also be responsible for supervision of the financial as well as the programmatic aspects of the grant when the funding agency does not have a separate staff person to perform this function such as a grants manager.

Program/Project Period. The total time interval during which the grant-supported activities may be carried out.

Progress Payment. The amount of the grant or contract paid by the grantor according to a regularly scheduled payment plan, such as quarterly, and usually contingent upon receipt of a written progress report or other indication of satisfactory work by the grantee.

Project Director/Principal Investigator. The person within the grantee organization who is responsible for the direction of a grant or nongrant-supported project and is accountable for the proper management and conduct of the financial, business, and substantive aspects of the project. Also sometimes known as project coordinator, program director, research director, or administrator.

Project Notification and Review System. See *OMB A-95*.

Project Officer. See *Program Officer*.

Proposal. A written document submitted to a funder that provides a detailed description of the project's objectives, activities, methods, operating plans, and budget. Also referred to as an application, particularly in cases where the funding agency requires that the request be submitted on its own application forms.

Regulations. Requirements of funding agency with respect to the rules that govern a particular program and with which grantees must be in compliance.

Reimbursement Formula. The basis upon which a grantee is paid by a grantor that relies upon some formula such as number of persons served, number of hours of service provided, or population characteristics (see *Formula Grant*).

Renewal Grant. A grant to continue a project for an additional period of time when the funding agency had not previously recommended or approved support for the project beyond the initial budget period. Renewal grants are competitive.

Research Project. A project whose primary purpose is to engage in studies, surveys, experimentation, evaluations, testing, or other forms of research to acquire and extend knowledge and contribute to policy and program decision making.

Revenue Sharing. Refers to grants for unrestricted use from the federal government to states and local governments.

RFP (Request for Proposal). A formal written announcement from a funding agency inviting competitive proposals for an available contract that sets forth the specifications and scope of the work and the product that is being sought.

Service Project. A project whose purpose is to provide a particular service or services to a group of participants as contrasted with research, training, planning, construction, or technical assistance projects.

Signature Card. A card signed by officials who are authorized to sign checks, purchase orders, vouchers, and other documents.

Site Visit. A formal visit to the site of a project by persons authorized by a funder to obtain firsthand information about a project, either prior to an award, during the project period, or in connection with renewal or continuation of funding.

Sponsor. Refers to the granting agency (see *Grantor*). Also used as an adjective, for example, in "sponsored research," to identify activities that are supported by sources outside the host organization.

Stipend. A payment made to an individual in a training program or participating in a project activity to defray the person's living and other costs associated with the period of training or participation, and not as a salary for services to be performed.

214

Glossary of Terms

Subcontractor. The organization or person that a project contracts with to perform a particular service to the project. Subcontractors are generally subject to all the requirements imposed on the project itself by a funding agency.

Subgrantee. An organization to which a project makes a grant (as contrasted with a subcontract) to perform particular services for the project.

Surplus Property. The General Services Agency of the federal government and many state governments offer surplus property to educational, health, and welfare organizations at minimal cost. The GSA sometimes has "excess" property which is property that federal agencies do not need and is offered to other federal agencies and sometimes to grantees. Excess property is usually in better condition than surplus property.

Technical Assistance Project. A project whose purpose is to provide some specific services to assist one or more other organizations with their operations, activities, programs, or management.

Terms and Conditions. All of the legal requirements that pertain to and are imposed on a grant or contract.

Third Party. An organization (or person) additional to the two main parties (the grantee and the grantor) involved in performing the work of a project usually as a subcontractor or a consultant performing contractual services.

Training Project. A project whose primary purpose is to use grant or contract funds to support training or educational activities for students, employees, prospective employees, or designated population groups.

Unobligated Balance. Unspent amount of funds that remain at the end of a budget period and against which there are no accrued expenses. These funds may have to be returned to the funder or may be applied to the subsequent grant period, if there is one, as a deduction or addition to the next grant at the discretion of the funder.

Voucher. A written order as part of a paper system to establish a record of requisitions, purchases of supplies and equipment, requests for travel and payments that require approval prior to being processed and paid.

Appendix A

Project Management

Resources

This appendix describes some of the books and articles that can provide project managers with a wide range of management information. It is divided into seven sections: General Management Resources; Accounting and Financial Management Resources; Marketing Resources; Legal Resources; Resources for Reports and Public Relations; Refunding Resources; and Evaluation Resources.

General Management Resources

Weiner, Myron E. *Human Services Management: Analysis and Applications.* Homewood, Ill.: The Dorsey Press, 1982, 640 pp.—One of the best up-to-date, comprehensive overviews of management theory and techniques as they apply to human services organizations. Includes chapters on financial management, personnel management, program management, the use of computers, and a fine analysis of the unreconcilable value tensions that face managers. There are only eight pages on projects, however.

Federal Grants Management Handbook. Washington, D.C.: The Grants Management Advisory Service, 2120 L Street, N.W., Suite 210, Washington, D.C. 20037—The most comprehensive service related to the rules and regulations that govern federal grant programs. The three-volume loose-leaf notebooks cover both basic material, as well as information on specific federal agency programs that can be ordered separately. A monthly update of "current developments" is included in the $105 annual charge.

Sladek, Frea E. and Stein, Eugene L. *Grant Budgeting and Finance: Getting the Most Out of Your Grant Dollar*. New York: Plenum Press, 1981, 328 pp.—One of the very few books devoted exclusively to the management of grants, this well done work focuses exclusively on financial management. Its orientation is to stretch grant dollars as far as possible by using money-saving and dollar-stretching techniques related to spending, cash flow, contacts with funders, "games playing," and the like. Persons interested in issues other than dollar efficiency may be concerned about some of the "tips" that would reduce salaries and might cut corners on program activities; but the authors are clear that their approach is to "trim" and "cut fat."

Grantsmanship Center News. Los Angles: Grantsmanship Center, 1031 South Grand Avenue, Los Angeles, Calif. 90015, $20 per year—A bimonthly magazine that covers a wide range of information regarding grants, grant administration, and administration of nonprofit organizations. The Center also runs workshops in proposal writing and management. The following is a list of helpful reprints related to management that are available from the Center: "Cost Accounting for Non Accountants," 12 pp.; "Employee Evaluation," 12 pp.; "The Process of Program Evaluation," 48 pp.; "Letting Go: The Difficult Art of Firing," 8 pp.; "Introduction to Accounting for Non-profits" (newly revised), 24 pp.; "An Overview of Office Management Procedures," 16 pp.; "Basic Guide to Salary Management," 24 pp.; and "Federal Surplus Property," 12 pp.

U.S. Government Publications—There are a number of government publications dealing with the management of federally-supported projects. Four of the principal ones are: *Grants Administration.* Department of Health and Human Services, Washington, D.C.: U.S. Government Printing Office, Washington, D.C., 20402. *National Science Foundation Grants Policy Manual.* Washington, D.C.: NSF Space, Supply and Communications, 1800 G. Street, N.W., Washington, D.C. 20550, March 1981 (also, *Grant General Conditions*). *NIH Grants Policy Guide.* Bethesda, Md.: U.S. Department of Health and Human Services, Associate Director of Extramural Research and Training, Building 1, Room 118; Bethesda, Md. 20014. *U.S. Public Health Grants Policy Statement.* October, 1976, Addendum, October, 1977.

The Public Management Institute, 333 Hayes Street, San Francisco, Calif. 94102, publishes a number of expensive manuals on how-to-do-it techniques, primarily for nonprofit organizations. These include: *Grants Administration; Bookkeeping for Nonprofits; Nonprofit Financial Management; Budgeting for Nonprofits; Managing Nonprofit Agencies for Results; Managing Nonprofit Staff for Results;* and *Successful Public Relations Techniques.*

Grants Magazine: The Journal of Sponsored Research and Other Programs. New York: Plenum Press—A quarterly periodical that includes excellent articles on obtaining grants and on the administration of grants, including research grants and service grants.

The Foundation News. Washington, D.C.: The Council on Foundations, Inc., 1828 L Street, N.W., Washington, D.C. 20036—A periodical primarily for foundation officials that lists foundation grants and includes articles about the problems and issues that are of concern to foundations.

Federal Grants and Contracts Weekly. Arlington, Va.: Capitol Publications, Inc., 1300 N. 17th Street, Arlington, Va., 22209—A weekly publication that summarizes developments in the grants field, including available RFPs, grant availability, and regulations in the broad field of education.

Sarri, Rosemary C. and Hasenfeld, Yeheskel, eds. *The Management of Human Services.* New York: Columbia University Press, 1978, 366 pp.—A reader dealing primarily with various aspects of social work administration and broad policy and program issues in the field of social welfare. In his chapter, "Demystifying Organizations" (pp. 105–20), Charles Perrow raises the question of why, with all the material developed on organizational theory, these ideas (ranging from human relations techniques to contingency theory) have had little effect in actual practice. He argues that the answer lies in the fact that the theories disguise the real functions of organizations. When organizations do not reach their goals, it is usually explained as a problem of resources, poor communication, poor coordination, and so on. Perrow suggests an alternative explanation: that is, organizations serve to meet the personal needs and interests of individuals and groups, often having little to do with accomplishing program objectives.

Fisher, John. *How to Manage A Non-Profit Organization.* Toronto: Management and Fund-Raising Centre Publishing Division, 1978, 214 pp., $16.50—A lightly written book that covers a wide variety of topics concerning the management of nonprofit organizations.

Anderson, Wayne F., Frieden, Bernard J., and Murphy, Michael J. *Managing Human Services.* Washington, D.C.: International City Managers Association, 1977—Aimed at the local governmental practitioner, this 591–page volume of articles surveys the broad range of issues related to the role of local government in the human services and the planning and administration of those programs. It contains illustrations from a variety of fields, such as social services, day care, and mental health. It does not include information on the management of special projects, nor does it contain much on the day-to-day techniques of program management, but it is a good overview of the field of governmental human service administration and planning issues.

Anthony, Robert N. and Herzlinger, Regina. *Management Control in Nonprofit Organizations.* Homewood, Ill.: Richard D. Irwin, Inc., 1975—Explains how the application of general management concepts should be adapted to the special

218

characteristics of nonprofit organizations and their orientation to clients, services, and the public.

Zallman, Gerald, ed. *Management Principles for Nonprofit Agencies and Organizations.* New York: AMACOM, American Management Associations, 1979—A general reader on the organization, planning, and control of nonprofit organizations.

Levin, Richard I. and Kirkpatrick, Charles A. *Planning and Control with PERT/CPM.* New York: McGraw-Hill Book Company, 1966, 179 pp.—A good explanation of the basic aspects of Program Evaluation and Review Technique (PERT) and Critical Path Method (CPM) providing a comprehensive understanding of these management tools as they are used in large-scale, nonrepetitive projects in business and construction.

Ugterhoeven, H.E.R. "General Managers in the Middle," *Harvard Business Review* 50 (March–April 1972): 75–85—Explains the differences in the characteristics and responsibilities between middle managers and managers at other levels. While this article does not address project managers as such, the material is applicable to some aspects of their managerial role.

Wile, Howard P. "Warning: This Grant May Be Hazardous To Your Health," in Burton J. Eckstein, *Handicapped Funding Directory: 1980-81 Edition,* Oceanside, N.Y.: Research Grant Guides, P.O. Box 357, Oceanside, N.Y., 11572—An interesting article that summarizes the liabilities and pitfalls facing a grantee as the result of the rules and regulations of funding agencies that add to the administrative burden of the grantee and can influence its program and operations.

Wilner, William and Hendricks, Perry B., Jr. *Grants Administration.* Arlington, Va.: National Graduate University, 1972—A guide to the organization of grants management offices.

Oleck, Howard L. *Nonprofit Corporations, Organizations and Associations,* 4th ed. Englewood Cliffs, N.J.: Prentice-Hall, Inc., $59.95—A forty-five chapter reference book that examines the legal characteristics of nonprofit organizations and how to comply with them. Covers a wide range of information from basic forms of by-laws to the nature of IRS decisions that affect nonprofit organizations. While not focused on projects or grant programs as such, there is a good deal of the general reference material that may be applied to projects lodged in nonprofit organizations.

Connors, Tracy Daniel. *The Nonprofit Organization Handbook.* New York: McGraw-Hill Book Company, 1980—A series of articles on the nonprofit sector, including a section on leadership, management, control, public relations, and fiscal management. Includes good articles on accounting principles and procedures.

Borst, Diane and Montana, Patrick J. *Managing Nonprofit Organizations*. New York: AMACOM, 1977—A useful group of articles covering various aspects of managing nonprofit organizations, including both governmental and voluntary agencies. Includes a section on "Project Management and Participatory Management" (pp. 207–59), but the papers in this section are geared to using the project approach as a way to deal with problems and inertia in the management of ongoing agencies and special program planning efforts rather than grant-supported activities.

The Federal Register. Washington, D.C.: Superintendent of Documents, U.S. Government Printing Office, Washington, D.C. 20402—Published five days a week, *The Federal Register* is the official government publication in which proposed and adopted rules, regulations, and guidelines which apply to all government grant programs are published. it is available in most libraries that maintain government publications.

Kaplan, Norman. "The Role of the Research Administrator," *Administrative Science Quarterly* 4 (1) (1959): 20–42—Administrators of research grants who handle the nonscientific aspect of the organization, such as budgeting and business management, are shown to have role problems. These managers are considered marginal by researchers even though they must often defend and explain the research and project activities. A proper reference group for grant business managers is hard to find since they are not accepted by either the scientists or by the larger business administration professionals.

Selbst, Paul L. "The Containment and Control of Organizational Crises," *Management Handbook for Public Administrators*. Edited by John W. Sutherland, New York: Van Nostrand Reinhold Company, 1978, pp. 843–878—A good explanation of the "crises" that face organizations and how managers can respond to them.

Handicapped Requirements Handbook. Washington, D.C.: Federal Programs Advisory Service, $80—A loose-leaf notebook and monthly updates of the federal government requirements and compliance materials in connection with Sections 504, 503, and 502 of the Rehabilitation Act of 1973.

Lawe, Theodore M. *How to Secure and Manage Foundation and Federal Funds in the 1980's*. Dallas, Texas: MRDC Educational Institute, 1980, 183 pp., $12.95—Focuses largely on the securing of funds.

Accounting and Financial Management Resources

Gross, Malvern, Jr. and Washauer, William, Jr. *Financial Accounting Guide for Nonprofit Organizations*, 3rd ed., New York: Ronald Press/John Wiley and Sons, 1979, 568 pp.—This is one of the most definitive guides to the accounting principles and techniques ranging from financial concepts to setting up books that apply to nonprofit organizations. It includes the AICPA accounting principles and financial reporting practices. Focused on the overall problems of nonprofit organizations, a good deal of the material can be adapted to apply to projects and grants. Written by two partners in the accounting firm of Price Waterhouse and Company.

Standards of Accounting and Financial Reporting for Voluntary Health and Welfare Organizations. New York: American Institute of Certified Public Accountants, 1211 Avenue of the Americas, New York, New York, 1974—The "official" statement of the AICPA on nonprofit accounting.

Johnson, Edward J. "The Makings of a Computer System for Sponsored Funds Administration," *Grants Magazine* 4 (4) (December 1981): 245–65—Explains the development of the computer system for financial administration and reports by the Research Foundation of the State University of New York.

Wehle, Mary M. *Financial Management for Arts Organizations.* Cambridge, Mass.: Arts Administration Research Institute, 1975, 163 pp.—An introductory manual that covers basic accounting and the use of financial data in decision making. Describes the special financial management issues that face organizations in the field of the arts.

Bookkeeping for Nonprofits. San Francisco, Calif.: Public Management Institute, 1979, $42.50—A loose-leaf workbook on how to establish and maintain a bookkeeping system. Includes many examples and forms.

Kenny, James T. "The Accounting Responsibilities of the Project Administrator," *Grants Magazine* 3 (4) (December 1980), New York: Plenum Press, pp. 227–231—An article that outlines the role of project directors in the area of financial management. Points out that in addition to technical supervision of activities, the project director must also assure that the project is properly integrated with the accounting and business management system of the larger institution and also has efficient internal financial systems in accordance with accepted accounting procedures.

Pearce, H. Richard "Finding the Ideal Cash Level," in Gerald Bisbee and Robert Vraciv, eds., *Managing the Finances of Health Care Organizations.* Ann Arbor, Mich.: Health Administration Press, 1980—Explains principles and methods for dealing with cash flow problems, including many tips regarding earning interest on a grant, obtaining advances, hedging against inflation, timing the issuance and clearance of checks, and the like.

Midgett, Elwin W. *An Accounting Primer.* New York: New American Library, 1969, 175 pp.—A handy guide to what accounting is all about.

Marketing Resources

There are very few resources specifically devoted to the marketing problems of organizations in the human service and social and behavioral science field. The three major resources are:

Kotler, Philip. *Marketing for Nonprofit Organizations.* Englewood Cliffs, N.J.: Prentice-Hall, 1975, 436 pp.—A good introduction to the use of marketing principles and methods by nonprofit organizations aimed at improving their ability to attract clientele, support and funds. This is the first major work in this field.

Rubright, Robert and MacDonald, Dan. *Marketing Health and Human Services.* Rockville, Md.: Aspen Systems Corporation, 1981—Explains how to apply marketing principles and methods to agencies in the human service field. Written with an understanding of the human services, this book focuses on how to select a series of marketing programs or projects and the way to develop and implement a marketing plan.

Rodos, David L. *Marketing for Nonprofit Organizations.* Boston: Auburn House, 1981, 572 pp., $24.95. A text on the application of marketing principles and methods to help achieve management objectives in nonprofit organizations.

Legal Resources

Yarmolinsky, Adam. "The Rights of Charitable Organizations and the First Amendment," *Grants Magazine* 3 (2) (New York: Plenum Press): 83–87—A good review of the grantee's rights derived from the first amendment provisions of the Constitution.

Cappalli, Richard B. *Rights and Remedies Under Federal Grants.* Washington, D.C.: The Bureau of National Affairs, 1979—A compendium of information about the legal rights of grantees and what can be done to remedy infringement on those rights.

Sell, Tim. "The Federal Grantee's Guide to the Privacy Act," in *Funding Review* 1 (4) (July/September 1981), Pocatello, Idaho: National Grant Development Institute—An excellent review of the Privacy Act of 1974 safeguarding information regarding individuals and providing the right of access to your own records. Also compares the relationship of the Privacy Act to the Freedom of Information Act.

Report and Public Relations Resources

Lefferts, Robert. *How to Prepare Charts and Graphs for Effective Reports*. New York: Barnes and Noble Books, 1981, 166 pp., $4.95—A step-by-step manual for nonartists describing how to prepare and use charts and graphs such as pie charts, bar charts, time charts, organization charts, flow charts, and various graphic techniques that add interest and emphasis to written reports.

Selby, Peter H. *Using Graphs and Tables*. New York: John Wiley and Sons, 1979—A self-teaching guide that focuses on how to interpret graphs and tables and their statistical meaning.

Schmid, Calvin F. and Schmid, Stanton E. *Handbook of Graphic Presentation*. 2nd ed., New York: John Wiley and Sons, 1979—A comprehensive survey of charts primarily directed toward the professional specialists in this field.

Editing Your Newsletter: A Guide to Writing Design and Production. Portland, Ore.: Coast to Coast Books, 2934 N.E. 10th Avenue, Portland, Ore. 97212, $7.50, 76 pp.—A guide to preparing an organizational newsletter.

Refunding Resources

There are many, many resources on preparing proposals and obtaining funding. A comprehensive listing of these resources can be found in:

Lefferts, Robert. *Getting A Grant in the 1980's: How to Write Successful Grant Proposals*. 2nd ed., Englewood Cliffs, N.J.: Prentice-Hall, 1982, 168 pp., $6.95—Includes step-by-step methods of preparing proposals for service projects and research projects. Includes a section listing resources for proposal presentation and locating funding sources.

Other widely-used books in this field include:

White, Virginia P. *Grants, How to Find Out About Them and What To Do Next*. New York: Plenum Press, 1975, 354 pp., $14.50.

Kiritz, Norman J. *Program Planning and Proposal Writing*. Los Angeles: The Grantsmanship Center, 1015 West Olympic Boulevard, Los Angeles, Calif. 90015, 48 pp., $2.45.

Krathwahl, David R. *How To Prepare a Research Proposal*. 2nd ed., New York:

Syracuse University Bookstore; 303 University Place, Syracuse, New York, 13210, 112 pp., $3.95.

Hall, Mary. *Developing Skills in Proposal Writing.* 2nd ed., Portland, Ore.: Continuing Education Publications, 194 pp., $12.50.

Evaluation Resources

There are numerous texts and other books on evaluation available in any university library. The following are a few selected resources that are primarily of an introductory nature.

Conducting Evaluations: Three Perspectives. New York: The Foundation Center, 1980, 60 pp.—Includes three papers that present different perspectives on evaluation: that of the foundation; that of an evaluator; and, that of grantees. An excellent annotated bibliography on evaluation research prepared by Peggy Sweitzer of the Foundation Center reviews the basic reference works in this field.

Evaluation News (EN). Newsletter of the Evaluative Network. University of Wisconsin-Milwaukee, Milwaukee, Wisconsin 53201.—A newsletter of the recent developments, publications, and activities in the field of evaluation.

Van Maanen, John. "The Process of Program Evaluation," *Grantsmanship Center News* (January/February 1979), Los Angeles, California: The Grantsmanship Center.—A 48-page reprint of this article is available from the Grantsmanship Center for $3.25. Discusses the evaluation process in a way that requires little research background.

Weiss, Carol H., ed. *Evaluating Action Programs: Readings in Social Action and Education.* Boston: Allyn and Bacon, Inc., 1972.—A group of twenty readings by experts in social program evaluation. One of the more widely used books, it is not designed as a how-to-do-it book but outlines the issues and language of the field of evaluation.

Rossi, Peter H., and Freeman, Howard E. *Evaluation: A Systematic Approach,* 2nd ed., Beverly Hills: Sage Publications, 1982.—A comprehensive examination of evaluation methods as applied to social programs. Includes procedures for planning programs, selecting participants, monitoring activities, and assessing program impact of ongoing as well as innovative programs.

Hawkridge, David; Campeau, Reggie L.; and Trickett, Penelope K. *Preparing Evaluation Reports: A Guide for Authors.* Pittsburgh: American Institute for Research, 1970.—A brief guide that is geared to evaluation of education programs but has good examples that can be adapted to the reporting of evaluations in other fields.

Washington, R.O. *Program Evaluation in the Human Services.* Lanham, Md.: University Press of America, 1980.—A good introduction to the basic language and design of program evaluation.

Klein, Rudolf. "Evaluation and Social Policy," *Evaluation and Program Planning,* vol. 5, no. 2, Elmsford, N.Y.: Pergamon Press, 1982.—An article that questions many of the usual technical assumptions about criteria that are used in evaluation.

Evaluation Review. Beverly Hills: Sage Publications.—Published six times a year, this journal often includes reports on the evaluation of specific projects that can be used as models in considering evaluation designs.

Morris, Lynn; Fitz-Gibbon, Carol; and Henerson, Marlene. *Program Evaluation Kit.* Beverly Hills: Sage Publications, 1978.—A series of eight short books on various aspects of evaluation, including a general handbook and specific books on design, goals and objectives, measurement of programs, measurement of attitudes, measurement of achievement, statistics, and report presentation.

Appendix B

Sample Federal Assurance of Compliance Forms

This appendix includes the forms and instructions used by federal grant agencies to assure that projects will comply with certain federal requirements in the course of their operations. These include: (1) Statement of Overall Assurance; (2) Assurance of Compliance with Title VI of the Civil Rights Act of 1964; (3) Assurance of Compliance with Section 504 of the Rehabilitation Act of 1973; (4) Assurance of Compliance with Title IX of the Education Amendments of 1972; and (5) Protection of Human Subjects.

Assurances

The Applicant hereby assures and certifies that he will comply with the regulations, policies, guidelines and requirements, including OMB Circulars No. A—95, A—102 and FMC 74—4, as they relate to the application, acceptance and use of Federal funds for this federally-assisted project. Also the Applicant assures and certifies to the grantor that:

1. It possesses legal authority to apply for the grant; that a resolution, motion or similar action has been duly adopted or passed as an official act of the applicant's governing body, authorizing the filing of the application, includ- ing all understandings and assurances contained therein, and directing and authorizing the person identified as the official representative of the applicant to act in connection with the application and to provide such addi-

tional information as may be required.

2. It will comply with Title VI of the Civil Rights Act of 1964 (P.L. 88–352) and in accordance with Title VI of that Act, no person in the United States shall, on the ground of race, color, or national origin, be excluded from participation in, be denied the benefits of, or be otherwise subjected to discrimination under any program or activity for which the applicant receives Federal financial assistance and will immediately take any measures necessary to effectuate this agreement.

3. It will comply with Title VI of the Civil Rights Act of 1964 (42 USC 2000d) prohibiting employment discrimination where (1) the primary purpose of a grant is to provide employment or (2) discriminatory employment practices will result in unequal treatment of persons who are or should be benefiting from the grant-aided activity.

4. It will comply with requirements of the provisions of the Uniform Relocation Assistance and Real Property Acquisitions Act of 1970 (P.L. 91–646) which provides for fair and equitable treatment of persons displaced as a result of Federal and federally assisted programs.

5. It will comply with the provisions of the Hatch Act which limit the political activity of employees.

6. It will comply with the minimum wage and maximum hours provisions of the Federal Fair Labor Standards Act, as they apply to hospital and educational institution employees of State and local governments.

7. It will establish safeguards to prohibit employees from using their positions for a purpose that is or gives the appearance of being motivated by a desire for private gain for themselves or others, particularly those with whom they have family, business, or other ties.

8. It will give the sponsoring agency or the Comptroller General through any authorized representative the access to and the right to examine all records, books, papers, or documents related to the grant.

9. It will comply with all requirements imposed by the Federal sponsoring agency concerning special requirements of law, program requirements, and other administrative requirements.

10. It will insure that the facilities under its ownership, lease or supervision which shall be utilized in the accomplishment of the project are not listed on the Environmental Protection Agency's (EPA) list of Violating Facilities and that it will notify the Federal grantor agency of the receipt of any communication from the Director of the EPA Office of Federal Activities indicating that a facility to be used in the project is under consideration for listing by the EPA.

The phrase "Federal financial assistance" includes any form of loan, grant, guaranty, insurance payment, rebate, subsidy, disaster assistance loan or grant, or any other form of direct or indirect Federal assistance.

11. It will comply with the flood in-

surance purchase requirements of Section 102(a) of the Flood Disaster Protection Act of 1973, Public Law 93–234, 87 Stat. 975, approved December 31, 1976. Section 102(a) requires, on and after March 2, 1975, the purchase of flood insurance in communities where such insurance is available as a condition for the receipt of any Federal financial assistance for construction or acquisition purposes for use in any area that has been identified by the Secretary of the Department of Housing and Urban Development as an area having special flood hazards.

12. It will assist the Federal grantor agency in its compliance with Section 106 of the National Historic Preservation Act of 1966 as amended (16 U.S.C. 470), Executive Order 11593, and the Archeological and Historic Preservation Act of 1966 (16 U.S.C. 469a–1 et seq.) by (a) consulting with the State Historic Preservation Officer on the conduct of investigations, as necessary, to identify properties listed in or eligible for inclusion in the National Register of Historic Places that are subject to adverse effects (see 36 CFR Part 800.8) by the activity, and notifying the Federal grantor agency of the existence of any such properties, and by (b) complying with all requirements established by the Federal grantor agency to avoid or mitigate adverse effects upon such properties.

ASSURANCE OF COMPLIANCE WITH THE DEPARTMENT OF HEALTH AND HUMAN SERVICES REGULATION UNDER TITLE VI OF THE CIVIL RIGHTS ACT OF 1964

_____(hereinafter called the "Applicant")
(Name of Applicant)

HEREBY AGREES THAT it will comply with title VI of the Civil Rights Act of 1964 (P.L. 88–352) and all requirements imposed by or pursuant to the Regulation of the Department of Health and Human Services (45 CFR Part 80) issued pursuant to that title, to the end that, in accordance with title VI of that Act and the Regulation, no person in the United States shall, on the ground of race, color, or national origin, be excluded from participation in, be denied the benefits of, or be otherwise subjected to discrimination under any program or activity for which the Applicant receives Federal financial assistance from the Department; and HEREBY GIVES ASSURANCE THAT it will immediately take any measures necessary to effectuate this agreement.

If any real property or structure thereon is provided or improved with the aid of Federal financial assistance extended to the Applicant by the Department, this assurance shall obligate the Applicant, or in the case of any transfer of such property, any transferee, for the period during which the real property or structure is used for a purpose for which the Federal financial assistance is extended or for another purpose involving the provision of similar services or benefits. If any personal property is so provided, this assurance shall obligate the Applicant for the period during which it retains ownership or possession of the property. In all other cases, this assurance shall obligate the Applicant for the period during which the Federal financial assistance is extended to it by the Department.

THIS ASSURANCE is given in consideration of and for the purpose of obtaining any and all Federal grants, loans, contracts, property, discounts or other Federal financial assistance extended after the date hereof to the Applicant by the Department, including installment payments after such date on account of applications for Federal financial assistance which were approved before such date. The Applicant recognizes and agrees that such Federal financial assistance will be extended in reliance on the representations and agreements made in this assurance, and that the United States shall have the right to seek judicial enforcement of this assurance. This assurance is binding on the Applicant, its successors, transferees, and assignees, and the person or persons whose signatures appear below are authorized to sign this assurance on behalf of the Applicant.

Date_____   _____
                                            (Applicant)

                                   By_____
                                      (President, Chairman of Board, or
                                        comparable authorized official)

_____

(Applicant's mailing address)

HHS–441
(12–64)

_____

Explanation Of

HEW FORM NO. 441, ASSURANCE OF COMPLIANCE WITH THE DEPART-MENT OF HEALTH, EDUCATION, AND WELFARE REGULATION UNDER TITLE VI OF THE CIVIL RIGHTS ACT OF 1964

Section 80.4 of the Department of Health, Education, and Welfare's Regulation effectuating Title VI of the Civil Rights Act of 1964 requires that every application to the Department for Federal financial assistance shall contain or be accompanied by an Assurance that the program or facility to be assisted will be conducted or operated in compliance with Title VI of the Civil Rights

Act and with all requirements imposed by or pursuant to the Department's Regulation.

Section 80.4 further provides that "the form of the foregoing Assurance and the extent to which like Assurances will be required of subgrantees, contractors, transferees, successors in interest and other participants," shall be specified by the responsible Department official. Under this authority, HEW Form No. 441 has been specified as the form of Assurance which shall apply to all applications for Federal financial assistance (except for continuing state programs which must meet the requirements of Section 80.4(b) and school districts availing themselves of Section 80.4(c) of the Regulation) submitted to the Department after January 3, 1965; also the circumstances have been specified under which an Applicant shall obtain comparable written Assurances of compliance from its subgrantees, contractors, and transferees. (See answers to Questions 11 and 12 below in this regard.)

HEW Form No. 441 constitutes a legally enforceable agreement to comply with Title VI of the Civil Rights Act of 1964, and with all requirements imposed by or pursuant to the Regulation of the Department of Health, Education, and Welfare issued thereunder. Applicants are urged to read the Department's Regulation before executing the Assurance.

The following explanation of the requirements of the Department's Regulation and the examples of the kinds of discriminatory practices prohibited by them are for the guidance of the Applicants.

1. *By executing the Assurance (HEW Form No. 441), what does an Applicant agree to do?*

A. The Applicant agrees to make no distinction on the ground of race, color, or national origin in providing to individuals any service, financial aid, or other benefit under any program receiving Federal financial assistance extended to the Applicant by the Department.

2. *What is meant by "distinction on the ground of race, color, or national origin"?*

A. "Distinction on the ground of race, color, or national origin" includes (1) any type of segregation, separate or different treatment, or other discrimination on the ground; (2) the imposition of any admission, enrollment quota, eligibility, or other requirement or condition which individuals must meet in order to be provided any service, financial aid, or other benefit under a program or to be afforded an opportunity to participate in a program, if the race, color, or national origin of individuals is considered in determining whether they meet any such requirement or condition; (3) the use of membership in a group as a basis of the selection of individuals for any purpose, if in selecting members of the group there is discrimination on the ground of race, color, or national origin; and (4) the assignment of personnel to provide services, or the assignment of times or places for the provision of services, on the basis of the race, color, or national origin of the individuals to be served. It does not, however, include distinctions on the ground of race, color, or national origin determined by the responsible Department official to be necessary to the conduct of research or experimental programs having as their primary objective the discovery of new knowledge concerning special characteristics of particular racial or other ethnic groups.

Sample Federal Assurance of Compliance Forms

HEW–441A (12/64)

3. *What is meant by "service, financial aid, or other benefit"?*

A. "Service, financial aid, or other benefit" under a program receiving Federal financial assistance includes any education or training, any evaluation, guidance, counseling, or placement service, any health, welfare, rehabilitation, housing, or recreational service, any referral of individuals for any of the foregoing services, any scholarship, fellowship or traineeship stipend or allowance, and any loan or other financial assistance or benefit (whether in cash or in kind), which is made available to individuals (1) with the aid of Federal financial assistance, or (2) with the aid of the Applicant's or of other non-Federal funds required to be made available for the program as a condition to the receipt of Federal financial assistance, or (3) in or through a facility provided with the aid of Federal financial assistance or the non-Federal matching funds referred to in (2).

4. *What requirements are placed on the use of facilities?*

A. The Applicant agrees to make no distinction on the ground of race, color, or national origin in making available to individuals the use of any land, building, equipment, or other facility leased, acquired, constructed, improved, or equipped with the aid of Federal financial assistance extended to the Applicant by the Department, including—

   (a) the use of any room, dormitory, ward, or other space in the facility;

   (b) the use of any equipment in the facility;

   (c) the use of any office, waiting room, restroom, eating, recreational, concession, or other accommodation or convenience provided in the facility;

   (d) the use of any facility not provided with the aid of Federal financial assistance if the availability of such facility is required as a condition to the receipt of Federal financial assistance for the Federally-assisted facility.

5. *What requirements are placed on the opportunities to participate in a program receiving Federal assistance?*

A. The Applicant agrees to make no distinction on the ground of race, color, or national origin in affording opportunities to individuals to participate (other than as employees) in any program receiving Federal financial assistance extended by the Department to the Applicant, including opportunities to participate—

   (a) as providers of any service, financial aid, or other benefit to individuals under the program (e.g., as physicians, surgeons, dentists, or other professional practitioners seeking the privilege of practicing in a Federally-aided hospital or other facility),

   (b) as conferees, observers, consultants, or advisers, or as members of advisory or planning groups, or

   (c) as volunteers (e.g., as voluntary workers, or as patients or other subjects of study or experimentation in research, survey, demonstration, or like programs).

6. *Does that mean that an Applicant who signs the Department's Assurance may nevertheless make distinctions among his employees on the basis of race, color, or national origin?*

231

A. Title VI of the Civil Rights Act does not concern itself with employment practices except where a primary objective of the Federal financial assistance is to provide employment. Thus, where a basic objective of the program is to provide employment, the Applicant's employment practices are subject to the Department's Regulation. However, even where this is not the case an Applicant may be precluded from engaging in any discriminatory employment practices under the provisions of Title VII of the Civil Rights Act, Executive Orders 10925 and 11114, and the Merit System Regulations.

7. When an Applicant's employment practices are covered by the Department's Regulation, what requirements must be met?

A. The Applicant agrees to make no distinction on the ground of race, color, or national origin in its employment practices (including recruitment or recruitment advertising, hiring, layoff or termination, upgrading, demotion, or transfer, rates of pay or other forms of compensation, and use of facilities) with respect to individuals seeking employment or employed under any program receiving Federal financial assistance extended to the Applicant by the Department, in those programs where a primary objective of the Federal financial assistance is to provide employment to such individuals. This includes programs under which the employment is provided—

(*a*) as a means of extending financing assistance to students or to needy persons,

(*b*) to students, fellows, interns, residents, or others in training for related employment (including research associates or assistants in training for research work), or

(*c*) to reduce unemployment or to provide remunerative activity to individuals who because of severe handicaps cannot be readily absorbed in the competitive labor market.

8. What effect will the Regulation have on a college or university's admission practices or other practices related to the treatment of students?

A. An institution of higher education which applies for any Federal financial assistance of any kind must agree that it will make no distinction on the ground of race, color, or national origin in the admission practices or any other practices of the institution relating to the treatment of students.

(*a*) "Student" includes any undergraduate, graduate, professional, or postgraduate student, fellow, intern, student, or other trainee receiving education or training from the institution.

(*b*) "Admission practices" include recruiting and promotional activities, application requirements, eligibility conditions, qualifications, preferences, or quotas used in selecting individuals for admission to the institution, or any program of the institution, as students.

(*c*) "Other practices relating to the treatment of students" include the affording to students of opportunities to participate in any educational, research, cultural, athletic, recreational, social, or other program or activity; the performance evaluation, discipline, counseling of students; making available to students any housing, eating, health, or recreational service; affording work opportunities, or scholarship, loan or other financial assist-

232

ance to students; and making available for the use of students any building, room, space, materials, equipment, or other facility or property.

9. *Does the Assurance of nondiscrimination apply to the entire operation of an institution?*

A. Insofar as the Assurance given by the Applicant relates to the admission or other treatment of individuals as students, patients, or clients of an institution of higher education, a school, hospital, nursing home, center, or other institution owned or operated by the Applicant, or to the opportunity to participate in the provision of services, financial aid, or other benefits to such individuals, the Assurance applies to the entire institution. In the case of a public school system the Assurance would be applicable to all of the elementary or secondary schools operated by the Applicant.

10. *What about a university which operates several campuses?*

A. Section 80.4(d)(2) of the Regulation provides for a more limited Assurance only where an institution can demonstrate that the practices in part of its operation in no way affect its practice in the program for which it seeks Federal funds. This would be a rare case.

11. *If an Applicant intends to make use of other individuals to help carry out the Federally-assisted program, does the requirement not to discriminate apply to such a subgrantee or contractor?*

A. It does. The Applicant must require any individual, organization, or other entity which it utilizes, to which it subgrants, or with which it contracts or otherwise arranges to provide services, financial aid, or other benefits under, or to assist it in the conduct of, any program receiving Federal financial assistance extended to the Applicant by the Department, or with which it contracts or otherwise arranges for the use of any facility provided with the aid of Federal financial assistance for a purpose for which the Federal financial assistance was extended, to comply fully with Title VI of the Civil Rights Act of 1964 and the Regulation of the Department of Health, Education, and Welfare issued thereunder.

12. *Must this Assurance of nondiscrimination by the subgrantee, etc., be in writing?*

A. In the case (1) of any contractual or other arrangement with another such individual or entity which will continue for an indefinite period or for a period of more than three months, (2) of any subgrant, or (3) of any conveyance, lease, or other transfer of any real property or structures thereon provided with the aid of Federal financial assistance extended to the Applicant by the Department, the Applicants shall obtain from such other person, subgrantee, or transferee, an agreement, in writing, enforceable by the Applicant and by the United States, that such other individual or entity, subgrantee, or transferee will carry out its functions under such subgrant, or contractual or other arrangement, or will use the transferred property, as the case may be, in accordance with Title VI of the Act and the Regulation will otherwise comply herewith.

13. *What obligations does the Applicant have to inform beneficiaries, participants, and others of the provisions of the Regulation?*

A. The Applicant must make available to beneficiaries, participants, and other interested persons information regarding the provisions of the Regulation and protections against discrimination provided under Title VI of the Civil Rights Act. The Department will issue shortly more detailed instructions on carrying out this phase of the Regulation.

14. *What obligations does the Applicant have to keep records and to make them available to the Department?*

A. From time to time, Applicants may be required to submit reports to the Department, and the Regulation provides that the facilities of the Applicant and all records, books, accounts, and other sources of information pertinent to the Applicant's compliance with the Regulation by made available for inspection during normal business hours on request of an officer or employee of the Department specifically authorized to make such inspections. More detailed instructions in this regard will also be forthcoming from the Department in the near future.

15. *Must separate Assurance forms be filed with each application?*

A. As a general rule once a valid Assurance is given it will apply to any further application as long as there is no indication of a failure to comply.

DEPARTMENT OF HEALTH AND HUMAN SERVICES ASSURANCE OF COMPLIANCE WITH SECTION 504 OF THE REHABILITATION ACT OF 1973, AS AMENDED

The undersigned (hereinafter called the "recipient") HEREBY AGREES THAT it will comply with section 504 of the Rehabilitation Act of 1973, as amended (29 U.S.C. 794), all requirements imposed by the applicable HHS regulation (45 C.F.R. Part 84), and all guidelines and interpretations issued pursuant thereto.

Pursuant to § 84.5(a) of the regulation [45 C.F.R. 84.5(a)], the recipient gives this Assurance in consideration of and for the purpose of obtaining any and all federal grants, loans, contracts (except procurement contracts and contracts of insurance or guaranty), property, discounts, or other federal financial assistance extended by the Department of Health and Human Services after the date of this Assurance, including payments or other assistance made after such date on applications for federal financial assistance that were approved before such date. The recipient recognizes and agrees that such federal financial assistance will be extended in reliance on the representations and agreements made in this Assurance and that the United States will have the right to enforce this Assurance through lawful means. This Assurance is binding on the recipient, its successors, transferees, and assignees, and the person or persons whose signatures appear below are authorized to sign this Assurance on behalf of the recipient.

This Assurance obligates the recipient for the period during which federal

Sample Federal Assurance of Compliance Forms

financial assistance is extended to it by the Department of Health and Human Services or, where the assistance is in the form of real or personal property, for the period provided for in § 84.5(b) of the regulation [45 C.F.R. 84.5(b)].

The recipient: [Check (a) or (b)]

a. ( )   employs fewer than fifteen persons;
   A73

b. ( )   employs fifteen or more persons and, pursuant to § 84.7(a) of
   A74   the regulation [45 C.F.R. 84.7(a)], has designated the following person(s) to coordinate its efforts to comply with the HHS regulation:

_____

Name of Designee(s) — Type or Print
C12   C42

Name of Recipient—Type or Print		Street Address or P.O. Box	
A12	A41	A42	A71

(IRS) Employer Identification Number		City	
A1	A11	B12	B41
B1	B11		
C1	C11		
		State	Zip
		B42	B71

I certify that the above information is complete and correct to the best of my knowledge.

_____   _____

Date   Signature and Title of Authorized Official
   B72   B77   B78

If there has been a change in name or ownership within the last year, please PRINT the former name below:

NOTE: The 'A', 'B', and 'C' followed by numbers are for computer use. Please disregard.

PLEASE RETURN ORIGINAL TO: Office for Civil Rights, HHS P.O. Box 8222, Washington, D.C. 20024.

HHS–541 (10/80)

Explanation Of

HEW FORM 639 A (3/77), ENTITLED "ASSURANCE OF COMPLIANCE WITH TITLE IX OF THE EDUCATION AMENDMENTS OF 1972 AND THE REGULATION OF THE DEPARTMENT OF HEALTH, EDUCATION, AND WELFARE IN IMPLEMENTATION THEREOF"

Section 901 of Title IX of the Education Amendments of 1972 provides that no person shall, on the basis of sex, be excluded from participation in, be denied the benefits of, or be subjected to discrimination under any education program or activity receiving Federal financial assistance. Section 902 of Title IX authorizes and directs the Department of Health, Education, and Welfare (hereinafter the "Department") to effectuate the nondiscrimination requirements of section 901 by issuing rules, regulations, and orders of general applicability. Pursuant to section 902, the Department has issued 45 C. F. R. Part 86 (hereinafter "Part 86") which became effective on July 21, 1975.

Section 86.4 of Part 86 requires that every application for Federal financial assistance for any education program or activity shall, as a condition of its approval, contain or be accompanied by an assurance from the applicant satisfactory to the Director of the Office for Civil Rights (hereinafter the "Director") that each education program or activity operated by the applicant and to which Title IX of the Education Amendments of 1972 and Part 86 apply will be operated in compliance with Part 86.

Section 86.4 also provides that the Director will specify the form of the assurance required and the extent to which such assurance will be required of the applicant's subgrantees, contractors, subcontractors, transferees, or successors in interest. Under this authority, HEW Form 639 A, (3/77) has been specified as the form of assurance which shall apply to all recipients of and applicants for Federal financial assistance subject to the provisions of Title IX and awarded by the Department.

HEW Form 639 A, (3/77) constitutes a legally enforceable agreement to comply with Title IX and all of the requirements of Part 86. Applicants are urged to read Part 86 and the accompanying preamble. The obligation imposed by Title IX and Part 86 are independent of, and do not alter, the obligation not to discriminate on the basis of sex imposed by Title VII of the Civil Rights Act of 1964 (20 U.S.C. 2000e *et seq.*); Executive Order 11246, as amended; sections 799A and 855 of the Public Health Service Act (42 U.S.C. 295h-9 and 298b-2); and the Equal Pay Act (29 U.S.C. 206 and 206 (d)).

PERIOD OF ASSURANCE

HEW Form 639 A, (3/77) is binding on a recipient for a period during which Federal financial assistance is extended to it by the Department. With respect to Federal financial assistance used to aid in the purchase or improve-

236

ment of real or personal property, such period shall include the time during which the real or personal property is used for the purpose of providing an education program or activity. A recipient may transfer or otherwise convey title to real and personal property purchased or improved with Federal financial assistance so long as such transfer or conveyance is consistent with the laws and regulations under which the recipient obtained the property and it has obtained a properly executed HEW Form 639 A, (3/77) from the party to whom it wishes to transfer or convey the title unless the property in question is no longer to be used for an education program or activity or the Federal share of the fair market value of such property has been refunded or otherwise properly accounted for to the Federal government.

An applicant or recipient which has submitted an HEW Form 639 A, (3/77) to the Director need not submit a separate form with each grant application but may, if the information contained therein remains accurate, simply incorporate by reference, HEW Form 639 A, (3/77), giving the date it was submitted. On the other hand, a revised HEW Form 639 A, (3/77) must be submitted within 30 days after information contained in the submitted form becomes inaccurate, even if no additional financial assistance is being sought.

OBLIGATION OF RECIPIENT TO OBTAIN ASSURANCES FROM OTHERS

As indicated in Article III, paragraph 2, of the Assurance, if a recipient subgrants to, or contracts, subcontracts, or otherwise arranges with an individual, organization, or group to assist in the conduct of an education program or activity receiving Federal financial assistance from the Department or to provide services in connection with such a program or activity, the recipient continues to have an obligation to ensure that the education program or activity is being administered in a nondiscriminatory manner. (See 45 C.F.R. 86.31.) Accordingly, the recipient must take reasonable steps to ensure that the individual, organization, or group in question is complying with Title IX and Part 86. These steps may include, but do not necessarily require, obtaining assurances of compliance from such subgrantees, contractors, and subcontractors in the form of, or modeled on, the HEW Form 639A, (3/77). These steps to require, however, such activities as may be reasonably necessary to monitor the compliance of these subgrantees, contractors, or subcontractors, regardless of whether they have submitted assurances to the recipient. If a recipient is unable to assure itself that any contractor, subcontractor, subgrantee, or other individual or group with whom it arranges to provide services or benefits to its students and employees does not discriminate on the basis of sex as described in Part 86, the recipient may not initiate or continue contracts, subcontracts, or other arrangements with that individual or group or make subgrants to it.

DEPARTMENT OF HEALTH AND HUMAN SERVICES	☐ GRANT ☐ CONTRACT ☐ FELLOW ☐ OTHER
PROTECTION OF HUMAN SUBJECTS ASSURANCE/CERTIFICATION/DECLARATION ☐ ORIGINAL ☐ FOLLOWUP ☐ REVISION	☐ NEW ☐ RENEWAL ☐ CONTINUATION APPLICATION IDENTIFICATION NUMBER (*If known*)

STATEMENT OF POLICY: Safeguarding the rights and welfare of subjects at risk in activities supported under grants and contracts from DHHS is primarily the responsibility of the institution which receives or is accountable to DHHS for the funds awarded for the support of the activity. In order to provide for the adequate discharge of this institutional responsibility, it is the policy of DHHS that no activity involving human subjects to be supported by DHHS grants or contracts shall be undertaken unless the Institutional Review Board has reviewed and approved such activity, and the institution has submitted to DHHS a certification of such review and approval, in accordance with the requirements of Public Law 93–348, as implemented by Part 46 of Title 45 of the Code of Federal Regulations, as amended, (45 CFR 46). Administration of the DHHS policy and regulation is the responsibility of the Office for Protection from Research Risks, National Institutes of Health, Bethesda, MD 20205.

---

1. TITLE OF PROPOSAL OR ACTIVITY

---

2. PRINCIPAL INVESTIGATOR/ACTIVITY DIRECTOR/FELLOW

---

3. DECLARATION THAT HUMAN SUBJECTS EITHER WOULD OR WOULD NOT BE INVOLVED
   - ☐ A. NO INDIVIDUALS WHO MIGHT BE CONSIDERED HUMAN SUBJECTS, INCLUDING THOSE FROM WHOM ORGANS, TISSUES, FLUIDS, OR OTHER MATERIALS WOULD BE DERIVED, OR WHO COULD BE IDENTIFIED BY PERSONAL DATA, WOULD BE INVOLVED IN THE PROPOSED ACTIVITY. (IF NO HUMAN SUBJECTS WOULD BE INVOLVED, CHECK THIS BOX AND PROCEED TO ITEM 7. PROPOSALS DETERMINED BY THE AGENCY TO INVOLVE HUMAN SUBJECTS WILL BE RETURNED.)

   - ☐ B. HUMAN SUBJECTS WOULD BE INVOLVED IN THE PROPOSED ACTIVITY AS EITHER: ☐ NONE OF THE FOLLOWING, OR INCLUDING: ☐ MINORS, ☐ FETUSES, ☐ ABORTUSES, ☐ PREGNANT WOMEN, ☐ PRISONERS, ☐ MENTALLY RETARDED, ☐ MENTALLY DISABLED, UNDER SECTION 6. COOPERATING INSTITUTIONS, ON REVERSE OF THIS FORM, GIVE NAME OF INSTITUTION AND NAME AND ADDRESS OF OFFICIAL(S) AUTHORIZING ACCESS TO ANY SUBJECTS IN FACILITIES NOT UNDER DIRECT CONTROL OF THE APPLICANT OR OFFERING INSTITUTION.

---

4. DECLARATION OF ASSURANCE STATUS/CERTIFICATION OF REVIEW
   - ☐ A. THIS INSTITUTION HAS NOT PREVIOUSLY FILED AN ASSURANCE AND ASSURANCE IMPLEMENTING PROCEDURES FOR THE PROTECTION OF HUMAN SUBJECTS WITH THE DHHS THAT APPLIES TO THIS APPLICATION OR ACTIVITY. ASSURANCE IS HEREBY GIVEN THAT THIS INSTITUTION WILL COMPLY WITH REQUIREMENTS OF *DHHS Regulation 45 CFR 46*, THAT IT HAS ESTABLISHED AN INSTITUTIONAL REVIEW BOARD FOR THE PROTECTION OF HUMAN SUBJECTS AND, WHEN REQUESTED, WILL SUBMIT TO DHHS DOCUMENTATION AND CERTIFICATION OF SUCH REVIEWS AND PROCEDURES AS MAY BE REQUIRED FOR IMPLEMENTATION OF THIS ASSURANCE FOR THE PROPOSED PROJECT OR ACTIVITY.

   - ☐ B. THIS INSTITUTION HAS AN APPROVED GENERAL ASSURANCE (DHHS ASSURANCE NUMBER _____) OR AN ACTIVE SPECIAL ASSURANCE FOR THE ONGOING ACTIVITY, ON FILE WITH DHHS. THE SIGNER CERTIFIES THAT ALL ACTIVITIES IN THIS APPLICATION PROPOSING TO INVOLVE HUMAN SUBJECTS HAVE BEEN REVIEWED AND APPROVED BY THIS INSTITUTION'S INSTITUTIONAL REVIEW BOARD IN A CONVENED MEETING ON THE DATE OF _____ IN ACCORDANCE WITH THE REQUIREMENTS OF THE *Code of Federal Regulations on Protection of Human Subjects (45 CFR 46)*. THIS CERTIFICATION INCLUDES, WHEN APPLICABLE, REQUIREMENTS FOR CERTIFYING FDA STATUS FOR EACH INVESTIGATIONAL NEW DRUG TO BE USED (SEE REVERSE SIDE OF THIS FORM).

THE INSTITUTIONAL REVIEW BOARD HAS DETERMINED, AND THE INSTITUTIONAL OFFICIAL SIGNING BELOW CONCURS THAT:
   EITHER ☐ HUMAN SUBJECTS WILL NOT BE AT RISK; OR ☐ HUMAN SUBJECTS WILL BE AT RISK.

Sample Federal Assurance of Compliance Forms

---

5. AND 6. SEE REVERSE SIDE

---

7. NAME AND ADDRESS OF INSTITUTION

---

8. TITLE OF INSTITUTIONAL OFFICIAL	TELEPHONE NUMBER
SIGNATURE OF INSTITUTIONAL OFFICIAL	DATE

HHS–596 (Rev. 5–80)

ENCLOSE THIS FORM WITH THE PROPOSAL OR RETURN IT TO REQUESTING AGENCY

---

5. INVESTIGATIONAL NEW DRUGS—ADDITIONAL CERTIFICATION REQUIREMENT

SECTION 46.17 OF TITLE 45 OF THE *Code of Federal Regulations states, "Where an organization is required to prepare or to submit a certification . . . and the proposal involves an investigational new drug within the meaning of The Food, Drug, and Cosmetic Act, the drug shall be identified in the certification together with a statement that the 30-day delay required by 21 CFR 130.3(a)(2) has elapsed and the Food and Drug Administration has not, prior to expiration of such 30-day interval, requested that the sponsor continue to withhold or to restrict use of the drug in human subjects; or that the Food and Drug Administration has waived the 30-day delay requirement; provided, however, that in those cases in which the 30-day delay interval has neither expired nor been waived, a statement shall be forwarded to DHHS upon such expiration or upon receipt of a waiver. No certification shall be considered acceptable until such statement has been received."*

INVESTIGATIONAL NEW DRUG CERTIFICATION

TO CERTIFY COMPLIANCE WITH FDA REQUIREMENTS FOR PROPOSED USE OF INVESTIGATIONAL NEW DRUGS IN ADDITION TO CERTIFICATION OF INSTITUTIONAL REVIEW BOARD APPROVAL, THE FOLLOWING REPORT FORMAT SHOULD BE USED FOR EACH IND: (ATTACH ADDITIONAL IND CERTIFICATIONS AS NECESSARY).

— IND FORMS FILED: ☐ FDA 1571,   ☐ FDA 1572,   ☐ FDA 1573

— NAME OF IND AND SPONSOR _____

— DATE OF 30-DAY EXPIRATION OR FDA WAIVER

    (FUTURE DATE REQUIRES FOLLOWUP REPORT TO AGENCY) _____

— FDA RESTRICTION _____

— SIGNATURE OF INVESTIGATOR _____ DATE _____

---

6. COOPERATING INSTITUTIONS—ADDITIONAL REPORTING REQUIREMENT

SECTION 46.16 OF TITLE 45 OF THE *Code of Federal Regulations* IMPOSES SPECIAL REQUIREMENTS ON THE CONDUCT OF STUDIES OR ACTIVITIES IN WHICH THE GRANTEE OR PRIME CONTRACTOR OBTAINS ACCESS TO ALL OR SOME OF THE SUBJECTS THROUGH COOPERATING INSTITUTIONS NOT UNDER ITS CONTROL. IN ORDER THAT THE DHHS BE FULLY INFORMED, THE FOLLOWING REPORT IS REQUESTED WHEN APPLICABLE.

USE FOLLOWING REPORT FORMAT FOR EACH INSTITUTION OTHER THAN GRANTEE OR CONTRACTING INSTITUTION WITH RESPONSIBILITY FOR HUMAN SUBJECTS PARTICIPATING IN THIS ACTIVITY: (ATTACH ADDITIONAL REPORT SHEETS AS NECESSARY).

INSTITUTIONAL AUTHORIZATION FOR ACCESS TO SUBJECTS

— SUBJECTS: STATUS (WARDS, RESIDENTS, EMPLOYEES, PATIENTS, ETC.) _____

_____

NUMBER _____ AGE RANGE _____

NAME OF OFFICIAL (PLEASE PRINT) _____

TITLE _____ TELEPHONE _____

NAME AND ADDRESS OF   _____
COOPERATING INSTITUTION   _____

                             _____

— OFFICIAL SIGNATURE   _____

NOTES: *(e.g., report of modification in proposal as submitted to agency affecting human subjects involvement)*

HHS 590 (Rev. 5–80) (Back)

Appendix C

Sample Financial Record-Keeping System[*]

The project's budget is developed in conformance with the specifications established by the sponsoring agency. There are six to eight major categories (for example, consultants, consumables, travel, and so forth) and within these areas, further divisions are made for specific items.

A journal page is maintained for each major category. At the time a requisition is submitted to the purchasing department for processing, the submission date, purchase requisition number, supplier and item description, and estimated cost are all entered into this journal. A copy of the requisition is logged in and kept in a separate file. When purchasing has ordered the item, a copy of the purchase order is sent to the project. The order number is then entered in the journal and the purchase order copy is attached to the requisition copy for future reference.

Once each month, each grant is sent an Account Expenditure Summary (AES), which is the computerized listing of all encumbrances and payments completed during the previous month. This is the only regular means the project has to know that invoices have been paid. All items entered in the journal for that month are double-checked against the AES. In addition, the actual amounts paid and the date they were paid are entered in the appropriate places. The total expended column is used to maintain a running total of the actual amounts paid.

In order to keep an accurate idea of the funds available to the project, a

* I am indebted to Jane Hazan, fiscal manager of the Program for Public and Community Services of the School of Social Welfare, State University of New York at Stony Brook, Stony Brook, New York, for preparing this explanation of a financial record system, the sample journal page, and monthly budget report, and to Stowe Hausner, director of the project, for her cooperation.

monthly budget report is completed (see table A-C1). This lists all items paid or requisitioned (encumbered) up until the date of the report. This allows patterns of spending to emerge and adjustments to be made if necessary. For example, at the six-month point in the budget year, the telephone budget had gone way over the halfway mark. To help rectify this, various phone lines were removed and staff were informed of the situation. In this way, the monthly telephone expenses were substantially reduced.

TABLE A–C1
Monthly Budget Report

As of 7/31						Program "A"
	Consultants	Equipment	Consumables	Travel	Rental	Other
Budgeted	50,000	0	Supplies—2,250 Books—1,250 TOTAL 3,500	6,400	0	16,500 (breakdown attached)
Spent or Encumbered	27,430		Supplies— 681 Books—1,000 TOTAL 1,681	3,935		14,715
Balance	22,570	0	Supplies—1,569 Books— 250 TOTAL 1,819	2,465	0	1,785

TABLE A–C2
Breakdown of "Other"

Item	Budgeted	Spent or Encumbered	Balance
Office Rental	$ 3,000	$ 2,750	$ 250
Postage	1,000	627	373
Xerox and Printing	4,400	1,847	2,553
Telephone	8,100	8,004	96
Miscellaneous (Advertisements, Video Rentals, Repairs)	0	1,487	(1,487)
TOTAL	$16,500	$14,715	$1,785

Sample Financial Record-Keeping System

TABLE A–C3
Journal Page

Budget — Supplies – 2250, Books – 1250   CONSUMABLES   B = Books and Films

Date Submitted	Purchase Request #	Purchase Order #	Supplier and Item Description	P.O. Amount	Amount Paid	Total Expended	Date Paid
10/13	219404	78069	IBM Direct—Ribbons & Tapes	69.75	69.75		12/18
10/13	219405	41444	B Child Welfare League—"Children as Parents"	9.00	9.00		11/6
10/22	219406	41533	B Mosby—"Helping People" (4)	50.00	54.28		12/18
11/17	232910	41812	B Columbia U Press—"Task CTR CSWK"	29.00	30.34		1/6
11/17	232911	41769	B Mosby—"Helping People" (4)	50.00	54.28		12/18
11/18	232912	41792	B Harper & Row—"Found. of Group Care"	24.50	26.00		1/4
10/20		IF181	Central Stores—Files, Binders, Staplers, etc.	63.13	60.09		12/15
1/12		IF373	Central Stores—Supplies	18.42	18.42		1/12
11/6		IF181	Central Stores—Calendars	12.80	10.71		12/15
12/1	232915	79573	Cooper's—Electric Heaters	44.92	53.90		1/11
12/3	232917	42034	B CWLA—Subscription	21.00	21.00		12/15
12/14	232920	42163	B Brookes Pub.—"Stress & Helping . . ."	9.95	11.28		1/21
1/4	232913	42395	B Boys Town—"Youth Helping Youth" (2)	5.00	5.00	424.05	2/8
1/4	232916	42369	B Harper & Row—"Comeback" (2)	24.04	21.64		4/5
1/4	232928	42604	B Reg. Comp. Rehab. Ctr.—"Operation . . ." (2)	12.50	12.50		5/4
1/21	240887	42619	Reg. Research Inst.—Oregon Material	55.00	55.00		2/4
2/1	240873	PC221	Ann Smith—Reimb. for Maps	2.25	2.25		2/10
2/18	240877	PC228	Mary Jones—Reimb. for Books	21.20	21.20		2/24
2/19	240878	42895	B Cont. Ed.-Suny Albany—Legal Books (100)	430.00	430.00		2/26
3/2	240879	43056	B Regional Research Inst.—Oregon Map	44.00	44.00		4/14
3/2	240880	43057	B Mosby—"Helping People"	42.00	44.78		5/4
4/26	240891	43678	Comm. Council—Directory	34.00	25.50	1,080.92	5/28
4/26	240892	50999	Coopers—Supplies	61.03	61.33		6/9
4/5		IF132	Central Stores	7.49	7.94		5/6
4/23	240885	43590	B NYU—Film Rental—"Interviewing"	64.00	64.00		5/26
4/30		IF927	Central Stores	105.56	105.56	1,319.75	4/9
5/17	240894		B Thomas Publ.—"Social Wk. Pract."—	Req. cancelled, couldn't find pub.			
6/5	240901		B Random House—"The Underclass"	35.00			
6/5	240910		Gestetner—Stencils, Paper	183.60			
6/8			Central Stores	73.23			
6/17	1322		Central Stores	16.00			
7/15	1638		Central Stores	5.06			
7/22	240913		B CWLA—Film Rental—"Abused Child"	35.00			
7/22	240912		Coopers—Calc. Ribbon & Nameplate	13.65			

Appendix D

Appendix D

Office of Management and Budget Circulars

This appendix includes five *Exhibits* as follows:

1. A listing of the OMB and Federal Management Executive circulars which establish the federal adminstrative requirements that affect grants. These circulars are listed by their number (for example, A–1) and are also indexed by subject (for example, Accounting). Copies of these circulars can be obtained by writing or calling the Office of Management and Budget, Executive Office of the President, Washington, D.C. 20503. (Circulars are often revised and you should request the latest version.)

2. A summary of OMB Circular A–110 which establishes uniform administrative requirements for grants and agreements with institutions of higher education, hospitals, and other nonprofit organizations.

3. A summary of OMB Circular A–102 which establishes uniform requirements for grants to state and local governments.

4. A summary of OMB Circular A–122 which establishes cost principles for nonprofit organizations.

5. A summary of OMB Circular A–21 which establishes cost principles for educational institutions.

Exhibit 1: Index of OMB Circulars

The following is the complete listing of all OMB circulars as of 1982. The listing is in two parts. The first part lists the circulars by number and subject. The second part is an index of subjects.

Office of Management and Budget Circulars

OFFICE OF MANAGEMENT AND BUDGET CIRCULARS

Table of Contents

Note: This Table of Contents lists the current Office of Management and Budget instructions of a continuing nature applicable to the departments and establishments.

As stated in Circular No. A-1, Bulletins will continue to be issued on matters of a one-time nature.

---

*Executive Order 11609 delegated to the Office of Personnel Management the functions in A-30, effective July 22, 1971. OMB will rescind this Circular when OPM issues superseding instructions.

** In accordance with Executive Order 11609, the General Services Administration assumed responsibility for the functions in OMB Circular A-48 (paragraph 3 only) (GSA Federal Travel Regulation, FPMR 101.7, May 1973).

Office of Management and Budget Circulars

Executive Order No. 11893, dated December 31, 1975, transferred responsibility for certain Federal Management Circulars from the Federal Supply Service of GSA to OMB. The following are the current OMB Circulars in this series.

Office of Management and Budget Circulars

OFFICE OF MANAGEMENT AND BUDGET CIRCULARS AND
FEDERAL MANAGEMENT CIRCULARS UNDER OMB JURISDICTION

Index

Note: This index arranges the current OMB Circulars and Federal Management Circulars under OMB jurisdiction by key words in the titles of the directives and by a limited number of broader captions. Those Circular Nos. preceded with 74- and 75- designate FMCs.

Office of Management and Budget Circulars

Office of Management and Budget Circulars

Exhibit 2: Excerpts and Summary of OMB Circular A-110

OFFICE OF MANAGEMENT AND BUDGET

[Circular No. A-110]

GRANTS AND AGREEMENTS WITH INSTITUTIONS OF HIGHER
EDUCATION, HOSPITALS, AND OTHER NONPROFIT ORGANIZATIONS

Uniform Administrative Requirements

JULY 1, 1976.

To the heads of executive departments and establishments.

Subject: Uniform administrative requirements for grants and other agreements with institutions of higher education, hospitals, and other nonprofit organizations.

1. *Purpose.*—This Circular promulgates standards for obtaining consistency and uniformity among Federal agencies in the administration of grants to, and other agreements with, public and private institutions of higher education, public and private hospitals, and other quasi-public and private nonprofit organizations. This Circular does not apply to grants, contracts, or other agreements between the Federal Government and units of State or local governments covered by Federal Management Circular 74-7.

2. *Effective date.*—The standards in the attachments to this Circular will be applied as soon as practicable but not later than January 1, 1977.

3. *Supersession.*—This Circular rescinds and replaces parts III and IV of the Appendix to Federal Management Circular 73-7, Administration of college and university research grants.

4. *Policy intent.*—The uniform standards and requirements included in the attachments to this Circular replace the varying and often conflicting requirements that have been imposed by Federal agencies as conditions of grants and other agreements with recipients.

5. *Applicability and scope.*—Except as provided below, the standards promulgated by this Circular are applicable to all Federal agencies. If any statute expressly prescribes policies or specific requirements that differ from the standards provided herein, the provisions of the statute shall govern.

The provisions of the attachments of this Circular shall be applied to subrecipients performing substantive work under grants that are passed through or awarded by the primary recipient if such subrecipients are organizations described in paragraph 1.

6. *Definitions.*

a. The term "grant" means money or property provided in lieu of money paid or furnished by the Federal Government to recipients under programs that provide financial assistance or that provide support or stimulation to accomplish a public purpose. The term "other agreements" does not include contracts which are required to be entered into and administered under procurement laws and regulations. Grants and other agreements exclude (a) tech-

255

nical assistance programs, which provide services instead of money, (b) assistance in the form of general revenue sharing, loans, loan guarantees, or insurance, and (c) direct payments of any kind to individuals.

b. The term "recipient" includes the following types of nonprofit organizations that are receiving Federal funds from a Federal agency or through a State or local government:

Public and private institutions of higher education; public and private hospitals; and other quasi-public and private nonprofit organizations such as (but not limited to) community action agencies, research institutes, educational associations, and health centers.

The term does not include foreign or international organizations (such as agencies of the United Nations) and Government-owned contractor operated facilities or research centers providing continued support for mission-oriented, large scale programs that are Government-owned or controlled, or are designed as federally-funded research and development centers.

7. *Requests for exceptions.*—The Office of Management and Budget may rant exceptions from the requirements of this Circular when exceptions are not prohibited under existing laws.

However, in the interest of maximum uniformity, exceptions from the requirements of the Circular will be permitted only in unusual cases. Agencies may apply more restrictive requirements to a class of recipients when approved by the Office of Management and Budget.

8. *Attachments.*—The standards promulgated by this Circular are set forth in the Attachments, which are:

Attachment A	Cash depositories.
Attachment B	Bonding and insurance.
Attachment C	Retention and custodial requirements for records.
Attachment D	Program income.
Attachment E	Cost sharing and matching.
Attachment F	Standards for financial management systems.
Attachment G	Financial reporting requirements.
Attachment H	Monitoring and reporting program performance.
Attachment I	Payment requirements.
Attachment J	Revision of financial plans.
Attachment K	Closeout procedures.
Attachment L	Suspension and termination procedures.
Attachment M	Standard form for applying for federal assistance.
Attachment N	Property management standards.
Attachment O	Procurement standards.

9. *Exceptions for certain recipients.*—Notwithstanding the provisions of paragraph 7 if an applicant/recipient has a history of poor performance, is not financially stable, or its management system does not meet the standards prescribed in the Circular, Federal agencies may impose additional requirements as needed provided that such applicant/recipient is notified in writing as to:

a. Why the additional standards are being imposed;

b. what corrective action is needed.

Copies of such notifications shall be sent to the Office of Management and

Office of Management and Budget Circulars

Budget and other agencies funding that recipient at the same time the recipient is notified.

10. *Responsibilities.*—Agencies responsible for administering programs that involve grants and other agreements with recipients shall issue the appropriate regulations necessary to implement the provisions of this Circular. All portions of such regulations that involve record-keeping and/or reporting requirements subject to the provisions of the Federal Reports Act and OMB Circular A–40 must be submitted to OMB for clearance before being introduced into use. Upon request all regulations and instructions implementing this Circular shall be furnished to the Office of Management and Budget. Agencies shall also designate an official to serve as the agency representative on matters relating to the implementation of this Circular. The name and title of such representative shall be furnished to the Office of Management and Budget not later than August 30, 1976.

11. *Inquiries.*—Further information concerning this Circular may be obtained by contacting the Financial Management Branch, Budget Review Division, Office of Management and Budget, Washington, D.C. 20503, telephone 395–3993.

JAMES T. LYNN,
Director.

ATTACHMENT A—Cash Depositories

Agencies can use their regular banking procedures for projects and a separate account is not required unless it is a condition of a letter-of-credit agreement.

ATTACHMENT B—Bonding and Insurance

Recipients can follow their own bonding and insurance procedures except in cases of contracts exceeding $100,000 in which cases the government must determine the adequacy of these arrangements.

ATTACHMENT C—Retention and Custodial Requirements For Records

Recipients may use their own record-keeping systems but must retain all records for at least three years.

ATTACHMENT D—Program Income

Defines program income as gross income of projects that are federally funded and requires accounting for such income.

ATTACHMENT E—Cost Sharing and Matching

Criteria and definitions to be used in determining matching funds and cost sharing are explained.

ATTACHMENT F—Standard for Financial Management Systems

Recipients may use their own financial management system as long as it (a) provides for accurate, current, and complete disclosure of financial results; (b) is consistent with federal reporting requirements; (c) identifies the source and application of funds; (d) effectively controls and accounts for funds; (e) compares outlays and budgeted amounts; (f) minimizes time between receipt and disbursement of funds; (g) is consistent with federal cost principles and grant conditions; (h) supports accounting records with source documents; and (i) provides for examinations in the form of audits.

ATTACHMENT G—Financial Reporting Requirements

Recipients must follow prescribed federal financial reporting requirements and complete federal forms including (a) Financial Status Report; (b) Report of Federal Cash Transactions; (c) Request for Advance of Reimbursement; and (d) Outlay Report and Request for Reimbursement for Construction Projects.

ATTACHMENT H—Monitoring and Reporting Program Performance

Recipients must monitor their performance, ensure timetables are met and performance goals are achieved. Progress and final reports must be submitted on actual program accomplishments, using quantitative data when possible (for example, unit costs), and reasons why goals were not met.

ATTACHMENT I—Payment Requirements

Describes methods of making payments to recipients by letter of credit, advance by treasury check, or reimbursement by treasury check and conditions under which these methods can be used.

ATTACHMENT J—Revision of Financial Plans

Establishes criteria and procedures for recipients to report deviations from budgets approved when an award is made to request approval for budget revisions.

ATTACHMENT K—Closeout Procedures

Federal sponsoring agencies must establish closeout procedures that assure prompt payment to a recipient when a project is completed. All reports from a project must be received within ninety days of completion (extensions may be granted).

ATTACHMENT L—Suspension and Termination Procedures

Federal agencies must establish procedures to terminate or suspend a grant when a recipient fails to comply with terms of the grant or other agreements, conditions, and standards. Reasonable notice must be given and all reasonable costs that could not be avoided must be allowed.

ATTACHMENT M—Standard Form for Applying for Assistance

Establishes form 424 as the standard form to apply for assistance.

ATTACHMENT N—Property Management Standards

Establishes standards for property furnished by the government or under a federal grant. Federal agency requirements must contain provisions that cover title to real property (land) equipment, patents, inventions, and copyrights.

Office of Management and Budget Circulars

ATTACHMENT O—Procurement Standards
Recipients may use their own procurement methods for obtaining equipment supplies and services subject to the standards set forth in this section.

Exhibit 3: Summary of OMB Circular A-102

UNIFORM ADMINISTRATIVE REQUIREMENTS FOR GRANTS TO
STATE AND LOCAL GOVERNMENTS

A 1979 publication of the Office of Management and Budget on *Financial Management of Federal Assistance Programs* describes Circular A-102 as follows:

OMB Circular A-102

What is Circular A-102?

Circular A-102 establishes uniform financial and other administrative requirements for grants to State and local governments. It promotes uniformity and consistency among Federal agencies in their administration of grants. It establishes uniform requirements in 16 areas. Only those specific requirements imposed by legislation establishing a grant program can take precedence over A-102.

The following are examples of some of the improvements brought about by Circular A-102:

— Before A-102 there was an application form for approximately every third program of the almost 500 programs eligible to State and local governments; now there is one.

— Before A-102, different reporting forms, averaging six pages in length, were as numerous as the application forms above. Now there are four, each only one page long.

— A multiplicity of records retention requirements have been reduced to one.

— Budget classification categories have been reduced from 103 to nine.

The following is a summary of the Circular.

a. *Cash depositories.* State and local governments can use their regular banking procedures, without any requirements for separate bank accounts, or special bank eligibility requirements. Use of minority banks is encouraged.

b. *Bonding and insurance.* Except as otherwise required by law, recipients can use normal bonding and insurance procedures for contracts of $100,000 or less. If the agency is certain that the Government's interests are adequately protected, the recipients' procedures may be used for contracts larger than $100,000. If that is not the case, construction contracts over $100,000 must have a 5% bid guarantee, 100% performance bond, and 100% payment bond. No other Federal requirements in this area should be imposed.

c. *Records retention.* Grantees may follow their own practices as long as they provide for retention of records for three years, to allow access for audit and public examination. If audit findings are not resolved, the records shall be retained beyond three years. The retention period starts when the annual or final expenditure report has been submitted or, for nonexpendable property, from the date of final disposition.

d. *Waiver of single State agency rules.* When requested by a State, Federal agencies should waive or remove "single State agency requirements." Such requirements set up impediments to effective administration. Future legislation should avoid single State agency requirements if possible.

e. *Program income.* States are not held accountable for interest earned on grant funds pending disbursement. Local units must return such interest to the Federal Government. Other income attributable to the grant should be used to increase the scope of the project, be deducted from the total project cost for the purpose of determining the amount in which the Federal Government will share or be applied toward the matching share (with Federal agency permission).

f. *Matching share.* Standards are established for determining the matching contribution. It can consist of charges which are project costs, including cash and "in-kind" contributions.

260

In-kind contributions must be necessary and reasonable, identifiable from the grantee's records, properly valued and not claimed for any other Federal program.

Specific guidelines are set forth for calculating the value of in-kind services provided by volunteers and contributions of materials, equipment, buildings, land and space.

g. *Standards for grantees financial management systems.* Standards are prescribed for financial management systems used for grant supported activities. Federal agencies will not impose requirements other than for current, accurate, and complete disclosure of financial results; adequate identification of source and application of funds; effective control and accountability for funds and property; comparison of actual and budgeted amounts; minimizing time elapsing between receipt and expenditure of funds; a cost allocation plan; and overall organization audits performed at the direction of the grantee. See Attachment "P" dealing with audits.

h. *Financial reporting requirements.* Four standard reporting forms are provided to replace the different forms previously required for each grant program.

1. *Financial status report*—To report status of funds for all nonconstruction programs.

2. *Federal cash transactions*—To monitor cash balances when funds are advanced to grantees by letter of credit or Treasury checks.

3. *Request for advance or reimbursement*—For all nonconstruction programs when advance letter of credit or predetermined advance payments are not used. May be submitted monthly.

4. *Outlay report and request for reimbursement*—For reimbursement on all construction programs. May be submitted monthly.

i. *Monitoring and reporting program performance.* Recipients will be held responsible for monitoring programs to assure that time schedules are met and that performance goals are being achieved. Periodic reports of progress, documented with quantitative data when possible, will be required. If goals are not being met, or costs are exceeding budget, these conditions must be reported.

Between reporting dates, grantees must report any unusual conditions or events that will affect achieving goals within the time period.

j. *Grant payment requirement.* A letter of credit will be used for all grants, except construction grants for which it is optional, when there is a continued relationship of at least 12 months, when the payment for a year would exceed $120,000, and the recipient's financial management system meets Federal standards.

Funds will be advanced when the annual amount is less than $120,000. Reimbursement will be used when there is not an adequate financial management system.

k. *Budget revision procedures.* For nonconstruction grants, prior Federal approval for budget revision must be obtained only when:

1. There is a change in the scope of objective, or a need for additional Federal funding.

2. The cumulative amount of transfers among object class categories or among programs, functions, or activities exceeds 5% or $100,000.

3. Indirect cost amounts are to be used for direct costs (if required by the Federal agency) or if the budget revision involves items requiring FMC 74-4 approval.

4. Recipients plan to transfer funds allocated for training to other categories of expenses.

Construction grants need approval for revisions only in the case of No. 1.

When Federal funds are expected to exceed needs by more than 5% or $5,000, the Federal agency must be notified.

l. *Grant closeout procedures.* Federal agencies must establish closeout procedures which provide for prompt payment by grantor or prompt refunds by grantee, reports within 90 days of completion, adjustment of the Federal share, accounting for Government property, and retaining the right of recovery until final audit.

Federal agencies must also develop procedures to be followed when the grantee does not comply with the grant agreement and the grant is terminated.

m. *Standard forms for applying for Federal assistance.* All State, local and tribal governments applying for all Federal grants will use the forms outlined in this attachment, with one exception. Most formula grants do not require grantees to apply for assistance on a project basis. Hence, these programs are not required to use the forms.

n. *Property management system.* Standards are prescribed governing the use and disposition of federally financed property. The grantees' property management procedures must provide for accurate records, bi-annual inventories, adequate maintenance and control, and proper sales procedures.

Each Federal agency must prescribe requirements for grantees covering real property. Such requirements will cover at a minimum:
— vesting title
— use of property in other projects
— disposition after use

In general, after using the property, the grantee will request disposition instruction from the Federal agency. The Federal agency shall observe the following rules: the grantee may compensate the Government and retain title, sell the property and pay the Government, or transfer title for the property back to the Government.

o. *Procurement Standards.* This Attachment was amended recently. It is anticipated that the amendment will reduce administrative cost, paperwork and other such factors which contributed to inefficiency, waste and delay in implementing assistance programs.

The following are the major changes:
(1) reaffirms the maximum reliance on State and local government grantees' management of their own procurement;

(2) directs grantor agencies to rescind nonconforming provisions of current agency subordinate regulations and limits the issuance of additional requirements;

(3) creates a grantee certification program to reduce the grantee agencies' burdensome preaward review of individual procurements;

(4) adds provisions to reduce the possibility of fraud or waste; and

(5) expands coverage addressing small, minority, women and labor surplus contracting.

263

Method of Procurement. The Attachment outlines four methods for making procurements under grants:

a. small purchase procedures;

b. competitive sealed bids (formal advertising);

c. competitive negotiation;

d. noncompetitive negotiation.

p. *Audit Standards.* Recent studies by the Joint Financial Management Improvement Program, the National Intergovernmental Audit Forum, the General Accounting Office, and others, point the way toward a new audit approach. The studies emphasized the fact that a State or local agency that had a number of individual grants could be subject to an audit of each grant. This is not only an uneconomical use of manpower, but fails to provide any overall judgment on the reliability or efficiency of the grantee organization. These recent studies indicate the need for a *total audit,* one in which an organization as a whole is audited, not just one individual grant or another.

This concept will require a great deal of interagency and intergovernmental cooperation. The audit work will be done using a single audit guide that meets the basic needs of all affected parties.

Recent Significant Changes—Total Audit Concept. Until recently, audits were covered in Attachment G. Now they will be covered by this new Attachment. Covering audits in a separate Attachment highlights the major importance ascribed to this facet of financial management. To summarize, the principal objectives in establishing the new requirements are twofold:

— reemphasizes that grantee audits are to be made on an organization-wide basis, rather than grant-by-grant.

— the provisions of this Attachment do not limit the authority of Federal agencies to make audits of a recipient organization. However, if independent audits arranged for by State and local governments meet the requirements prescribed, all Federal agencies shall rely on them, and any additional audit work should build upon the work already done.

Exhibit 4: Excerpts and Summary of OMB Circular A-122

OFFICE OF MANAGEMENT AND BUDGET

Circular A-122, "Cost Principles for Nonprofit Organizations"

[Note: This reprint incorporates corrections published at 46 FR 17185, Tuesday, March 17, 1981.]

AGENCY: Office of Management and Budget.

ACTION: Final Policy.

SUMMARY: This notice advises of a new OMB Circular dealing with principles for determining costs of grants, contracts, and other agreements with nonprofit organizations.

The Circular is the product of an interagency review conducted over a two-year period. Its purpose is to provide a set of cost principles to replace existing principles issued by individual agencies. These have often contained varying and conflicting requirements, and created confusion among agency administrators, auditors, and nonprofit officials. The new Circular will provide a uniform approach to the problem of determining costs, and promote efficiency and better understanding between recipients and the Federal Government.

EFFECTIVE DATE: The Circular becomes effective on issuance.

FOR FURTHER INFORMATION CONTACT: Palmer A. Marcantonio, Financial Management Branch, Office of Management and Budget, Washington, D.C. 20503, (202) 395-4773.

SUPPLEMENTARY INFORMATION: Before the Circular became final there was extensive coordination with the affected nonprofit organizations, professional associations, Federal agencies and others. All interested persons were given an opportunity to comment on the proposed Circular through informal consultations and a notice in the Federal Register. In response to our requests for comment, we received about 100 letters from Federal agencies, nonprofit organizations, associations, and other interested members of the public. These comments were considered in the final version of the Circular. There follows a summary of the major comments and the action taken on each.

In addition to the changes described, other changes have been made to improve the clarity and readability of the Circular. To the extent possible, we have tried to make the language of this Circular consistent with that of cost principles for educational institutions (Circular A-21), and State and local governments (Circular 74-4).

Summary of Significant Changes:

Set forth are changes that have been made in the final Circular as a result of public comments. The more significant changes to the basic Circular and Attachment A include:

1. Paragraph 2. "Supersession" was added to the basic Circular to make it clear that this Circular supersedes cost principles issued by individual agencies.

2. Paragraph 4 of the basic Circular has been amended to make it clear that the absence of an advance agreement on any element of cost will not in itself affect the reasonableness of allocability of that element. Also, this paragraph was amended to make it clear that where an item of cost requiring prior approval is specified in the budget, approval of the budget constitutes approval of the cost.

3. Paragraph 5 of the basic Circular has been changed to remove any doubt as to which nonprofit organizations would not be covered by the Circular. Now, Appendix C to the Circular lists all exclusions.

4. Paragraph 8 was added to the basic Circular to permit Federal agencies to request exceptions from the requirements of the Circular.

5. Paragraph E.2. was added to Attachment A to cover the negotiation and approval of indirect cost rates, and to provide for cognizance arrangements.

The more significant changes to Attachment B to the Circular include:

1. Paragraph 6, *Compensation for Personal Services,* was modified to:

a. Permit Federal agencies to accept a substitute system for documenting personnel costs through means other than personnel activity reports.

b. Clarify provisions covering the allowability of costs for unemployment compensation or workers' compensation, and costs of insurance policies on the lives of trustees, officers, or other employees.

c. Make unallowable any increased costs of pension plans caused by delayed funding.

d. Delete a paragraph dealing with review and approval of compensation of individual employees.

2. Paragraph 7, *Contingencies,* was changed to make it clear that the term "contingency reserves" excludes self-insurance reserves or pension funds.

3. Paragraph 10 was modified to provide that the value of donated services used in the performance of a direct cost activity shall be allocated a share of indirect cost only when (a) the aggregate value of the service is material, (b) the services are supported by a significant amount of the indirect cost incurred by the organization, and (c) the direct cost activity is not pursued primarily for the benefit of the Federal Government. Provisions were also added to this paragraph for the cognizant agency and the recipient to negotiate when there is no basis for determining the fair market value of the services rendered, and to permit indirect costs allocated to donated services to be charged to an agreement or used to meet cost sharing or matching requirements.

4. Paragraph 13, *Equipment and Other Capital Expenditures,* was changed. Capital equipment is now defined as having an acquisition cost of $500 and a useful life of more than two years.

5. Paragraph 24, *Meetings, Conferences.* The prior approval requirement for changing meetings and conferences as a direct cost was deleted. A sentence was added to make it clear such costs were allowable provided they meet the criterion for the allowability of cost shown in Attachment A.

6. Paragraph 26, *Organization Costs,* was amended to provide that organization costs may be allowable when approved in writing by the awarding agency.

7. Paragraph 28, *Page Charges in Professional Journals,* was revised to provide that page charges may be allowable.

Office of Management and Budget Circulars

8. Paragraph 36, *Public Information Service Costs,* was modified to make public information costs allowable as direct costs with awarding agency approval.

9. Paragraph 42, *Rental Costs,* was rewritten to:

a. Make it clear that rental costs under leases which create a material equity on the leased property are allowable only up to the amount that the organization would have been allowed had it purchased the property; e.g., depreciation or use allowances, maintenance, taxes, insurance, etc.

b. Clarify the criteria for material equity leases.

10. Paragraph 50, *Travel Costs,* was amended to delete the prior approval requirement for domestic travel. In addition to the above, a number of editorial changes were made to the original document.

Suggested Changes Not Considered Necessary.

Comment. Several respondents questioned the provision that, for "less than arm's length" leases, rental costs are allowable only up to the amount that would be allowed had title to the property been vested in the grantee organization. In their opinion this rule will result in unnecessary cost to the Federal Government, since it would encourage an organization to lease space on the commercial market at a higher rate.

Response. The cost principles are designed to cover most situations; however, there are always exceptions that must be considered on a case-by-case basis. The Circular contains a provision for Federal agencies to request exceptions.

Comment. Several respondents questioned why interest is not an allowable cost, since it is an ordinary and necessary cost of doing business.

Response. It has been a longstanding policy not to recognize interest as a cost. However, this policy has recently been revised for State and local governments in Circular 74–4, with respect to the cost of office space. The revision provides that "rental" rates for publicly owned buildings may be based on actual costs, including depreciation, interest, operation and maintenance costs, and other allowable costs. This revision was under consideration for some time. It was studied extensively by OMB, the General Accounting Office and others, and considerable analysis went into its formulation. Suggestions for extending it to nonprofit organizations would have to be examined with equal care. This has not yet been done; and we were reluctant to further delay issuance of this Circular.

Comment. Several respondents questioned why public information costs were not allowable as an indirect cost.

Response. Public information costs are often direct services to an organization's other programs. They are allowable, however, as a direct charge when they are within the scope of work of a particular agreement.

Comment. One respondent suggested that smaller grantees be excluded from complying with the Circular.

Response. Similar rules for the 50 selected items of cost would be needed regardless of the size of the grantee. To the extent possible, the Circular provides simplified methods for smaller grantees.

Comment. One respondent said the requirements of the Cost Accounting Standards Board should be applied to cover contracts with nonprofit organizations.

Response. It is unlikely that the type of grantees covered by this Circular would have contracts large enough to be covered by the CASB. In the event that they do, however, the regulations of the CASB would apply.

Comment. One respondent said the allocation of indirect cost to donated services would pose a tremendous difficulty to the organization. The organization relies on a corps of approximately 8,000 committee members to carry out obligations in response to Government requests. There is no employer relationship in the arrangements for this assistance, nor are there committee members normally reimbursed for such services. Further, it was pointed out the committee members spend many thousands of hours outside the organization's premises conducting research.

Response. It would appear that this type of committee arrangement would not be considered in the determination of the organization's indirect cost rate provided that Federal agreements do not bear an unreasonable share of indirect cost. However, the cognizant agency will be responsible for evaluating the allocation of indirect cost where there are committee-type arrangements on a case-by-case basis.

Comment. One respondent suggested that wherever possible the language in the *Federal Procurement Regulations* be used for nonprofit organizations.

Response. The language in the *Federal Procurement Regulations* was designated primarily for commercial firms, and is not necessarily well suited to nonprofit organizations. At the suggestion of the General Accounting Office, the nonprofit cost principles were written to conform as closely as possible to those of educational institutions (Circular A–21), and State and local governments (Circular 74–4).

John J. Jordan,
Chief, Financial Management Branch.

[Circular No. A–122]

June 27, 1980
To The Heads of Executive
Departments and Establishments
Subject: Cost principles for nonprofit organizations.

1. *Purpose.* This Circular establishes principles for determining costs of grants, contracts and other agreements with nonprofit organizations. It does not apply to colleges and universities which are covered by Circular A–21; State, local, and federally recognized Indian tribal governments which are covered by Circular 74–4; or hospitals. The principles are designed to provide that the Federal Government bear its fair share of costs except where restricted or prohibited by law. The principles do not attempt to prescribe the extent of cost sharing or matching on grants, contracts, or other agreements. However, such cost sharing or matching shall not be accomplished through arbitrary limitations on individual cost elements by Federal agencies. Provision for profit or other increment above cost is outside the scope of this Circular.

2. *Supersession.* This Circular supersedes cost principles issued by individual agencies for nonprofit organization.

3. *Applicability.* a. These principles shall be used by all Federal agencies in

determining the costs of work performed by nonprofit organizations under grants, cooperative agreements, cost reimbursement contracts, and other contracts in which costs are used in pricing, administration, or settlement. All of these instruments are hereafter referred to as awards. The principles do not apply to awards under which an organization is not required to account to the Government for actual costs incurred.

b. All cost reimbursement subawards (subgrants, subcontracts, etc.) are subject to those Federal cost principles applicable to the particular organization concerned. Thus, if a subaward is to a nonprofit organization, this Circular shall apply; if a subaward is to a commercial organization, the cost principles applicable to commercial concerns shall apply; if a subaward is to a college or university, Circular A–21 shall apply; if a subaward is to a State, local, or federally recognized Indian tribal government, Circular 74–4 shall apply.

4. *Definitions.* a. *"Nonprofit organization"* means any corporation, trust, association, cooperative, or other organization which (1) is operated primarily for scientific, educational, service, charitable, or similar purposes in the public interest; (2) is not organized primarily for profit; and (3) uses its net proceeds to maintain, improve, and/or expand its operations. For this purpose, the term "nonprofit organization" excludes (i) colleges and universities; (ii) hospitals; (iii) State, local, and federally recognized Indian tribal governments; and (iv) those nonprofit organizations which are excluded from coverage of this Circular in accordance with paragraph 5 below.

b. *"Prior approval"* means securing the awarding agency's permission in advance to incur cost for those items that are designated as requiring prior approval by the Circular. Generally this permission will be in writing. Where an item of cost requiring prior approval is specified in the budget of an award, approval of the budget constitutes approval of that cost.

5. *Exclusion of some nonprofit organizations.* Some nonprofit organizations, because of their size and nature of operations, can be considered to be similar to commercial concerns for purpose of applicability of cost principles. Such nonprofit organizations shall operate under Federal cost principles applicable to commercial concerns. A listing of these organizations is contained in Attachment C. Other organizations may be added from time to time.

6. *Responsibilities.* Agencies responsible for administering programs that involve awards to nonprofit organizations shall implement the provisions of this Circular. Upon request, implementing instruction shall be furnished to the Office of Management and Budget. Agencies shall designate a liaison official to serve as the agency representative on matters relating to the implementation of this Circular. The name and title of such representative shall be furnished to the Office of Management and Budget within 30 days of the date of this Circular.

7. *Attachments.* The principles and related policy guides are set forth in the following Attachments:

Attachment A—General Principles
Attachment B—Selected Items of Cost
Attachment C—Nonprofit Organizations Not Subject to This Circular

8. *Requests for exceptions.* The Office of Management and Budget may grant

exceptions to the requirements of this Circular when permissible under existing law. However, in the interest of achieving maximum uniformity, exceptions will be permitted only in highly unusual circumstances.

9. *Effective Date.* The provisions of this Circular are effective immediately. Implementation shall be phased in by incorporating the provisions into new awards made after the start of the organization's next fiscal year. For existing awards the new principles may be applied if an organization and the cognizant Federal agency agree. Earlier implementation, or a delay in implementation of individual provisions is also permitted by mutual agreement between an organization and the cognizant Federal agency.

10. *Inquiries.* Further information concerning this Circular may be obtained by contacting the Financial Management Branch, Budget Review Division, Office of Management and Budget, Washington, D.C. 20503, telephone (202) 395-4773.

James T. McIntyre, Jr.,
Director.

Attachment A to Circular A-122 establishes the general principles used in determining whether costs are allowable and covers the following:

"A. Basic Considerations
1. Composition of total costs
2. Factors affecting allowability of costs
3. Reasonable costs
4. Allowable costs
5. Applicable credits
6. Advance understandings
B. Direct Costs
C. Indirect Costs
D. Allocation of Indirect Costs and Determination of Indirect Cost Rates
1. General
2. Simplified allocation method
3. Multiple allocation base method
4. Direct allocation method
5. Special indirect cost rates
E. Negotiation and Approval of Indirect Cost Rates
1. Definitions
2. Negotiations and approval of rates"

Attachment B to Circular A-122 defines the principles to be applied in determining the allowability of costs for fifty items as follows:

1. Advertising costs
2. Bad debts
3. Bid and proposal costs (reserved)
4. Bonding costs
5. Communication costs

6. Compensation for personal services
7. Contingency provisions
8. Contributions
9. Depreciation and use allowances
10. Donations
11. Employee morale, health and welfare costs and credits
12. Entertainment costs
13. Equipment and other capital expenditures
14. Fines and penalties
15. Fringe benefits
16. Idle facilities and idle capacity
17. Independent research and development (reserved)
18. Insurance and indemnification
19. Interest, fund raising, and investment management costs
20. Labor relations costs
21. Losses on other awards
22. Maintenance and repair costs
23. Materials and supplies
24. Meetings, conferences
25. Memberships, subscriptions, and professional activity costs
26. Organization costs
27. Overtime, extra-pay shift, and multishift premiums
28. Page charges in professional journals
29. Participant support costs
30. Patent costs
31. Pension plans
32. Plant security costs
33. Preaward costs
34. Professional service costs
35. Profits and losses on disposition of depreciable property or other capital assets
36. Public information service costs
37. Publication and printing costs
38. Rearrangement and alteration costs
39. Reconversion costs
40. Recruiting costs
41. Relocation costs
42. Rental costs
43. Royalties and other costs for use of patents and copyrights
44. Severance pay
45. Specialized service facilities
46. Taxes
47. Termination costs
48. Training and education costs
49. Transportation costs
50. Travel costs

Exhibit 5: Excerpts and Summary of OMB Circular A-21

The following is the announcement of OMB Circular A–21 and a list of the contents of this circular.

OFFICE OF MANAGEMENT AND BUDGET

CIRCULAR A-21—COST PRINCIPLES FOR EDUCATIONAL INSTITUTIONS

This notice revises Federal Management Circular 73–8. It will be renumbered OMB Circular No. A–21. The revision originated from recommendations made by the Department of Health, Education, and Welfare after urging by the House and Senate Appropriations Committees.

On March 10, 1978, the Office of Management and Budget published a proposed revision in the FEDERAL REGISTER for comment. In response to the publication, we received approximately 300 letters from Members of Congress, Federal agencies, university administrators, faculty members, professional associations, and members of the public.

There follows a summary of the major comments grouped by subject, and a response to each, including a description of any changes made as a result of the comment. In addition to the changes described specifically, other changes have been made to improve clarity, readability, and precision, and to reduce the burden of compliance as much as possible.

For further information, contact Mr. John J. Lordan, Chief, Financial Management Branch, Office of Management and Budget, New Executive Office Building, 726 Jackson Place, N.W., Washington, D.C. 20503, (202) 395–6823.

PURPOSE

Comment. Several commentators pointed out that the proposed revision contained too much detail, and that it seemed to establish cost accounting procedures and instructions, rather than cost accounting principles.

Response. In our opinion, the revision does not change the fundamental nature of the Circular. It provided for more consistent treatment of costs, and clarifies many provisions that were considered too vague and which left the way open to widely varying interpretations. This subject is covered in more detail below in specific comments on other sections of the Circular.

Comment. Several commentators had a favorable reaction to the provision which says that agencies are not expected to place additional restrictions on individual items of cost.

Response. This provision remains in the Circular.

APPLICABILITY

Comment. Several commentators agreed with the provision which extends regulations of the Cost Accounting Standards Board to federally funded research and development centers operated by universities. This was a coordinated action with the CASB, which has exempted other work at universities from coverage.

Response. This provision remains in the Circular.

EFFECTIVE DATE

Comment. Several commentators pointed out the need for adequate time for implementation. Some suggested a two-year transition period.

Response. The Circular now establishes an effective date of October 1, 1979, and says that implementation will begin in the institution's first fiscal year beginning after that date. This can be speeded up or extended with the agreement of the cognizant Federal agency. We would expect this provision to be used to assure an orderly phase in of new provisions such as the accounting for tuition remission and specialized service facilities.

DEFINITION OF TERMS

Comment. Many commentators stated that "other sponsored activities" should not include agricultural extension programs, which has been cited as an example.

Response. This example has been removed from the Circular and we are now studying a request to exempt this program from coverage by the Circular.

INDIRECT COSTS

Comment. Many commentators objected to the inclusion of a standard allocation method to be used for each of the categories of indirect cost.

Response. The Circular has been revised to more clearly state that the standard allocation method is used only in the absence of a cost analysis study, or a mutual agreement between the institution and the cognizant agency on use of a different method.

Comment. Several commentators argued that it was inequitable to allocate depreciation on certain capital improvements on a standard base of unweighted headcount of students and employees.

Response. The unweighted headcount base has been replaced by a full-time equivalent base.

Comment. As proposed, the modified total direct cost base consisted of salaries and wages, fringe benefits, materials and supplies, travel, and subgrants and subcontracts up to $5,000 each. Several commentators proposed an increase in the dollar level of subgrants and subcontracts. Suggestions ranged from $10,000 to $50,000.

Response. The amount has been raised to $25,000.

Comment. A number of commentators objected to the use of the number of sponsored agreements as the standard base for allocating the costs of sponsored projects administration.

Response. The standard allocation base has been changed to modified total direct costs.

LIBRARY EXPENSES

Comment. Many commentators objected to the unweighted headcount base for allocating library expenses.

Response. The unweighted headcount base has been changed to the full-time equivalent base.

STUDENT ADMINISTRATION AND SERVICES

Comment. Several commentators objected that the Circular would not recognize student administration and service costs as applicable to the sponsored agreements. They contended that these services benefit all students, including those employed by the institution.

Response. The standard base for allocating student service costs would call for allocation to the instruction function, and subsequently to any sponsored agreement in that function.

DETERMINATION AND APPLICATION OF INDIRECT COSTS OR RATES

Comment. Several commentators objected to the use of modified total direct cost as the standard base for allocating indirect costs to sponsored agreements.

Response. The definition has been modified to include all subgrants and subcontracts up to $25,000 each.

COMPENSATION FOR PERSONAL SERVICES

Comment. Several commentators objected to the frequency of personnel activity reports.

Response. Compared to present requirements, frequency has been reduced from monthly to once an academic term. Also, the Circular has been clarified to explain that employees whose salaries and wages are not charged direct, or not involved in the distribution of indirect costs would not be included in the reporting system.

Comment. Several commentators criticized applying the monitored workload system only to professional employees.

Response. Introducing the monitored workload concept for professional employees recognizes that their activities cannot be measured with the same degree of accuracy as nonprofessionals. We believe that the monitored workload alternative represents a good balance between reducing paperwork and achieving an acceptable level of accountability.

DEPRECIATION AND USE ALLOWANCES

Comment. Several commentators stated that the requirement for a physical equipment inventory every two years was burdensome.

Response. The two-year inventory requirement remains. However, it has been clarified to recognize that statistical sampling techniques may be used in making the inventory. We believe an institution wishing to recover depreciation or use allowances on equipment must take the normal business precaution of assuring by physical inventory that the equipment is still on hand.

EQUIPMENT AND OTHER CAPITAL EXPENDITURES

Comment. Many commentators recommended that the definition of equipment be changed from an acquisition cost of $300 and a useful life of more than one year. The most common suggestion was $500 and a useful life of more than two years.

Response. The Circular has been amended to define equipment as tangible personal property having a useful life of more than two years and an acquisition cost of $500 or more per unit.

SCHOLARSHIPS AND STUDENT AID COSTS

Comment. Some commentators objected to the provision that tuition remission for student employees be treated as a direct charge to sponsored agreements.

Response. The Circular would not prohibit tuition remission as an indirect cost in all cases. It would require that tuition remission be treated as a direct or indirect cost in accordance with the actual work being performed. This is consistent with the general rules stated earlier in the Circular and with basic principles of cost accounting.

Comment. Some commentators stated that the tuition remission provision would discriminate against out-of-state students. Since the tuition they would ordinarily pay at State universities is higher than that of in-state students, their remission would be higher, thereby encouraging research faculty to favor in-state graduate assistants.

Response. The Circular has been modified to permit tuition remission to be charged on an average rate basis.

SPECIALIZED SERVICE FACILITIES

Comment. Many commentators objected to the inclusion of "animal resources centers" as a specialized service facility.

Response. "Animal resource centers" has been deleted as an example, but may be treated as a specialized service facility as circumstances dictate at each institution.

Comment. Many commentators cited the possibility that including indirect costs in the charges for specialized service facilities might raise the apparent cost of the services to such a high level that research faculty would decline to use them. They also cited unique situations where it might be appropriate to recover less than the full cost of a specialized service facility.

Response. The Circular provides that normally charges for these services should include both direct and indirect costs. It allows for exclusion of indirect costs where not material in amount.

VELMA N. BALDWIN,
Assistant to the Director
for Administration.

EXECUTIVE OFFICE OF THE PRESIDENT,
OFFICE OF MANAGEMENT AND BUDGET,
Washington, D.C., February 26, 1979.

(Circular No. A-21, Revised]

To the Heads of Executive Departments and Establishments.
Subject: Cost principles for educational institutions.

1. *Purpose.* This circular establishes principles for determining costs applicable to grants, contracts, and other agreements with educational institutions. The principles deal with the subject of cost determination, and make no attempt to identify the circumstances or dictate the extent of agency and institutional participation in the financing of a particular project. The principles are designed to provide that the Federal Government bear its fair share of total costs, determined in accordance with generally accepted accounting principles, except where restricted or prohibited by law. Agencies are not expected to place additional restrictions on individual items of cost. Provision for profit or other increment above cost is outside the scope of this Circular.

2. *Supersession.* The Circular supersedes Federal Management Circular 73-8, dated December 19, 1973. FMC 73-8 is revised and reissued under its original designation of OMB Circular No. A-21.

3. *Applicability.*

a. All Federal agencies that sponsor research and development, training, and other work at educational institutions shall apply the provisions of this Circular in determining the costs incurred for such work. The principles shall also be used as a guide in the pricing of fixed price or lump sum agreements.

b. In addition, Federally Funded Research and Development Centers associated with educational institutions shall be required to comply with the Cost Accounting Standards, rules and regulations issued by the Cost Accounting Standards Board, and set forth in 4 CFR Ch. III; provided that they are subject thereto under defense related contracts.

4. *Responsibilities.* The successful application of cost accounting principles requires development of mutual understanding between representatives of educational institutions and of the Federal Government as to their scope, implementation, and interpretation.

5. *Attachment.* The principles and related policy guides are set forth in the Attachment, "Principles for determining costs applicable to grants, contracts, and other agreements with educational institutions."

6. *Effective date.* The provisions of this Circular shall be effective October 1, 1979. The provisions shall be implemented by institutions as of the start of their first fiscal year beginning after that date. Earlier implementation, or a delay in implementation of individual provisions, is permitted by mutual agreement between an institution and the cognizant Federal agency.

7. *Inquiries.* Further information concerning this Circular may be obtained by contacting the Financial Management Branch, Budget Review Division, Office of Management and Budget, Washington, D.C. 20503, telephone (202) 395-6823.

JAMES T. MCINTYRE, JR.,
Director.

Office of Management and Budget Circulars

PRINCIPLES FOR DETERMINING COSTS APPLICABLE TO GRANTS, CONTRACTS, AND OTHER AGREEMENTS WITH EDUCATIONAL INSTITUTIONS

TABLE OF CONTENTS

5. Sponsored projects administration.
6. Library expenses.
7. Student administration and services.
8. Offset for indirect expenses otherwise provided for by the Government.

G. DETERMINATION AND APPLICATION OF INDIRECT COSTS RATE OR RATES

1. Indirect costs pools.
2. The distribution basis.
3. Negotiated lump sum for indirect costs.
4. Predetermined fixed rates for indirect costs.
5. Negotiated fixed rates and carry forward provisions.

H. SIMPLIFIED METHOD FOR SMALL INSTITUTIONS

1. General.
2. Simplified procedure.

J. GENERAL PROVISIONS FOR SELECTED ITEMS OF COSTS

1. Advertising costs.
2. Bad debts.
3. Civil defense costs.
4. Commencement and convocation costs.
5. Communication costs.
6. Compensation for personal services.
7. Contingency provisions.
8. Deans of faculty and graduate schools.
9. Depreciation and use allowances.
10. Donated services and property.
11. Employee morale, health, and welfare costs and credits.
12. Entertainment costs.
13. Equipment and other capital expenditures.
14. Fines and penalties.
15. Fringe benefits.
16. Insurance and indemnification.
17. Interest, fund raising, and investment management costs.
18. Labor relations costs.
19. Losses on other sponsored agreements or contracts.
20. Maintenance and repair costs.
21. Material costs.
22. Memberships, subscriptions, and professional activity costs.
23. Patent costs.
24. Plant security costs.
25. Preagreement costs.
26. Professional services costs.
27. Profits and losses on disposition of plant equipment or other capital assets.

28. Proposal costs.
29. Public information services costs.
30. Rearrangement and alteration costs.
31. Reconversion costs.
32. Recruiting costs.
33. Rental cost of buildings and equipment.
34. Royalties and other costs for use of patents.
35. Sabbatical leave costs.
36. Scholarships and student aid costs.
37. Severance pay.
38. Specialized service facilities.
39. Special services costs.
40. Student activity costs.
41. Taxes.
42. Transportation costs.
43. Travel costs.
44. Termination costs applicable to sponsored agreements.

K. CERTIFICATION OF CHARGES

Index

Index

Index

Index

Notice of Award, 50

Objectives: adherence to, 138–139; outcome, 140; process, 140; program management by, 139; refining, 139–140; relationship to activities, 142

Office of Management and Budget (OMB), 48–49, 50, 53, 64; approval of data forms, 64–65; circulars, 72, 244–279; clearance of research instruments, 64–65

"Open" systems, 33

Organizations: analysis, 15; interdependency, 10; strategy of, 5

Overspending, 79, 181–183

"Paper trail," 70

Paragraphing, 104

Participant observation, 37

Participants: problems in selection of, 80–81; protection of human research subjects, 80

Patent and invention clause, 63

Patents: grant agency policies, 63; host agency policies, 63

Patient care rates, establishment of, 92

Payment request, 94

Performance, communicating and reporting on, 41–42

Performance report form, 151, 152

Performance reporting techniques, 149–151

Personal contact, staff of funding and host agencies, 87

Personality clashes, 16

Personalized folders, for site visits, 120

Personnel, cost-sharing arrangements for, 65

Personnel management, structural approach to, 16

Personnel procedures, 33

Philanthropy, 48

Policies and procedures, conflicting interpretations of, 84

Postaward site visits, purposes of, 112

Preparation responsibilities, assignment of, 100

Principal investigator: defined, 61; NIH policies regarding, 61

Privacy Act, 96

Problem analysis, systematic approaches, 76–79

Procurement, "open and free competition" in, 67

Profit-making firms, contracts and, 51–52

Program activities: focusing, 138; management of, 129–166

Program budget, 172–175

Program direction: assigning responsibility, 142–143; components, 129–130; focusing, 138; managing crises, 151–153; objectives as basis for, 138–139; and performance reporting techniques, 149–151; refining project activities, 142; refining project objectives, 139–140; relating objectives and activities, 142; and timetables, 143–149

Program Evaluation Review Techniques (PERT), 20, 23, 148–149

Program objectives, 78; behavioral terminology in, 21; less measurable, 21; quantitative measurement of, 21

Program, Planning, Budgeting Systems (PPBS), 20

Program report principles: clarity, 95; consistency, 95–96; interest and impact, 96; relevance/responsiveness, 95

Program reports: and freedom of information act, 59; information required in, 59

Program/research performance: monitoring of, 58–59; reporting on, 58–59

Index

Index

Social organizations, obstacles inherent in, 22

Social Security Act, 54

Space allocation, relationship problems over, 82

"Span of control," 135

Special projects: characteristics of, 13; contradictory attitudes toward, 26; financial dependence of, 24; goal achievement, 19-22; and host agency relationships, 25-29; implementation of, 17-19; increased utilization of, 9; management implications, 13; structural nature of, 15-17; time-limited duration of, 22-24

Special report requirements, 61

Staff: communication with, 39, 42; justifying qualifications of, 80; organization of, 36-38; public recognition of, 40; recruitment and selection, 132-134; task-oriented supervision of, 137

Staff activities, management of, 129-166

Staff management: adopting leadership style, 130-132; components, 129; orientation of, 134-136; recruitment and selection, 132-134; staff meetings, 136-137; task-oriented supervision, 137

Staff meetings, 136-137; content of, 40

Staff members: and host agency, 27; job stability and, 27

Staff morale, 6, 21

Staff organization: functional, 135; geographic decentralization model, 135; on-target population basis, 135

Staff and project structure, organization of, 134-136

Staffing and personnel issues, 80

State agencies: auditing units of, 60; and block grants, 54

State governments, and grant requirements, 49

State laws, and freedom of information, 57

Statistics, in reports, 96

Statute of Charitable Uses, 47

Standards of Accounting and Financial Reporting for Voluntary Health and Welfare Organizations, 176

Structural approach: to personnel management, 16; to project management, 15-17

Structural characteristics, major problems generated by, 16

Subgrant management, 68

Subpoenas, records subject to, 58

Subsystems: functional, 33; of host agency, 33; managerial, 33; research, 33

Success measurement, use of objectives as criteria for, 20

Support, acknowledgment of, 62

Survey instruments, slowness in approval of, 81

Systems: general, 33; human, 33; management information, 33; "open," 33; sub, 33

Table of contents, 105

Task-oriented supervision, 137

Tasks, grouping of, 37

Tax Reform Act (1969), 49

Taylor, Frederick W., 10

Technical assistance project, 52

Telegraph, 3

Temporary Society, The, 8

Termination, appeal against, 92

Third Wave, The, 8

Theory X, 131n

Theory Y, 131n

Thesaurus, 103

Thompson, P. H., 10

Timetables: components, 22-23; as management tool, 143-149; negative consequences of adherence to, 23

Title 45, Public Welfare, Sub-title A, 49

Title page: sample, 105; use of, 104

Toffler, Alvin, 8